A CULTURAL HISTORY OF MONEY

VOLUME 5

A Cultural History of Money
General Editor: Bill Maurer

Volume 1
A Cultural History of Money in Antiquity
Edited by Stefan Krmnicek

Volume 2
A Cultural History of Money in the Medieval Age
Edited by Rory Naismith

Volume 3
A Cultural History of Money in the Renaissance
Edited by Stephen Deng

Volume 4
A Cultural History of Money in the Age of Enlightenment
Edited by Christine Desan

Volume 5
A Cultural History of Money in the Age of Empire
Edited by Federico Neiburg and Nigel Dodd

Volume 6
A Cultural History of Money in the Modern Age
Edited by Taylor C. Nelms and David Pedersen

A CULTURAL HISTORY OF MONEY

IN THE AGE OF EMPIRE

Edited by Federico Neiburg and Nigel Dodd

BLOOMSBURY ACADEMIC
LONDON • NEW YORK • OXFORD • NEW DELHI • SYDNEY

BLOOMSBURY ACADEMIC
Bloomsbury Publishing Plc
50 Bedford Square, London, WC1B 3DP, UK
1385 Broadway, New York, NY 10018, USA
29 Earlsfort Terrace, Dublin 2, Ireland

BLOOMSBURY, BLOOMSBURY ACADEMIC and the Diana logo are trademarks of
Bloomsbury Publishing Plc

First published in Great Britain 2019
Paperback edition published in 2023

Copyright © Bloomsbury Publishing, 2019

Federico Neiburg and Nigel Dodd have asserted their right under the Copyright, Designs and
Patents Act, 1988, to be identified as Authors of this work.

For legal purposes the Acknowledgments on pp. 13 and 71 constitute an extension
of this copyright page.

Series design: Raven Design
Cover image: *The OP Spectacles*, pub. 1809 (hand coloured etching), Cruikshank, George
(1792–1878) (© Private Collection/The Stapleton Collection/Bridgeman Images)

All rights reserved. No part of this publication may be reproduced or transmitted in any
form or by any means, electronic or mechanical, including photocopying, recording, or
any information storage or retrieval system, without prior permission in writing from
the publishers.

Bloomsbury Publishing Plc does not have any control over, or responsibility for, any
third-party websites referred to or in this book. All internet addresses given in this book
were correct at the time of going to press. The author and publisher regret any
inconvenience caused if addresses have changed or sites have ceased to exist,
but can accept no responsibility for any such changes.

A catalogue record for this book is available from the British Library.

A catalog record for this book is available from the Library of Congress.

ISBN: PB Set: 978-1-3503-6718-0
HB: 978-1-4742-3740-6
PB: 978-1-3503-6579-7
ePDF: 978-1-3502-5354-4
eBook: 978-1-3502-5353-7

Series: The Cultural Histories Series

Typeset by RefineCatch Limited, Bungay, Suffolk
Printed and bound in Great Britain

To find out more about our authors and books visit www.bloomsbury.com
and sign up for our newsletters.

CONTENTS

List of Illustrations — vii
Notes on Contributors — ix
Series Preface — xi

Introduction: Monetary Landscapes of the Nineteenth Century — 1
Federico Neiburg and Nigel Dodd

1 Money and Its Technologies: Inventing the Future through Money—Images of Monetization in Nineteenth-Century American Patents — 15
Juan Pablo Pardo-Guerra

2 Money and Its Ideas: Colonial Currencies, Money Illusions — 35
G. Balachandran

3 Money, Ritual, and Religion: Reason, Race, and the Re-Enchantment of the World — 57
Bill Maurer

4 Money and the Everyday: Paper Money, Community, and Nationalism in the Antebellum US — 73
Michael O'Malley

5 Money, Art, and Representation: "T'was only a balloon"—Seeing and Satire in the Cultural History of Money — 97
Nicky Marsh

6 Money and Its Interpretation: The Century of Mobility
  and Acceleration and Its Money   123
  Leopoldo Waizbort

7 Money and the Issues of the Age   147
  Nigel Dodd

NOTES   165
BIBLIOGRAPHY   171
INDEX   185

LIST OF ILLUSTRATIONS

CHAPTER 1

1.1	Patent for a money box, 1876.	23
1.2	Patent for a mechanical money box, 1877.	25
1.3	Patent for a coin assorting device, 1900.	27
1.4	Patent for a street car money handling mechanism, 1874.	29
1.5	Patent for a pneumatic tube despatch system, 1901.	31

CHAPTER 3

3.1	Thomas Nast, "The American River Ganges," *Harper's Weekly*, September 1871.	61
3.2	One-rin coin, Meiji Emperor Year 16, 1883, Japan.	62
3.3	Thomas Nast, "Milk Tickets for Babies in Place of Milk," in *Robinson Crusoe's Money*, 1876.	65
3.4	"The Administration's Promises Have Been Kept," 1900.	67

CHAPTER 4

4.1	Reproduction of a Shinplaster Note, *Baltimore Sun*, June 13, 1839.	81
4.2	Thomas Satterwhite Noble, "The Price of Blood," 1868.	85

4.3	Commercial Shinplaster Currency, 1863.	88
4.4	Reproduction of Shinplaster Note, *Baltimore Sun*, November 21, 1839.	89

CHAPTER 5

5.1	William Hogarth, "Some of the Principal Inhabitants of ye Moon," 1788.	100
5.2	William Dent, "Public Credit or the State Idol," 1791.	101
5.3	Francis Jukes, "Stock Exchange," 1785.	105
5.4	"The national parachute," 1802.	107
5.5	George Cruikshank, "The Land of Promise!!!," 1811.	108
5.6	Thomas Howell Jones, "The Reign of Humbug!!," 1825.	108
5.7	Edward Williams Clay and Henry R. Robinson, "The Times," 1837.	109
5.8	Charles Jay Taylor, "Coxey's Paternalism," 1894.	111
5.9	Louis Dalrymple, "The 'advance-agent of prosperity' on the road," 1896.	111
5.10	*The Wizard of Oz*, first published 1900.	118

NOTES ON CONTRIBUTORS

G. Balachandran teaches at the Graduate Institute of International and Development Studies, Geneva. His research engages South Asia and the Indian Ocean in a global frame spanning labor, capital, and entrepreneurship. His books include *John Bullion's Empire: British Gold Problems and India between the Wars* (1996, 2013, 2015) and *Globalizing Labour? Indian Seafarers and World Shipping, c. 1870–1945* (2012).

Nigel Dodd is a Professor of Sociology at the London School of Economics. His latest book, *The Social Life of Money*, was published by Princeton University Press in 2014.

Nicky Marsh is Professor of Twentieth Century Literary Studies at the University of Southampton. She works on literary and cultural representations of money and financial markets. She is the author of *Money, Speculation and Finance in Contemporary British Fiction* and co-editor of *Show Me the Money: The Visual Image of Finance* and *Literature and Globalization*.

Bill Maurer is Professor of Anthropology and Law, and Dean of the School of Social Sciences, at the University of California, Irvine. He writes widely on money and payment technologies, alternative economies, and the relationships among money, technology, and law.

Federico Neiburg is Professor of Social Anthropology at the Federal University of Rio de Janeiro (Museu Nacional), Brazil, Principal Investigator at the Brazilian Science Research Council and Coordinator of the Research Group on Culture and Economy (NuCEC, www.nucec.net).

Michael O'Malley is Professor of History at George Mason University. He is the author of *Face Value: The Entwined Histories of Money and Race in*

America; Keeping Watch: A History of American Time, and co-editor of *The Cultural Turn in US History*.

Juan Pablo Pardo-Guerra is an Assistant Professor in Sociology at the University of California, San Diego. His research interests include markets, finance, art, and challenges and possibilities of emerging data sciences.

Leopoldo Waizbort is Professor of Sociology at the University of São Paulo (USP), Brazil, and Researcher of the Brazilian National Council of Scientific Research (CNPq). He is the author of *As Aventuras de Goerg Simmel* (2000, 3rd ed. 2013) and *A passagem do Três ao Um: Crítica Literária—Sociologia—Filologia*.

SERIES PREFACE

When the British Museum decided in 2012 to redesign Room 68, the hall containing objects from its Department of Coins and Medals, its curators made a bold departure from how numismatic material had conventionally been displayed. Rather than cases filled with rows upon rows of gold, silver, and bronze coins of European antiquity, the new gallery design featured all manner of objects, not limited to coin or paper currency, capturing the history of transactional artifacts and infrastructures from shells to mobile phones. Each case had a theme: cases on one side of the gallery spotlighted money's institutional supports and issuing authorities, while cases on the other underscored all the myriad ways people use money, not just for exchange or payment but for ritual or religious observance, political contestation, adornment, and storytelling.

The intention in preparing these six volumes was to provide readers with a similar experience, inviting them into the wonder-cabinets of money in all its variegation, multiplicity, and complexity. What emerges is money's irreducible plurality, the multiple stories it tells. Money opens windows into plural economic and moral worlds, too, worlds of value and evaluation, wealth and worth. Never merely coin, cash, or credit rendered in strictly economic terms, money is so much more than the old couplet would have it: "Money is a matter of functions four: a medium, a measure, a standard, a store." Instead, money is always also a medium of communication, a set of instruments with which people exchange messages with one another—about price, to be sure, but also about political conviction and authority, fealty, desire, or disdain. And money is a method of memorializing the past so that relations established among people, institutions, the gods, and the ancestors can be carried forward through the present and into near, distant, and imaginary futures.

Money is in this sense both irredeemably "cultural" and "historical," and so it is apt that this six-volume Cultural History of Money should spotlight money's relation to religion, technology, the arts and literature, everyday life, metaphysical interpretation, and a wide variety of issues of the age. While many contributors to the first several volumes are numismatists and archaeologists, trucking in the material evidence of coin and bullion, the volumes also contain contributions from scholars of digital infrastructures, literary and legal historians, and science fiction scholars, sociologists and anthropologists, economists and artists.

Archaeologists have long bemoaned the fact that the great majority of ancient coins in museums and private collections today were unearthed without any data having been collected on their surrounding context, rendering much of the ancient and even more recent past a mystery. Even where the context for a particular find is present, its interpretation is always ambiguous. In the contemporary period, money is surrounded by context—cables and wireless signals, data protocols and computer servers, lobbying groups' and legislators' voluminous writings, television soap operas and online social media. Yet just as with ancient hoards, we have difficult escaping our own assumptions about what money is, what people do with it, and the style with which they do so.

Take a basic plastic credit card transaction at a physical till. How many users of this everyday payment device would be able to explain how it works? How would a museum curate this technological assemblage? Moving from the simple act of paying to more involved interactions with money, how might an archaeologist of the future deduce, for example, the practice in some central Asian Muslim immigrant communities known as the "Imam Zamin," which consists of wrapping of a coin in a piece of cloth tied about the upper arm to protect a traveler? Or the practice from around 2005–2009 of what people called "doing tuning"(튜닝하다) to a transit card in Seoul, Korea—dissolving the plastic payment card with acetone so as to remove the radio-frequency identification (RFID) antenna and chip, and creatively stitching it into one's pocketbook, bracelet, or the elbow patches of one's blazer, so you can breeze through the turnstile, with style?

Trapped in our own "coin consciousness," we assume money has to be, or that its value should be found in, a tangible thing, despite the fact that our own interactions with it are increasingly dematerialized in digital networks. We hold on to bullionist conceptions of money's worth, despite our bearing continuous witness to its fluctuations based on prevailing political whims. We think of money as abstract, even as we use it in the most concrete and interpersonal relations. We believe money equilibrates values, rendering goods and services commensurable with one another measured on one scale of value, even as we use money to demarcate difference—national difference, religious difference, intergenerational difference, differences in class, race, and gender.

The periodization of these volumes is somewhat arbitrary but still Eurocentric. The selection of authors and themes is intended to help disturb this Western-oriented history by globalizing it and insisting on bringing into the frame its political, imperial, and often racial dynamics.

The chapters in these volumes capture money's complexities in both substance and form. In substance, insofar as they attempt a cross-cultural, transhistorical survey of money technologies and cultures that will illuminate its variability and complexity. In form, in that each volume takes up the same thematic areas, but in reading across the volumes one will discover that these themes are themselves complicated by having different eras' understandings of said theme juxtaposed with other eras' often incompatible understandings. Like a ledger book, then—one of the most basic manifestations of money's record-keeping devices—the volume can be read "down," reading the chapters within one historical period, and "across," reading the affiliated thematic chapters from volume to volume. What emerges is an affirmation that money itself is a cultural history.

Bill Maurer, General Editor
University of California—Irvine

INTRODUCTION

Monetary Landscapes of the Nineteenth Century

FEDERICO NEIBURG AND NIGEL DODD

The Age of Empire does not refer to a steady state but to a time of huge global transformations. The emerging world system gained new modulations and intensities. Empires existed long before, but nineteenth-century Imperialism was a new worldwide assemblage that implied new geographies of power, new technologies of domination, and a new configuration of colonialism. At the same time, the nation state, an entirely new political unit, was developing almost everywhere, first in the ancient colonies of the Americas and the Caribbean, later in Europe and Asia, and later still, falling under the scope of the next volume in this collection, in Africa. As a result, there emerged new frontiers, fluxes, landscapes, and new "sociability thresholds" to use the concept proposed by Georg Simmel at the end of the period (Simmel 1910 [1945]).

Besides large-scale geopolitical transformations, technological innovations were also important. These included new technologies to govern the monetary flows, to store money, to identify and separate true money from false. They made it possible to unify markets and global monetary exchanges, and ultimately, to attain the "Enlightenment utopia" of the *doux-commerce* (Hirschman 1982) and a single, worldwide system of measures (Darnton 1989). This made it possible to imagine a universal monetary standard: the gold standard, implemented, albeit partially, in diverse metropolises and colonies between the second quarter of the nineteenth century and the First World War. Technological changes that were crucial to the development of money in the nineteenth century included electricity and oil, photography and cinema, the telegraph, telephone, bicycles, cars, trains, balloons and airplanes, "universal exhibitions." These were accompanied by an intellectual infrastructure that consisted of new, rational scales of measurement, and novel—increasingly homogenous—perceptions of space and time.[1] Technological innovations also made it possible to standardize coinage and more importantly, for the first time in a generalized form, to print money: paper currencies founded purely on trust without any intrinsic metallic value. The principles of monetary production and exchange increasingly became a technical task for the emerging "science" of economics: "Currency is to the science of economy what the squaring of the circle is to geometry, or perpetual motion to mechanics," wrote Jevons in his mammoth *Money and the Mechanism of Exchange* (Jevons 1896: vi).

In terms of "progress" these massive transformations were inevitably ambivalent in their consequences. On the one hand, acceleration, fluidity, and communicability gave fresh impetus and meaning to liberal utopias of a laissez-faire world characterized by the "natural" rhythms of free trade. In Britain, John Stuart Mill's *On Liberty* (1859) championed the cause of the individual over and against the "tyranny of the political rulers" (Mill 2015: 5), and argued that "both the cheapness and the good quality of commodities are most effectually provided for by leaving the producers and sellers perfectly free, under the sole check of equal freedom to the buyers for supplying themselves elsewhere" (Mill 2015: 92). On the other hand, these vast changes gave rise to dystopian images of a world without magic, a hyper-rational iron cage (Weber 1905 [2001]). "The fate of our times is characterized by rationalization and intellectualization and, above all, by the disenchantment of the world," wrote Weber in "Science as a Vocation" (1917) (Weber 1917 [1991]: 155). In a similar vein, Simmel argued that this emerging world order of rational monetary exchange—later described by David Frisby as the "mature money economy" (in Simmel 1908 [2011]: xx)—was characterized by new forms of individualism that were simultaneously both empowering and profoundly alienating, marked by an "over-growth of objective culture" wherein the individual "becomes a single cog as over against the vast overwhelming organization of things and forces which gradually take out of his hands everything connected with progress, spirituality and value" (Simmel 1903 [2002]: 18).

The social sciences, especially economics, that began to emerge towards the end of the nineteenth century at universities in Germany, Austria, Great Britain, France, and the United States created concepts for thinking about and acting on money and the social world. Thus, the origin myth of modern money acquired scientific form and legitimacy (Menger 1892 *apud* Dodd 2014: 17; Graeber 2011; Maurer 2006). This was deemed to be healthy money, good, strong, and civilized money (see Neiburg 2010). It was money *ab initio*, without any fixed point in the past, evolving spontaneously from the "primitive" and spatially restrictive universe of barter towards forms of money that were essentially abstract, fluid and empty. This abstract money was really a mixture between what is observed in the present and what is projected into the future as an ideal—Simmel described it as the "pure concept" of money (see Dodd 2014: 317)—and which served, simultaneously, as a means of payment, a unit of measure and a store of value; a money for multiple ends, a generic medium of exchange, pure abstraction, and pure quantity: an evolutionist and double-faced cosmology (Sahlins 1996). The contrast in these ideological representations of the monetary landscape in the "age of empire" is stark and clear, and goes to the heart of two very distinct images of the nature and societal effects of money: on one hand, free markets, peaceful and fluid, fuelled by fiat and convertible currencies; on the other, a degraded humanity, corroded by the acid of money, which depersonalizes, creating pure and interchangeable individuals, quantified lives "only" valued in money.[2]

As Simmel persuasively argued in "The Metropolis and Mental Life" (1903), the emergence of the "mature money economy" during the mid- to late nineteenth century went hand in hand with an intense of widespread process of urbanization. Modern, abstract forms of money—increasingly, paper—were a huge stimulus to the commercial vibrancy of the city. The consequences were both intellectual—or cultural—and structural. Life in cities required an increasingly calculating attitude among citizens: the money economy of the city "filled the daily life of so many people with weighing, calculating, enumerating and the reduction of qualitative to quantitative terms" (Simmel 1903 [2002]: 13). Urban concentrations grew to a new scale, founded on new infrastructures such as the markets and train stations made of steel and glass that began to compete in grandeur with the ancient palaces. These metropolises became inhabited by people who increasingly had (and could only have) access to goods through money (through purchasing), and who obtained (and could only obtain) money by selling their own labor for wages (see Marx 1849, Chapter 2; Ellison 1983).[3] From the viewpoint of the metropolis, money was everywhere—even in its absence, as experienced in the landscapes of the new urban poverty, occupied by the unemployed, those without wages (Castel 2017).

Despite the massive forces and ideals of homogenization and stabilization that characterized the nineteenth century, however, nothing *was* homogenous or stable. The Age of Empire was also an age of upheaval, fluidity, uncertainty, and incessant transformation. "All that is solid melts into air," as Marx and Engels wrote in 1848.[4] Money was integral to this overriding atmosphere of disturbance and disorder, as can be observed in the plural and complex monetary landscapes that spread everywhere, not only on the margins of the global system (on the so-called "peripheries" of modernity) but also in the old and new metropolises and in new geopolitical units such as the nation state—always some distance from attaining the ideal of "for each national market its own currency." Much the opposite in fact: everywhere we can observe arrangements (singular, complex, tense, hierarchical) of national currencies, imperial currencies, colonial currencies, monetary unions, systems of fixed exchange between currencies (currency board systems), currencies for specific commercial circuits, currencies issued by merchants (shinplasters, cowries, glass beads, and many other forms), units of account separated from means of payment, currencies of infinite variety, materials, and scales. Despite the immense power and homogenizing effects of the "forces of modernization" throughout the nineteenth century, monetary multiplicity and diversity were ever present—as indeed they continue to be through to the present day (Dodd 2014; Zelizer 1994).

Hence nothing is quite so new (or *purely* new) as the various modernisms announce. As always, looking back, we must deal with singular and complex assemblages with their own multiple historicities in which varied temporal layers coexist, articulating diverse meanings of the past in the present, distinct concepts of time and history. Money itself is a memory bank (Hart 2001), and a highly multifaceted one: each currency, like every unit of measure, in each specific context of interaction, comprising a singular historical synthesis (Mintz 1961).

The texts assembled in this volume offer a vision of the cultural history of money during the nineteenth century which is nuanced by a double perspective that unfolds in the various explored themes. This is a perspective that is attentive, on the one hand, to the complex entanglement of erudite and popular monetary practices, ideas, and ideals; and on the other, to the structural (and structuring) tensions that characterize all monetary spaces in the nineteenth century, caught as they were between *unifying* forces and agencies such as those of the national and imperial states, or the companies that control large commercial circuits who are keen to see monetary *homogenization* to reduce duties and facilitate exchanges; and agencies and forces that favor *dispersion*, the *multiplication* of money, and the discrepancies between the monetary functions cited above: the *multiplication* of pure units of account, the *autonomization* of means of payment, the invention (and reinvention) of new forms of storing values.

These tensions were inherently political. On the side of centralization, state agencies whose main model in the nineteenth century would become the central banks (among many others, the Banque de France, created in 1800, and the Federal Reserve in the United States, created in 1917), along with the large transnational companies and globalized private banks, and "houses" like the House of Rothschild (Kuper 2001), transformed over the period into a model of a new player of globalized finance. On the side of monetary dispersion and multiplication, agencies and profits distributed among a seemingly infinite number of brokers (Guyer 2004), actants of fragments of networks and multiscalar exchanges (each adjective that qualifies a scale is destabilized by another, exposing continuities and disjunctures between them: local, national, imperial, state, global, etc.).[5]

The chapters in this volume offer decentered perspectives of these tense universes in motion, opening windows onto small details (of everyday monetary theories and practices) and situating them within large-scale processes. It is not a question of accompanying, much less proposing, "theories of money," but instead of radicalizing a perspective that is both inductive and comparatist, so as to allow an appreciation of the peculiarities of social forms and monetary sensibilities through the identification of ruptures as well as continuities. The wealth of approaches is potentialized by the transdisciplinary and transnational character of the enterprise: sociologists, anthropologists, historians of money, the arts and literature, situated in diverse institutional contexts (contemporary centers and peripheries), discerning and illuminating landscapes in all their minute singularity, providing clues that highlight a surprising outcome: by avoiding any kind of anachronism, they demonstrate the extreme familiarity between the traces of the nineteenth-century monetary universes (their concepts, practices, sensibilities, and infrastructures) and those of "our own" contemporaneity.

HOMOGENIZATION AND MULTIPLICITY

Unlike the evolutionist cosmology formulated over the nineteenth century which narrates a continuous movement of civilizational homogenization, monetary landscapes are varied, unstable, and ambiguous. Rather than evolving, historical forms of money were increasingly layered and intermingled. As G. Balachandran shows us in Chapter 2 of this volume, old imperial currencies continued to live on, evincing an enormous cultural resilience, inserting and reinventing themselves even after losing their status as official currencies or even after ceasing to be coined. Such is the case of the Spanish doubloon, issued until 1849 and which remained in use for decades afterwards in the old colonies of the Americas that by then already had their own national currencies. This is the case too of the Maria Theresa thaler, which lost its status as the official currency of Austria in 1858 but continued to be used, even a century later, in commercial circuits as far afield as Northeast Africa and South Asia (Kuroda 2007).

Even though the monetary theories that were dominant in the old and new metropolises postulated the ideal of an exclusive currency for each (national or imperial) monetary space (Helleiner 2003a), during the nineteenth century, in all corners of the planet, one can actually observe the coexistence of various currencies, demonstrating that, as Nigel Dodd formulates in Chapter 7, far from being natural, the relationship between state, society, and currencies is contingent and always contested. As Dodd shows, in political terms, money in the nineteenth century was often caught between the ideological "push" of major theories and ideas (such as the gold standard, bimetallism, monetary union, and the idea of incontrovertible paper) on the one hand, and the pragmatic "pull" of "realpolitik" on the other.

Dodd also points to different monetary modulations on land and sea. The latter is a space of conflict and competition between currencies of consolidated or declining empires and the currencies of new powers, like the dollar, which expanded its planetary influence at the same time as it became consolidated as a national currency in the United States. The Spanish–American war (1898) is usually the main marker of the emergence of the dollar as a reference currency in competition with European currencies in the Caribbean, Central America, and soon after in South America, as well as in the South Pacific where the dollar began to compete with the Indian rupee and especially with the Japanese yen, created in 1871 and that had acquired a certain hegemony after the Sino-Japanese war. The dollarization of Cuba occurred in 1898; in the Philippines the currency board system between the peso and the US dollar was implanted in 1901. Close to the end of the nineteenth century, the monetary landscape also began to be inhabited by new figures and new agencies designing and implementing these neocolonial devices: "money doctors" and "monetary missions" spreading the good news, recommending and imposing policies for market liberalization and monetary stabilization and homogenization, taking as a reference the US dollar and, later on the horizon, the gold standard (Rosenberg 2003; Drake 1994; Helleiner 2003b).

When we leave the tides and coasts and move inland, deep into the continental interiors, the monetary landscapes change once more. Other currencies are encountered, other scales and other conversions, as described too by the heroes of the new colonialism themselves, such as, for example, the expeditions of Livingston and Stanley (Pallaver 2009: 22), or the caravans of the east of Africa. "Black dollars" (as the Maria Teresa thaler used to be named), cowries, glass beads, and so many others (Leer Weiss 2005; Mwangi 2001; Pallaver 2009, 2015). Currencies were issued by both states and merchants. Money therefore circulated within multidimensional and differentiated spaces that articulated social hierarchy and value: strong and higher denomination currencies among the elites, weak and lower denomination currencies among the ordinary poor (Helleiner 2003a: 27). Money's circulation also marked out interfaces and thresholds (Guyer 2004) between internal and external markets, and between different currencies, units of measure, and scales. Spaces that are relationally productive and also multipliers and distributors of profits.

As Michael O'Malley demonstrates in Chapter 4, this hierarchized plurality is not exclusive to the peripheral monetary landscapes. He describes how in the United States, throughout the nineteenth century and irrespective of the series of prohibitions, all kinds of printed small denomination paper notes circulated.

These were issued by shopkeepers, merchants, saloons, restaurants, and business of all kinds, nicknamed shinplasters. By 1850, more than 9000 different kinds of paper money were in circulation, contributing to the shaping of monetary landscapes inhabited by poor people, fueling trade and credits. The parallel circulation of different currencies expressed and reinforced social inequalities: among the white population, strong currencies; among the black population, shinplasters. In fact, as O'Malley shows, the fabulous sums in shinplasters made possible the economic lives and identities of the poor, women, people of color, the "underclass" (also see O'Malley 2012).

Efforts to homogenize these plural monetary universes took various and multiple lines of approach. One such attempt, mentioned above, was to ban other currencies to the benefit of the official (or state) currencies. Another was the creation (and imposition) of common, national, or supranational monetary spaces such as the Latin Monetary Union, formed in 1865 by Italy, Belgium, France, and Switzerland, or the Scandinavian Monetary Union, created in 1873 (for a discussion of the politics of monetary unions in the nineteenth century, see also Dodd in Chapter 7); or the monetary spaces that emerged from banking reforms: in 1901, for example, the former Banque du Sénégal was transformed into the French Banque de l'Afrique Occidental; in 1894 the first Bank of British West Africa was established with jurisdiction in the colonies of Nigeria, Gold Coast, Sierra Leona, and Liberia. A third instance was the implementation of the already-mentioned currency board systems, which sprang up at the end of the nineteenth century, both in Africa (for example, the East and West Currency Board Systems, with the British pound and the French franc as reference, respectively; Fuller 2009) and in Central America and the Caribbean, where, as remarked earlier, the presence of the US dollar was spreading.

The cosmopolitan quality of monetary landscapes is revealed in few other places so clearly as in the (old and new) vertices articulating the nineteenth-century world system (Mintz 1984). One of these "complicated places" (Geertz 2004), Haiti, serves as an example. As throughout the plantation and post-plantation universe (Mintz 1964), Haiti was a plurimonetary space in which various imperial (*heavy* or *hard*) currencies circulated along with a multitude of other (*light* or *soft*) currencies, among them the gourde, the national Haitian currency first issued after the revolution of independence (1804). Over the course of the nineteenth century, the value of the gourde was calculated using a fixed equivalence system (one without any official legal existence but that existed *de facto*, we could say, in the culture and the markets). According to this system, a French franc was equal to five gourdes.[6] After US military occupation of the country in 1915, this equivalence was maintained, taking the currency of the new metropolis as a benchmark, now within the legal framework of a currency board stipulating that a US dollar was equal to five gourdes. The complexity of the monetary culture shaped in the process can still be seen today in the existence of the Haitian dollar whose parity is five gourdes to one Haitian dollar—the *dolà*, in Creole, a concept, an imaginary currency, a pure unit of account that serves to calculate most transactions, connecting temporalities, markets, and commercial circuits that go far beyond the national territory (Neiburg 2016).

Central banks, monetary unions, and fixed parities between currencies were just some of the different devices designed to govern (in the Foucauldian sense) currencies and, with them, flows and people. As demonstrated by the chapters in this volume, various debates unfolded concerning the nature and governance of money over the course of the nineteenth century. Here we can mention just three. The first discussed the issue of the viability of the new nations and new currencies; territorially-based monetary normalcy (Helleiner 2003a) was one of the principles of nationalism (Hobsbawm 1989: 30–44): were Wales, Ireland, or Scotland viable nations from an economic and monetary viewpoint? How should a pertinent and viable monetary area be defined?[7] The second was the debate between the advocates of so-called bimetallism (which allowed the equivalent use of silver and gold) and the advocates of the gold standard, established first in Britain (1821), later in the United Province of Canada (1853), in Newfoundland (1865), Germany (1871), the US (1879), Japan (1895), etc. The third debate reactualized the origin myth of modern money, opposing strong and weak currencies, as contained in the so-called Gresham law ("bad money drives out good") formulated in the mid-nineteenth century. Symptomatic of the era covered here, the law is attributed to the Scottish merchant and lawyer Henry Dunning Macleod, who supposedly named his law referring a discussion that had taken place some three centuries earlier concerning the purity of the metal used in English shillings and the quality of British coinage. Sir Thomas Gresham, a financial agent and consultant to the sixteenth-century English Crown, had been one of the protagonists of the controversy (Macleod 1855–56).[8]

CONCEPTS AND DEVICES

The formulation of concepts for thinking about money and the design of devices for governing it, the debates over its nature, the effects of monetization on human relations and on people, grew hugely in intensity over the nineteenth century, impacting not only the field of the sciences but also that of the humanities and arts. Some devices, like those described at the end of the previous section, were intended for large-scale collectives like nations, empires, or colonies. Others focused on the monetary education of the public, especially the poor. These sought to teach people how to cope with money (or its scarcity) on a day-to-day basis, organize budgets, administrate wages and debts, count currencies, and increasingly calculate everything in monetary values (including objects, services, and people).[9] Governments, companies, and unions negotiate wages, calculate variations in the "cost of living" quantified in percentages and currencies, specialize in numbers, and educate and are educated in economics. In the US the movement of "home economy" spread at the same time as a rise in women's participation in politics and the management of money (Skocpol 1995). "Domestic sciences" were created, intended to educate farm wives in running their households. The American Home Economics Association was founded in 1889.

In Chapter 6, Leopoldo Waizbort provides a panorama of these debates in the German-speaking world, showing how one of their vectors was the need of intellectuals to capture the dizzying speed of changes. The acceleration of time and the fluidity of connections were related to the intensifying presence of money in everyday life, reaching spheres of human experience that invoked the existence of new specialists: history, culture, politics, economics, science, society, and the psyche (the mind or the soul, terms that were also circulating at that time).

In the human sciences that were then emerging, the landscape altered with the birth of the social sciences, including economics. One of the key debates that led to the birth of modern economics was the *Methodenstreit* (the "battle of methods") that occurred between 1880 and 1890 in the German universe and that would have long-term consequences for the forms of thinking about and acting on the economy and currencies in economics and in other social sciences. Simplifying, on one side the German economist Gustav Schmöller, leader of what at that time was called the "cultural historical school," an advocate of the use of inductive methods to understand social facts; on the other side, Carl Menger, one of the principal names of the so-called Austrian school of economics and one of the first formulators of the marginalist theory— alongside William Stanley Jevons in England, and Marie-Esprit-Léon Walras in Switzerland and France (for a discussion of the implications of this debate for the theory of money, see Ingham 2004).

Waizbort sheds light on a central figure of this landscape, an outsider who remained equidistant from these controversies, despite having been a central figure in the creation of the first sociology society in Germany in 1909: Georg Simmel. His chapter focuses on what perhaps was the *magnum opus* of the period in terms of a multifaceted study of money, *The Philosophy of Money* (Simmel 1900 [2005]). Seemingly infinite in scope, the book provides a complex phenomenology of money explicitly situated in the experience of European modernity and life in the major metropolises in which everything seems to be in motion. Landscapes inhabited by individuals for whom, as Waizbort recalls, money would attain the ideal of Esperanto as a language that everyone can speak and understand, a universal language produced by humans (or by God? or by the Devil?), homogenous and commensurable pure quantities, each currency of the same value supposedly equivalent to all their peers ("a dollar is a dollar"), an ideology that took shape in the nineteenth century far beyond Germany, of course.

God and the Devil, a double-faced cosmology consolidated over the nineteenth century, as Bill Maurer also shows us in Chapter 3 apropos the tensions between the supposed decline in religion in the face of the rise of that cold, amoral, and increasingly transcendent entity: the market. Religion, political order, and money were blended in multiple ways during the period. From French secularism and the modernizing reforms of the Ottoman Empire, which tailored modern finance with Islam, to the secularized Shintoism characteristic of Meiji Japan, the unifying tendencies of Hinduism and the new forms of Protestantism, like Methodism or Mormonism, which extended their influence especially among the working classes, first in England and the United States, later in various other corners of the planet through missionary action and the revivalist sentiment that impregnated religious experience (contrary to the liberal creed of the end of religions). Maurer also shows how at the conceptual level some of the major monetary debates of the period were heavily imbued with religious eschatologies and doctrines. The creation of fiat currencies, on paper like the greenbacks, the establishment of universal equivalents (like the gold standard), demanded positions to be adopted on the ontological "reality" of money, and its representative or referential character (Neiburg and Guyer 2017; Neiburg and Guyer 2018). After all, as Maurer shows, rather than being "hostile worlds" (Zelizer 1994), money and religion have historically been (and continue to be) co-constitutive.

Symbol, language, concept, medium; money was all of these and much more in the social landscapes of the nineteenth century. It was also an engine, a field of innovations and speculations, an expanding frontier, both "real" and fictionalized. New universes of loans and finances, virtual currencies, intrinsically linked to illusion, mobility, and continuous time (that which "is money"). In Chapter 5 of this volume Nicky Marsh focuses on images of balloons and bubbles, which in the critical satire of the period were ontologically associated with credit and money. English-language authors like Jonathan Swift, Edgar Allan Poe, and Frank Baum of *The Wizard of Oz* described the shifting nature of currencies, emphasizing the airiness of the rapid circulation of money and the expansion of finance, with the bubble acquiring a theoretical and metaphorical status in the representation of money—according to Marsh, an amplified sense of money's enduring imaginary reality, something at once both entirely real (a physical token) and highly aerial (an idea, an object to believe in).

Balloons were also technological devices. The satire is also a critique of the ongoing technological revolutions. Means of transport and communication, large works that connect different parts of the planet (the Suez Canal in 1869, the Panamá Canal in 1881–1914), forms of mining and saving gold without which the ideal of the universal equivalent (the gold standard) would have been impossible. Indeed, the nineteenth century was also the time of the "gold rushes". The most intense of these occurred in the United States (California and

Alaska), Australia (the Victorian Gold Rush) and South Africa (the Witwatersrand Gold Rush). Hundreds of thousands of people moved about in search of golden money, cities, railroads, infrastructures for food supplies and the extraction, storage, and distribution of thousands of tons of gold (Limebeer 1935), new legal instruments that established ownership of the mines, payment of taxes, and measurement of the quality of the precious metal.

As Juan Pablo Pardo-Guerra relates in the first chapter of this volume, money mobilizes a set of technological devices to calibrate the quality of the metal used in currencies, to identify true and false monies, to separate genuine and spurious money, to ban counterfeit, to make coins and print bills, to save money in the new banks and in family houses (i.e. the toy money boxes that also functioned as pedagogical and moral devices intended to cultivate good use of money), to handle money in the new department stores (cash machines were first patented in 1879),[10] and to transfer monies from colonial lands to metropolises, facilitating their integration into global fluxes of capital and transnational money markets. Pardo-Guerra observes a crucial and surprising vertex in the link between money, innovation and perceptions of time: patents, which became widespread from the 1830s, especially after the Civil War. Dreams of saving, dreams of containment, and dreams of ontology, patents are devices that connect the government of monetary landscapes, the materiality of money and the future projections of individuals and families.

MULTIPLE PASTS AND PRESENTS

In his classic *The Great Transformation*, written in the context of the Second World War, Karl Polanyi qualifies the period spanning from 1815 to 1914 as "the century of peace" but stresses its relative character: new empires, national states, the redefinition of colonial relations, slavery (the last country to abolish the practice was Brazil in 1888), "seas of blood" everywhere:

> The Ottoman, Egyptian, and the Sherifian empires broke up or were dismembered; China was forced by invading armies to open her door to the foreigner, and in one gigantic haul the continent of Africa was partitioned. Simultaneously, two Powers rose to world importance: The United States and Russia. National unity was achieved by Germany and Italy; Belgium, Greece, Romania, Bulgaria, Serbia, and Hungary assumed, or reassumed, their places as sovereign states on the map of Europe. An almost incessant series of open wars accompanied the march of industrial civilization into the domains of outworn cultures. Russia's military conquests in Central Asia, England's numberless Indian and African wars, France's exploits in Egypt, Algiers, Tunis, Syria, Madagascar, Indo-China, and Siam.
>
> —Polanyi 1941 [2001]: 5–6

Hence, it amounts far more to a "pragmatic peace," sustained by the ideas of order and progress, the gold standard, the self-regulated market and the liberal state. An authentic "satanic mill" (Polanyi 1941 [2001]: 35) fed by money, which, nonetheless "society resists," Polanyi argues, albeit only to attenuate the pace of transformations and the suffering caused by changes.

In the large capitalist metropolises (like London, Berlin, Moscow, or Chicago) the price of time and labor is negotiated (wages and the extending of the working day). Unions, parties, and other collectives are transformed into spaces in which money is breathed, the "cost of living" is calculated and priced, numbers and currencies are discussed, other possible worlds are imagined. As Maurer suggests in Chapter 3, attempts proliferated to "reenchant" the world with other moralities, other definitions of the public, other monies. As Dodd argues in Chapter 7, the outcome was an explosion of new theories and ideas about the nature and value of money, and new ways of organizing and regulating its production and exchange. Critical thought and libertarian utopias proliferated, competing (and sometimes surprisingly converging) with ideas of the self-regulated market, focusing (for example) on the idea of "labour money" advocated by the English writer John Ruskin, the French theorist Pierre-Joseph Proudhon's proposals for a Bank of the People, and the German economist and activist Silvio Gesell's arguments in favor of "decaying" money. Hovering in the background to all of their works were the debates on socialism, was surely the figure of Karl Marx, and the nascent social democracy, growing in Europe and the Americas, but still timid in the East.

This volume of the *Cultural History of Money* does not aim to cover the "totality" of the planet-wide monetary universe of the nineteenth century. This is an infinitude of landscapes that cannot be illuminated within the confines of the seven chapters presented here. There are absences here: including, for instance, deeper views on the monetary dynamics of the Far East or Eastern Europe. Any pretension to produce a map at real-life scale would, however, evidently be impossible, even more so if, as we try to show in these pages, monetary landscapes are understood to be far from being exclusively territorial. Despite the widespread ideal of territorial currencies in the nineteenth century, they contain various other scales, multiple agencies, agents and perspectives. Exploring this pluri-scalar form (and avoiding Eurocentric or Anglocentric viewpoints as far as possible), the chapters that we present here display a surprising confluence: they make explicit the contemporary resonances of nineteenth-century monetary landscapes, the broth of a world that is and appears to be our own too. Fluidity and acceleration (see Waizbort, Chapter 6), dematerialization (see Marsh, Chapter 5), technologies that support images of the present and promises of the future (see Pardo-Guerra, Chapter 1), multiple and hierarchized landscapes, stretched between persistent heterogeneity and unification (see Balachandran, Chapter 2, O'Malley, Chapter 4 and Dodd, Chapter 7).

The Age of Empires shapes people tensioned between money's acidity, which anonymizes and individualizes, and relational productivity, which turns individuals into relational people, while also enabling the existence of human collectives. Political and moral tensions and ambivalences involve the social and cultural life of the money of our recent ancestors of the nineteenth century and of ourselves still today, shaping multiple pasts and multiple presents.

ACKNOWLEDGMENTS

We would specially like to thank Catherine Eagleton for her generous inputs on the first steps of this project and Bill Maurer for his encouragement during the long process to make this volume.

CHAPTER ONE

Money and Its Technologies

Inventing the Future through Money—Images of Monetization in Nineteenth-Century American Patents

JUAN PABLO PARDO-GUERRA

Weber's Protestants teach us something we sort of already know: money conjures the imagination of the future and the moral fallibilities of the present (Weber 2002). A coin saved today is a compulsion paused—but it is, too, a thoughtful contribution to a greater project, whether a special purchase by a thrifty child at FAO Schwartz on a rainy weekend or a one-way ticket to spiritual salvation. Money is a promise, an expectation, a possibility, a deferred potential present. Money is, in this very specific sense, a future in your pocket.

In this chapter, I want to think of the temporal orientation of money not through money itself but through the devices and paraphernalia associated to its keeping, use, and making. That money is thoroughly technological is obviously clear to the contemporary reader. Salaries are often paid in electrons and magnetization, read and modified through circuits and processors, represented on plastic, paper, and metal. Money *is* technology, not only in its substance but also in its essence, enframing our modern experiences through distinct (though by no means single) forms of valuation (Zelizer 1994).

Here, though, I am not so much concerned with "money-as-a-technology" (a topic that has an extensive literature (see Maurer 2015, Coeckelbergh 2015)), as with the technologies that money fostered in the nineteenth century. If a technology, money requires supports—infrastructures of monetization that stabilize its use and circulation. As with the digital payment systems and global transaction networks that animate electronic money in the early twenty-first century (Bátiz-Lazo et al 2014, Stearns 2007), nineteenth-century money existed in relation to a growing network of objects, designs, and things that collectively distilled what monies meant and what was expected from them for the future. These machines were vivid expressions of the understandings, anxieties and promises associated with money and its place in societies where capitalism and monetization were rapidly expanding across everyday life. And as such, they are the objects of this brief excursion.

In considering how technologies referenced the meanings of money, I will furthermore focus on *imagined* rather than actual things. With this, I want to doubly stress the promissory character of money, firstly through how it signals a particular future-orientation, but secondly in how it elicits designs about the future, promises of how promises will be produced and handled. So while this is a chapter on the technologies of money, it is rather more specific. Instead of actually-existing things, I look into the checkered history of patents about money in order to see how this double promise—one of technology, one of money—speaks of the meanings of monies, societies, and their conjoined paths.

PATENTS AND THEIR (UN)REALIZED FUTURES

As central features of the modern intellectual property regime, patents represent both the bounties of innovation and the countless failures of invention. Originally introduced in the late Middle Ages and early Renaissance as monopolies granted by monarchs to inventors over the fruits of their invention, patents became central instruments for the legal protection of property in the seventeenth and eighteenth centuries. When the control over intellectual products became important in the nascent capitalist economies of modern Europe, patents rose into undisputed terrains for defining and contesting ownership over designs that could, in theory, be profitably exploited by entrepreneurial minds.

This is not to say that all patents materialize into innovations. Cliometricians may use the frequency of patenting as a measure of innovation (Streb 2016), of the creative powers of industry and entrepreneurialism. Yet much evidence exists that patents more often than not fail to reach the point of application (in the field of biotechnology, for example, the consulting firm Ernst & Young estimates that fewer than ten percent of the patents reach the market). In some cases, patents merely serve the purpose of claiming a potentially useful innovation to deter possible competitors (Heller and Eisenberg 1998); in most other cases, they are clearly fancies of the imagination (a nineteenth-century patent for spectacles for chickens, meant to protect them from aggressive pecking from other chickens, stands as a notable example).

Independently of whether patents result or not in a material contribution to the world, they clearly index the dreams and preoccupations of their makers. For example, in the United States, where the patent system is almost as old as the nation itself, patentability is couched in terms of practical utility: in addition to not being merely hypothetical, a patent must solve a problem of some sort, introducing a "useful process, machine, article of manufacture, or composition of matter, or any new and useful improvement thereof" (United States Patent Office 2017) into possible circulation. Establishing utility is predicated on creating a clear distinction between problems and non-problems, things that preoccupy the inventor with things that do not. Effectively, in order to be patentable, a design must demonstrate some form of improvement, a rationale, a logic, a contribution; it requires shifting the state-of-art through a proposed solution.

While individualizing as most forms of property are, patents are necessarily tied to a larger infrastructure of knowledge-making. In establishing "novelty" with respect to a "state-of-art," for example, patents create linkages and comparisons, provenances of authors, claims, and previous inventions that generate the boundaries of patentability. That patents are associated with individuals rather than the larger contexts from which they derive is, in many ways, an artifact of legal work. As anthropologist Marilyn Strathern alerts, patents truncate the social networks where problems are constituted, claims contested, and knowledge developed (Strathern 2001). This form of intellectual property "points simultaneously to an item or technique made available to knowledge, authorizing its use and circulation, and to the knowledge, on which claims are made, which has made it into an item or technique" (Strathern 2001: 20). As such, patent records are not simply disentangled indicators of punctuated innovation trajectories but rather telescopes into possibly existing futures shared by collectives through their knowledges past and present. This is how I interpret patents in this chapter: not as signaling moments of invention by individuals, but rather as nodes that condense how the possibly existing futures of money were imagined across societies.

For the purpose of this chapter, I constrain my analysis to American patents from *c.* 1860 to 1915. The rationale for this is threefold. The first motive is historical. Patents in the United States were arguably closer to the construction of a national entrepreneurial project than their equivalents elsewhere. The modern patent system might have originated in Europe (as in England, where Henry VI notionally issued the first patent in 1449, although the practice was formalized in the Statue of Monopolies of 1624), but it was generally costly (patent fees for England in 1860 were approximately four times the annual per capita income). In England, the hierarchies of class drove the logic of invention. This was certainly not obvious in the United States, where the protection of intellectual property was enshrined in the Constitution and the powers it conferred on Congress to "promote the Progress of Science and the useful Arts by securing for limited Times to Authors and Inventors the exclusive Right to their respective Writings and Discoveries." If anything, the American patent system was designed around slightly less steep entry standards than its European equivalents: whereas in 1860 filing fees in Europe averaged about 400 US dollars per patent, the costs in the United States were significantly lower at 30 dollars. The patent system in America was, as Zorina Khan (2005) writes, carefully calibrated to promote social and economic welfare, and entangled with the imagery of invention, merit and democracy of the young nation.

A second reason is monetary. Much of the early monetary history of the United States was marked by the political debacle of currency in relation to bimetallism: from the Colonial and Continental Currencies of the eighteenth century to the bills issued by free state banks in the 1830s, the forms of general-purpose monies available to the American public were multiple and underpinned by their convertibility into gold or silver. Triggered by the constraints and pressures of the Civil War, however, the United States government issued a new monetary standard in 1861, initially by transforming $50,000,000 of debt into Treasury notes, convertible on demand, and that became legal tender and underpinned the notes of national chartered banks. These so-called "greenbacks" signaled an important transformation in the politics of money and currency: the consolidation, perhaps, of a particular and slightly more contemporarily capitalist way of thinking about the economy in relation to state and society. Unlike bullionists, greenbackers located value not in the convertibility of a note into gold but, rather, in "exchangeability as a basis for confidence" (Carruthers and Babb 1996). The value of currency emanated from the institutional status of government; money was "a creature of law," rather than an intrinsic value derived from scarcity and nature. For my analysis, this matters critically since the period that I cover is defined by the issuance of the United States Note and the simultaneous use of the gold coin. Bullionist concerns about the status of money did not disappear with the adoption of the greenback—the metaphors animating bitcoin today serve as striking indicators of the continuity of these concerns. In the imaginations of inventors from the period we should thus expect to find both a concern for institutions as well as references to the intrinsic value of the rare. Monetarist history also informs the endpoint of this period: 1915 marks the creation of the Federal Reserve System that has defined the makeup of currency ever since.

A third consideration is eminently practical. Patents existed in the United States since 1791 but are mostly unavailable from before 1836, when a fire destroyed the records of the United States Patent Office. Like most historical records, patents are tied to their physical qualities as legal instrumentalia, and in the case of the United States, are curtailed by the eventfulness of history itself. That the corpus informing this paper was segmented in this way should not affect the quality of the results, though: the loss of early American patents (though important in historical terms) does not overlap with the critical inflection points of the intertwined institutional history of money and patents in the United States.

The patents that I examine in the following pages are bounded by these three constraints. Nevertheless, they address how people at the time, caught between the claims of bullionists and greenbackers, imagined how money ought to be measured, handled, stored and produced. These patents were part of the infrastructures of money that nineteenth-century inventors dreamt up in their minds and perhaps built in their shops—and that, as truncated elements in a larger network, spoke of the anxieties, desires, hopes and afflictions that American societies had about the nature and future of money itself. Patents and money were linked by dreams, and by examining the former we can understand the world that societies built around the latter.

THE DIMENSIONS OF MONEY IN NINETEENTH-CENTURY AMERICAN PATENTS

What do patents say of money? Throughout the corpus, money emerges as a clear rationale for innovation. Whether a hog-killing bed that sought to reduce the "great deal of money" lost with previous methods of slaughter (US712579A; Nicholson and Blanchard 1902), or the method for forming beaches that reduced the "vast sums of money [. . .] expended in dredging along coast-lines" (US715557A; Cushing 1902), pecuniary concerns are notable argumentative elements in establishing the novelty of inventions. I am not so much interested in these but in identifying the broad themes that structured the content of shared imaginaries about money. The first is necessarily about currency itself, that is, about the stability of money as an object of exchange.

Dreams of Ontology

Money is decidedly an abstraction (Ingham 2004), yet money-stuff grounds its everyday experience. The obduracy of money matters tremendously, even in the space of digital electronic payments systems. Think of credit cards. A recent trend among American banking institutions has been the production of premium credit cards that are tactilely distinguishable from their competition. In 2016, for example, the American bank JP Morgan Chase & Co. issued a new, premium, high-fee credit card. Unlike other cards offered by the bank's its competitors and that used plastic as the substrate for the chips and magnetic tapes, Chase opted for an undisclosed alloy. The "card's metal composition," wrote a popular internet resource, is "clearly part of the appeal. Only a handful of other credit cards are metal, including the American Express Centurion Card, commonly known as the AmEx 'black card,' which is typically available only to millionaires, billionaires and celebrities." Technically identical to the average plastic (digital bytes do not discriminate their substrate), Chase's premium card was materially unique.

Of course, other forms of currency are not free from the constraints of the physical. Exchanged on average about 110 times per year (or about every three days), a one-dollar bill is prone to the forces and frictions of the wallet, purse, cash register, bundle, and forgotten drawer (Leibbrandt 2009). The stuff of money matters with such a hectic existence. A telling report from the United State's National Research Council on the future of banknotes observes the importance of substrate, form, color and tactile qualities (National Research Council 1993). This was not merely a matter of printing and design but, as the council noted, of harnessing the most advanced technologies available to the Treasury: "microelectronics, nanotechnology, molecular electronics, materials, photonics, and magnetics should not only be followed but also encouraged by supporting technical work that is focused on deriving very sophisticated but inexpensive, reliable, accurate, inconspicuous devices to assist visually disabled people in recognizing, denominating, and perhaps authenticating U.S. banknotes" (NCR 1993).

It is not entirely surprising that some of the patents in the collection were aimed at guaranteeing the authenticity of currency. They were, so to speak, devices of ontology that sought to discriminate between true and false money: some patents were dreamt as devices that would allow testing the authenticity of money. This practice, so common today in the tills of small vendors where large denomination bills are confirmed under ultraviolet lamps, was particularly important in the nineteenth century. Greenbacks provided some guarantee of stability, for example, but the sphere of currency was invariably occupied by a panoply of notes produced by the National banks. Earlier in the country's history, guaranteeing the authenticity of a bill was a matter of political concern. When Congress issues the Continental Currency, for example, a strategy of Britain was to produce high quality fakes that would devalue the country's newfangled money supply. In the late nineteenth century this was no longer the case, though fakes—both of coins and notes—remained an important problem.

One set of patents tackled this ontological question through substrate (much in the same way as the National Research Council above). The question of money's value could be resolved by printing and minting it on particularly "virtuous" materials. For coins, the solution was obvious. As most of the coinage at the time was based on gold and nickel, telling fake from true was a matter of distinguishing between different alloys. Through physics, the weight and dimensions of a particular coin could be used to corroborate its authenticity. As a patent from 1900 noted, "Genuine coins usually differ perceptibly in weight from those which are spurious or counterfeit, the specific gravity of the metal of which coins are composed being different from the specific gravity of pieces of base metal of corresponding diameter and thickness" (US688839A; Evard 1901). A rather contrived apparatus could thus be fashioned to automatically discriminate genuine from counterfeit coins.

Notes were slightly more complicated. Some patents consisted of methods or devices meant to facilitate determining the genuineness of bank notes. One device introduced by Isabella Cohen in 1909 involved a rather simple set up where a note was easily placed under a powerful magnifying glass for inspection. This and other devices, however, delegated much of the work of telling things apart to the relatively untrained eye of their operators. Other patents tackled this problem by investing in the production of notes. A host of technologies at the time relate to printing and engraving techniques specifically engineered with bank notes in mind; yet others refer to issues of design that would make the production of counterfeits difficult. A patent by an English inventor filed in 1911 in the United States, for example, involved:

> a lined ground-work (which may be subsequently overprinted in any suitable manner) having upon it letters, figures, or devices of a distinguishing character which are of the same tint as the ground-work, but produced in lines at angles to the lines thereof, so that such distinctive letters or the like are almost invisible in connection with the groundwork, and absolutely invisible when overprinted, and in the use in conjunction with a surface so printed of a lined screen or surface, the lines or marks upon which hear such relation to the lining or marking of the ground-work, that when the said screen is in juxtaposition to the printed surfaces, the said distinguishing marks will be rendered visible notwithstanding the overprinting.
> —US1002600A

An earlier patent from 1895 similarly considered using a geometric pattern to prevent forgeries (USD248090). Others focused on substrate: as a patent from 1910 shows, methods for producing specialized paper with added "small sheets of paper or of fibrous materials cut out in various shapes" (US964014A) in sufficient quantity and with enough consistency were also solutions to the problem of money's stability.

Dreams of Saving

The corpus also reveals a number of patents for "toy moneyboxes." Money containers, coin hoarders, and other devices for storing currency are certainly ancient inventions. Archeological evidence shows that storing monies in containers is as old as money itself. These humble devices are nevertheless important indicators of broader patterns in society. Storing can take many forms, and patterns of storage-use are revealing for what they say about the relation of the stored good to conceptions about its cultural meanings and value. By studying the medieval moneyboxes stored in cesspits in Edam in the Netherlands, Zuijderduijn and van Oosten (2015) show patterns of savings that indicate the rise of Protestantism and its particular philosophy of money and accumulation, as well as the widespread introduction of mandatory insurance schemes for craft guilds. Saving money might have been an apt strategy under the Roman Catholic church, but the practice lost some credence as the Netherlands transitioned into forms of social organization that, associated to a Protestant logic, and collectivized risks.

By focusing on saving practices, Zuijderduijn and Oosten (2015) highlight the disciplining character of moneyboxes: these technologies were meant to elicit particular forms of behavior and dispositions towards the use (and withdrawal) of money, punctuated by moral concerns about responsibility, uncertainty, and rights. The inventions that we see in nineteenth-century American patents are not different in this respect. These "toy" moneyboxes had the concrete objective of fomenting specific disciplines of money keeping among users who happened to be particularly young. They involved pedagogies of thrift, ways of behaving around currency deemed to be morally adequate. Consider one of the simplest patents in the dataset, filed in 1876 by Robert Kane of Cambridgeport, Massachusetts:

> The nature of my invention consists of a hollow obelisk provided with a slot in one side [Figure 1.1] and is designed to serve as a savings or money bank for children. It is constructed, preferably, of tin. The base or pedestal is struck up, and the sides are separate pieces, molded as shown, with two of the four parts somewhat wider, for the purpose of making a lap-joint at the corners, as represented. The parts are then united with solder.
> —USD9231S

This simple object was not for adults but for children, one among a panoply of devices and institutions meant to develop habits of saving among a younger generation of Americans. Concerns with thrift were common in (patently moralized) discussions about money at the time (Zook 1920). Many often connected to specific educational projects. Writing in the *Annals of the American Academy of Political and Social Science* in 1920, the economist Alvin Johnson stressed thrift as a "public service and a private virtue" acquired through practice. "Most men who have learned to practice (sic) thrift have been little influenced by theory and exhortation. They have been much influenced by environing conditions that make saving and investment as easy and natural as spending" (Johnson 1920: 233–4). Kane's little tin savings

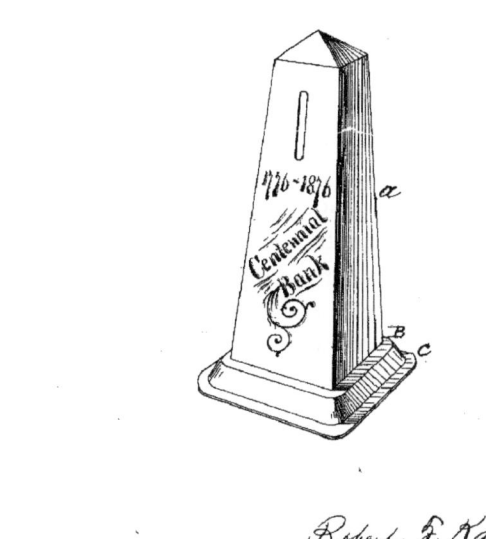

FIGURE 1.1: Patent for a money box, 1876. Courtesy of the US Patents office.

box was just one way of producing habits by materializing of some of these conditions.

The imagination of moneyboxes as instruments for creating habits of the purse is perhaps clearer in another patent. A filing from 1877 by John Hall, also of Massachusetts, was as much a device to store money as one to invest trust in savings institutions. Moneyboxes are unavoidably small in scale. While not necessarily individualistic (after all, several members in a household or community can use the same moneybox for some collective purpose), they are ill designed for larger forms of accumulation. A piggy bank is simply not a bank. An economy of savings requires much more than mattresses and hollow clay figures—it needs banks whose deposits are circulated and multiplied rather than stored. In the late nineteenth century trusting in banks was a fraught investment. Banking crises were common at the time—in the panics of 1857 and 1873, several hundred banks failed, without insurance covering the deposits of their customers—and so confidence in their survival was meek. Hall's invention deposited both money and trust. His improvement on the design for a toy moneybox was decorated as a miniature bank, topped with "mechanical figure representing a cashier, adjusted to receive and deposit the money in the bank, forming a toy for the amusement of children and a safe deposit for small coins" (USRE7614E) (Figure 1.2).

Following a similar, though slightly less decorative logic, a design from 1899, a mechanical depository by Morris Mengis of New York, sought to facilitate a culture of savings. His invention was:

> chiefly designed for use in coöperation with savings banks to receive the smaller deposits as made by children or others preparatory to their deposition in the bank and passing to the credit of the depositor upon the books of the institution, although, as will be obvious, the improved device may be employed in coöperation with charities and other institutions to receive contributions or payments which may be made thereto, the object of the invention being to provide or produce a simple, reliable, and convenient mechanical depository for the above-named purposes which in addition to receiving the money that may be deposited shall automatically return to the depositor a receipt for or other acknowledgment of the exact amount contributed, paid, or deposited.
>
> —US631024A; Mengis 1889

Mengis' device was part of a larger family of money-counting technologies that meant to facilitate accumulation, particularly of coins. What matters from these technologies, though, is what they reflected about nascent moralized visions of money and money keeping. Mengis, like Hall, Kane, and a host of other patent assignees, understood the distributed accumulation of money as conforming to a larger pattern of institutional behavior. Savings were habituated, trained into; they were channeled, from the toy moneyboxes of children, to the automated devices of receiving and tallying that banks made available; and from these, they fed the vaults of organizations that banked on trust. These devices, however humble, represented fragments of a growing infrastructure of everyday monetary circulation. They were the gateways, connectors, and tubes upon which the economy of the future was imagined to flourish.

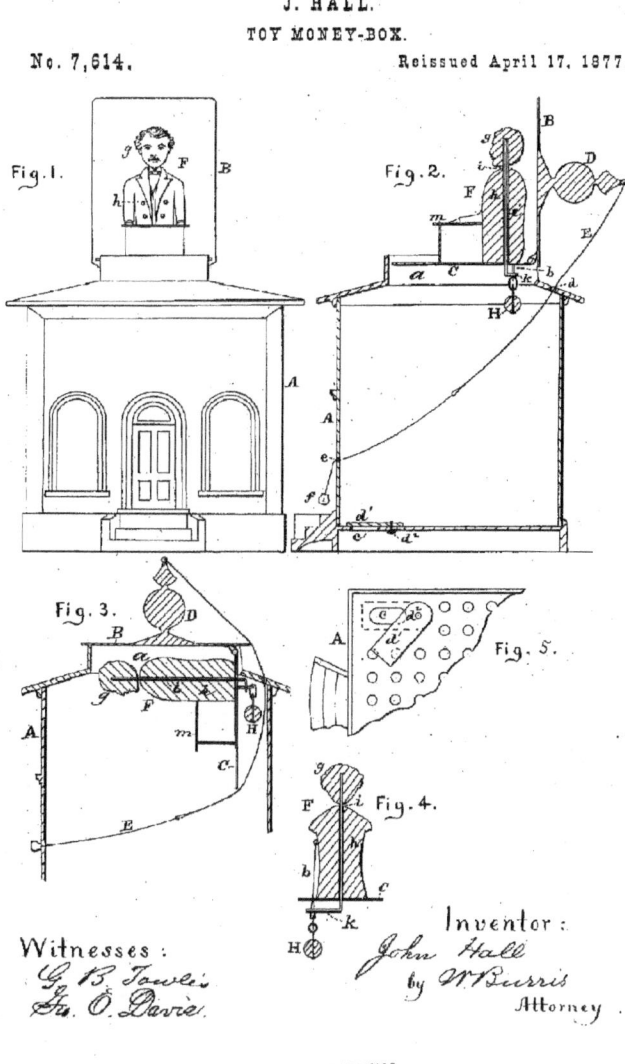

FIGURE 1.2: Patent for a mechanical money box, 1877. Courtesy of the US Patents office.

The larger objective of these technologies of saving was also visible in their iconography. National currencies are key to the construction of national identities—just like internal markets were tied to political projects to create the boundaries of an exchange economy within the confines of the modern state, the designs of national currencies were meant to buttress specific symbols of idealized nations (Helleiner 1998, Polanyi 1957). This symbolic quality was also relevant to the technologies of money. Although primarily utilitarian, patents were often charged with the imagery of the nation. In the years surrounding the first centennial of the American Revolution, for example, patents reflected patriotic themes: Kane's moneybox was inscribed with the legend "Centennial Bank 1776–1876," and an 1875 patent by Candide Croteau involved "a toy moneybank, having the form and appearance of the tower of Independence Hall, Philadelphia" (USD8655). These little devices made the national economy as much as the symbols printed and mint on currency.

Dreams of Containment

Inventions for accumulation were important features of the iconosphere of nineteenth-century money-use. But just as accumulation was a recurrent theme, so was money's mobility. We often speak of money through metaphors of liquids and flows—we think of movements of capital, of monies running from bank to purse, between consumers and producers, or across nations and governments. The idea of leakage is invariably linked to this metaphor. Like a poorly conserved Philip's hydraulic model of the economy, a system of monetary transfers can be beset by holes, poor connections, and sites of loss—whether physical, as in the case of systems used to move money and currency across space, or social, as in corruption and theft that move monies in unexpected ways.

One family of inventions corresponded to money-counting technologies. For instance, starting with the first patent in 1879 by James Ritty of Ohio, novel designs of cash registers were filed frequently throughout the late nineteenth and early twentieth centuries. These technically sophisticated apparatuses integrated sorting, storage, and reporting functions through a combination of levers, gears, bells, and springs (e.g. US817725A, US678218A, and US754961A; Osborn 1906; Bassett 1901; Baynes 1904). Related to these devices, patents also reveal a growth of designs meant to automatically organize currency according to its denomination. Thus, in 1900, Sanford Boyd patented a coin sorting, delivering and recording apparatus that was intended for:

> handling money, and has for one of its objects to provide a simple, inexpensive, and highly-reliable apparatus for expeditiously assorting and delivering coins of various denominations and other money, and one which is calculated to record the reception of each coin or other piece of money and the discharge thereof, so as to enable the proprietor of a place of business to ascertain at the close of each business day or other desired period the amount of money placed in and the amount removed from the apparatus.
>
> —US655544A; Boyd 1900 (Figure 1.3)

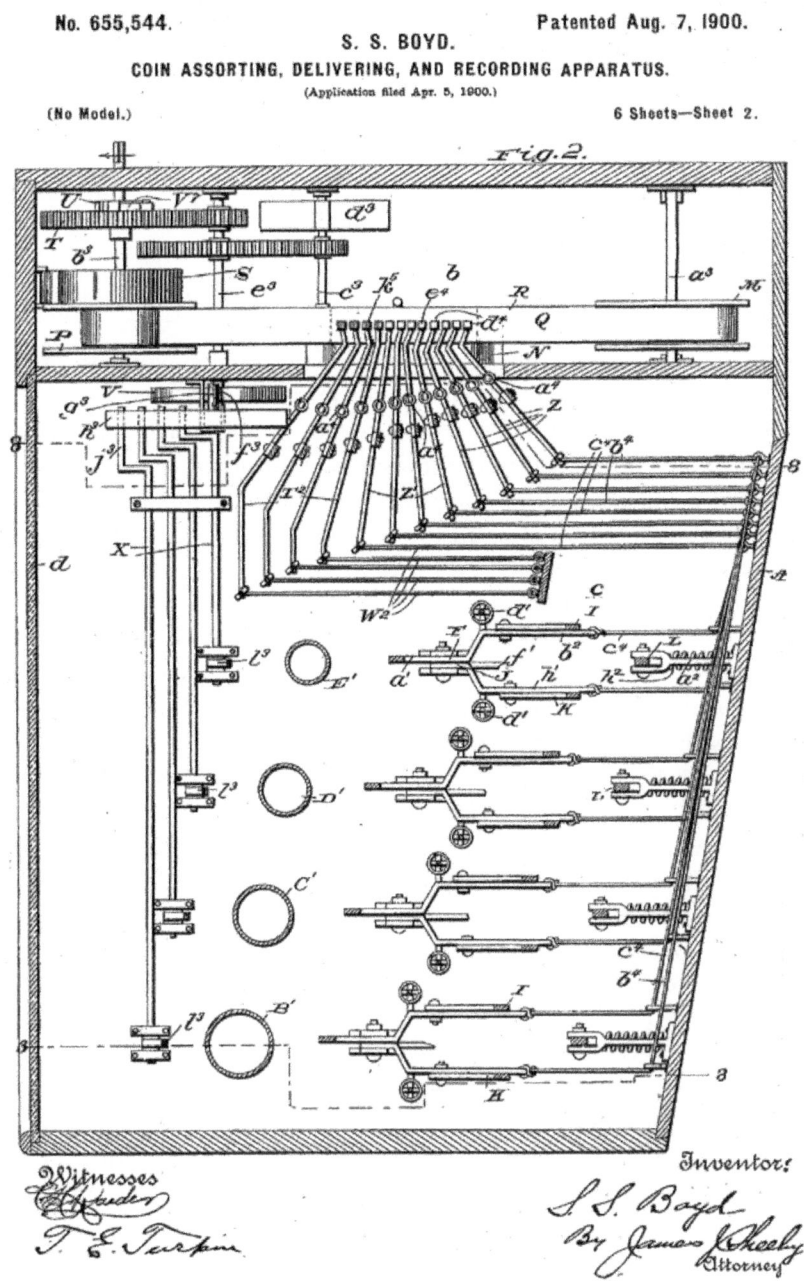

FIGURE 1.3: Patent for a coin assorting device, 1900. Courtesy of the US Patents office.

A similar patent from 1902 for a checking apparatus:

> afforded [restaurant owners the] opportunity of readily inspecting the amount of [payments collected by waiters] before it is deposited in the receptacle therefor, which shall permit of the proprietor or manager readily ascertaining, at any time the total amount paid in by the waiter or other employee and which shall be cheap and simple in construction and not liable to get out of order.
>
> —US715122A; Nelson 1902

Containing money implied much more than storage in moneyboxes: it required accounting for its movement and change through time.

A notable characteristic of the patent corpus is the presence of inventions that sought to avoid leakages in the transmission of money. One set of patents clearly shows a concern to limit the interactions between humans and currency so as to avoid the temptation of customers to short-change the business, or of workers to skim the cash register to the detriment of the owners. For example, although they were not monetary technologies, streetcars were designed with money in mind. A patent from 1861 by John Stephenson of New York shows this well. The improvement in his design of a streetcar was partly based on the introduction of a device that allowed the conductor to collect the fare of the passengers without having to handle coinage or move (USRE6059E; Oastoe 1874) (Figure 1.4). Stephenson's patent gave the driver some opportunities to illicitly retrieve money from the fare box, but this was a problem soon solved by other patents that introduced slightly more hermetic designs that made withdrawals cumbersome if not impossible. Also in 1861, Horace Tupper and John Slawson filed a patent for a fare box that, in addition to facilitating counting the coins deposited by travellers in a more efficient and less error-prone fashion, was designed with a money drawer flanked by "a couple of guard-slides [. . .] so as to prevent felonious abstraction of the fare" (USRE6689E; Ttjppee 1875). This was also the logic behind other, similar patents, including a 1901 system through which "money-bags may be effectually closed and sealed to retain the contents thereof against unauthorized opening" (US688671A; Nason 1901), a pressure-activated electronic burglar alarm for "for any kind of closed spaces, such as apartments, money-chests, and the like" (US657672A; Petternel 1900), and a traveler's "treasure belt" designed for "Carrying Money, Diamonds, or other Valuables" (US297268A; Kepley 1884).

Some inventions were more overtly related to metaphors of leakage. One is salient: the pneumatic tube, invented in England in the 1830s and used in the London Stock Exchange as early as 1856. A patent from 1901 by Maurice Anderson of Chicago, Illinois, provides an example. Contributing to existing designs of pneumatic tubes, Anderson's invention was aimed at:

MONEY AND ITS TECHNOLOGIES

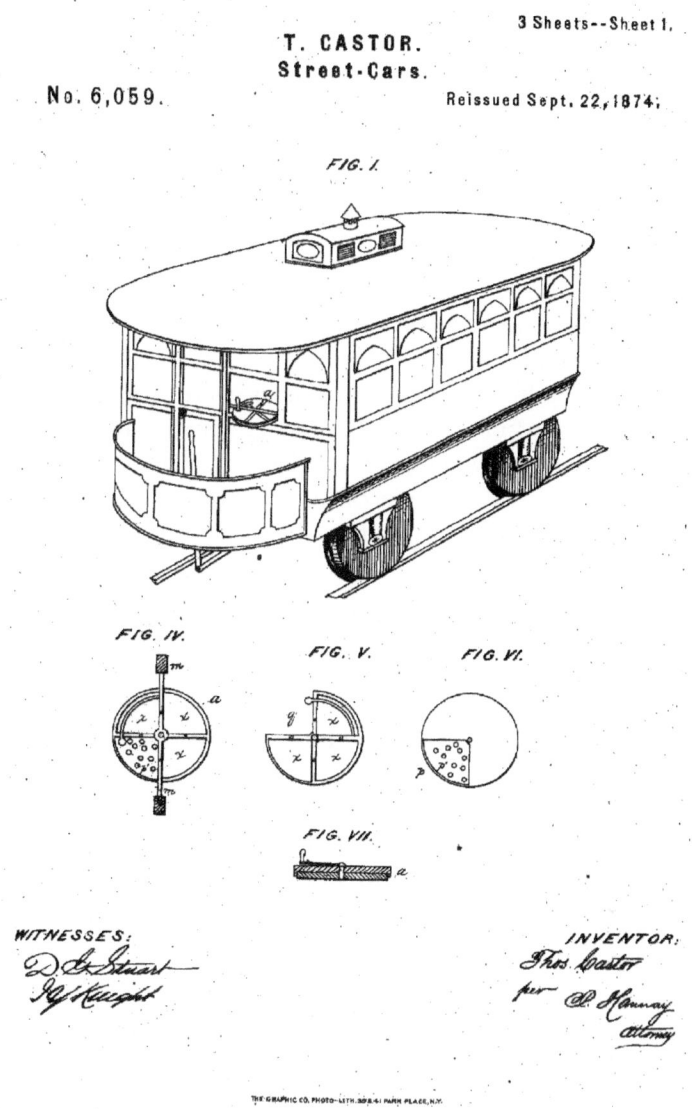

FIGURE 1.4: Patent for a street car money handling mechanism, 1874. Courtesy of the US Patents office.

such systems as are used in stores for facilitating the handling of money and the like. In such systems, for example, a series of tubes run to a central station, generally the cashiers desk, from different parts of the store, and one person or cashier attends to a series of these tubes, removing the money from the cashboxes and returning the proper change, due. Experience has shown that the cashier often inserts the wrong cashbox in the wrong return-tube, so that it may be returned to a point entirely different from that from which it was received. This causes confusion and delay and often loss of money to the proprietors of the store. One of the objects of my present invention is to insure the proper return of the cashboxes to the points from which they were received, and thus avoid all these difficulties.

Anderson's invention, like others based on the original design of the pneumatic tube, demonstrates how patents imagined the infrastructures of money and society in the nineteenth century (Figure 1.5). Pneumatic tubes were not used only to move money between cashiers and the back office; they could as easily distribute notes, memorandums, and objects of small weights within and across buildings. Pneumatic tubes were infrastructural, making money and information comparable. They foregrounded an economy that was right around the corner, where control over the flows of data, over the organization of files and the design of information, was as important as the production of objects for consumption.

Money, Everywhere

Of course, part of this comparability had to do with the growing availability and use of currency in American life. By the end of the century, currency was widely in circulation, facilitating the multiplication of uses and applications of devices that somehow interfaced with money. This is clear in the patents analyzed for this chapter. In addition to devices intended to guarantee the value, accumulation, and mobilization of money, the collection is populated by numerous examples of coin-operated valves, knobs, tellers, and objects that monetized very specific actions. In 1900, for example, the English inventor Frederick John Beaumont patented a coin operated lavatory lock in the United States (US656082A; Beaumont 1900). Earlier, in 1899, Charles Burton of New Haven, Connecticut, filed a design for a prepayment mechanism for gas meters (US647803A; Burton 1900). And, in the same year, Adolph Linick of Chicago patented a coin-controlled medical battery (US641309; Linick 1900).

CULTURES OF MONEY, FOR THE FUTURE

The past is incredibly modern and the records of the United States Patents Office confirm this historical intuition. Money was prolific, inspiring trays, boxes, printing mechanisms, gadgets and a host of devices that—though rarely materialized—revealed a public fascination with coins, bank notes, and other forms of currency.

Yet the collection also shows that, just as money was everywhere, so were its meanings, multiplying across inventors and their imaginations. Money was far

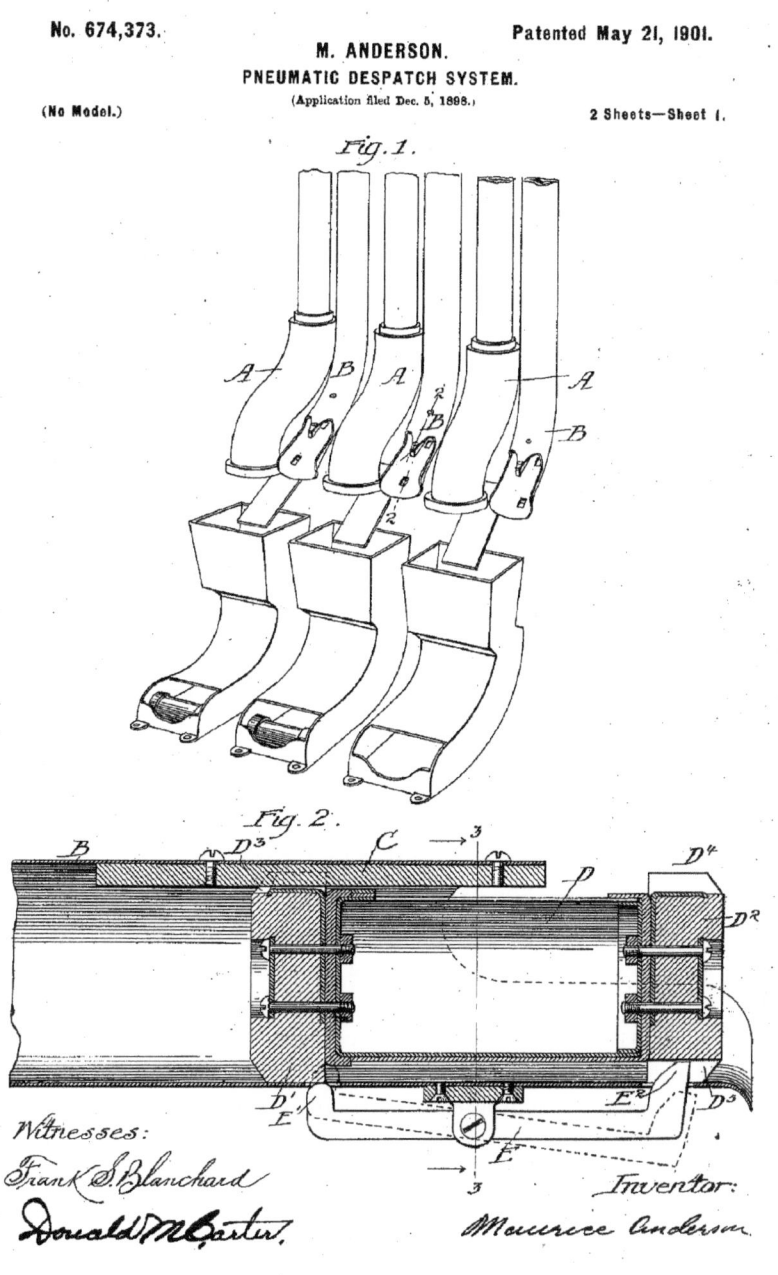

FIGURE 1.5: Patent for a pneumatic tube despatch system, 1901. Courtesy of the US Patents office.

from being a single, stable entity. For some, even the bullionists who saw in coins of silver and gold true value, money could stand as exercises in nation building. Such were the moneyboxes that, through patriotic imagery and crystalized pedagogy, sought to build trust in private institutions (banks) that were meant to play a greater role in the public sphere. For others, money was a problem of design and stabilization—its worth was not problematized by greenbacks and its claims upon the state but by reproducibility, by the relative ease with which someone could counterfeit a bill and with it disturb the true value of currency. For these inventors, design rather than chemistry was the solution, highlighting in intricate ways the symbolic primacy of the state and its chartered National banks in facilitating the flow of money. And for some more, money was a problem of hydraulics, of containment and leaks. For these entrepreneurs, the problem was building a society around money, whether through streetcar architectures that facilitated fare collection, or boxes that made theft particularly difficult, or through tubes and devices that mobilized physical currency across space.

It is interesting, then, that no-one really challenged the inevitability of money. Monetization was not something that was only happening in the homes and streets of the country, but as much in the minds of the makers of things for the future. This proclivity towards monetization was notable in specific devices that made the world commensurate to currency. Consider devices that sought to transform work tasks into discrete bits of quantifiable labor time. Like Thompson's clocks, these devices materialized the disciplines of capitalist work. One such device, filed in 1900 by Franklin Gilson, then presented:

> an apparatus for determining the wage cost of work done in factories and other industrial establishments where it is desirable or necessary to ascertain the cost of time spent by each operative on a certain job or piece of work. In-such establishments operatives of different degrees of skill are employed for various kinds of work, and the wages paid thereto vary accordingly, so that it has hitherto been necessary in figuring the cost of a certain piece of work to determine the length of time spent by each operative thereon and then to calculate the wage cost according to the value of each operatives time. This has required a large clerical force in factories or workshops of any considerable size and has added greatly to the cost of production.
> —US689301A; Gilson 1901

This patent distills the logic of capitalism and its drive towards monetization. Like the clocks that animated E.P. Thompson's (1967) discussion of the emergence of capitalism through the re-orientation of work from tasks to clock time, this little device disciplined both capitalist and worker, parceling out time into fractions that needed little calculation to convert into expenses. But this was precisely the imaginary of money in patents: as currency proliferated in the late nineteenth century, as it opened doors, from safes and lavatories, to vaults and vending devices, it also transformed the value of time, work, and experience in uncanny and unpredictable ways (cf. Zelizer 1994).

This is precisely why these patents matter: they show us a past that imagined and created the economic forms of the present. Gilson's clock is not too different in function from current systems that monetize minor tasks (a popular app called TaskRabbit, for example, allows users to hire local handymen and housekeepers for discrete bits of work, monetizing their labor through matching algorithms) or from devices meant to promote some sort of thrifty economy of time among their users (the app RescueTime also serving as an example that allows clients to automatically track their use of work time throughout the day). And in this, the patents reveal capitalism as a product of imagination (Beckert 2016). Certainly, the designs of moneyboxes, vending machines and other sorts of devices were tied to a dense web of innovators, previous patents, and companies seeking to profit from the market. Yet thinking that these networks determined the future would be incorrect. These patents do not show the technology of the past tracing the paths of the societies of the future, simply because patents are not technologies. They are promises. They are ways of thinking about what could be, rather than what necessarily is. The lessons we learn from them are thus simple: in how people imagined the containment, movement, and use of money, they were imagining the societies to come, the one that they would build through shifted actions and novel institutions (when most of these patents were filed, Silicon Valley was nowhere near San Jose, California). The forms of capitalism that were to come a century later were imagined much earlier. They were made material, if not through success of innovations, at the very least through the anxieties and aspirations of now long-forgotten inventors.

CHAPTER TWO

Money and Its Ideas

Colonial Currencies, Money Illusions

G. BALACHANDRAN

Ideas about money remain bound up with notions about financial specialization and development largely deriving from nineteenth-century conceptions of modernity and progress. While definitions may vary, greater "financialization" tends to be associated with the deepening of capitalism and hence, after a fashion, with pushing the boundaries of "progress." A term of relatively recent currency, "financialization" in rich countries with relatively diversified economies no longer indexes merely the relative size of securities markets or their depth and liquidity. Since the last two decades this bar has risen to denote a capacity for financial innovation, described usually by the presence of actors and institutions engaged in financializing transactions; decomposing, commodifying, and securitizing financial transactions; creating markets and other arbitrage solutions across time, space, asset classes, or riskiness; and laws, regulations, and regulatory environments conducive to these activities (Krippner 2005). The 2008 financial crisis and its aftermath may appear to have stemmed this tide. Doubtless such moments are significant. But there is no sign yet that powerful market incumbents and financial establishments have lost their power to veto any alternative forward-looking trajectories that might emerge, or filter and mold how they might be scaled up, nor apparently of a let up in the "dividuating" effects of "deep financialization" and their social implications (Appadurai 2016).

"Financialization" follows in a trajectory whose usual starting point is the supposed introduction of money and the unsheathing of its irresistible universalizing logic. As Maurer (2006) has noted, even when it advances new insights or challenges conventional distinctions between money in modern and non-modern societies, the social science scholarship on money can seem to conform to "comforting plotline[s] ... about the impact of money on 'traditional' societies and the dehumanizing and homogenizing effects of monetary incursion on ... life in our own society." In consequence "social inquiry provides both an analysis and a folk theory about money in the capitalist West" (Maurer 2006: 17). From the perspective of historical method, the folk theory seems to run even deeper. It can inform philosophical thought relating money as a universal metaphor within overlapping semantic fields in the ancient past. Anthropologists, and even historians, are liable to "uncover" them in the rest of the world, in relations between the "West and the rest," and in tracing their pasts. Consequently, a challenge in exploring nineteenth- and twentieth-century projects bearing on money is to be alert to their continuities and discontinuities without, however, prefiguring the present moment in financial capitalism. Is there a way to think about money in the past without reprising the "classical account of the invention and impact of modern money"? How could one resist the "compulsion to circle back" to the classical account, or avoid unfolding this story as if it were a feature of the money form itself (Maurer 2006: 17)?

Nearly a quarter century ago the editors of a pioneering collection of essays on the political geography of money lamented the neglect of money in social sciences besides economics. They attributed the neglect to a "continuing focus... upon the static and tangible," a scholarly "thrall to... 'productionism'," and a reluctance to engage with emerging forms of power and political economies. The editors were themselves not insensitive, disavowing any suggestion that they and the contributors "subscribe[d] to the view that money ... [was] all-important" or that it should be analyzed "independently of ... the productive economy and its governing institutions" (Corbridge and Thrift 1994: 1–3). Since then research on money has expanded across the disciplines though perhaps not quite in the integrated and integrating way that Corbridge and Thrift might have hoped for, yet for the most part without disturbing the classical account.

While generalizations oversimplify, some broad trends nevertheless seem worth noting. By and large, with notable exceptions especially among Africanists, historical interest in money tends to take its cues from the related economics scholarship. In political, social, and cultural history, perhaps because of assumptions about money's universalizing logic, its supposed "passivity" or "neutrality" (a term with multiple usages including interchangeably with "passivity"), or even its technical nature, money, along with banking and finance, tends rather to be taken for granted, as some kind of a backdrop. This backdrop may occasionally blow on to the stage, but changes in it also quickly recede and stay in the background. As Corbridge and Thrift note, money and politics are not mutually exogenous. As the rich Africanist scholarship dealing with money reveals, histories and pathways of money in individual societies can often be very different. They also illuminate that histories of money cannot only be about money. To assume otherwise, historically wall money off from how it is used, adapted, managed, "reformed" or, for want of a better term, manipulated, or stylize its relations with politics and society by reference to some presumed norms, would simply mean reinforcing money's axiomatic relocation to an abstract and impersonal space characterized by its own internal logics and laws. A likely danger in this for histories of money, particularly in the late-nineteenth and twentieth centuries, is of merely amplifying dominant contemporary voices, notably here influential Western bankers confronting multiplying claims on the state, including by other powerful voices of capital, or battling to stem the democratic tide, and especially after the First World War, insulating the world of money and credit from the pressures and demands of an expanding franchise (Balachandran 1994). The convention of money as a "magic instrument" which, in Engels' words, can "change at will into everything desirable and desired," opens up to two possible perspectives. In one, money crystallizes relations between all commodities in one commodity, in the other ("money fetishism"), commodities become mere reflections of money (Goux 1990: 94). As with commodities, so, in this chapter, with currencies: in regard to them norms of universal money could portend claims to knowledge, monopoly, and power.

Conflicts even in the West over money, monetary standards, monetary policies, currency pegs, exchange rates and so on serve as a caution against the flattened political and material relationships that theoretical accounts of the spread of money generally presuppose. By an interesting but largely unremarked coincidence, universal and voluntarist conceptions of money came to the fore in social theory at almost the same time that states were claiming or asserting sovereign national moneys and competing empires were eyeing and building their own currency spheres. Despite privileging money's universal form, neither functional nor sociological approaches are entirely context-blind when it comes to specifying money or interpreting its relationships. But the contexts tend to be limited, and along with specifications and relationships, stylized to reproduce a fairly narrow telos about money. Functional definitions of money and monetary aggregates (M1 through M4) can seem elastic, even if seemingly narrow, and modular within a vertical telescopic form. Yet they are hardly separable from their short-term operational contexts or the institutional implications of objectives such as enhancing the "effectiveness" of monetary policy. In the functionalist view, the operational utility of the monetary aggregates M1 through M3 or M4 traces an arc of "progress" to which sociological interpretations are not unsusceptible though, in looking beyond functional attributes, they insightfully open out to a wider "liquidity" spectrum of instruments and assets that they may also periodically update (e.g. Bryan and Rafferty 2007; 2016). But the determinism implicit in money's supposed capacity to bridge or commensurate and impersonalize, which depends on its ability to change form, is liable to obscure the conditional and contingent nature of the spectrum, or even its "materiality." This has long been a dark spot in studies of financial markets, sometimes reflected in operational discussions of counterparty risk, accounting procedures, contingent liability provisions and capital adequacy norms for banks, and otherwise only briefly illumined by headline stories of "rogue traders" causing their firms millions of dollars in losses through unhedged trades. Even in financial markets, let alone around its fuzzy edges and in the liminal spaces between financial and other markets, as the 2008 crisis most recently demonstrated and even popular cinema reminds us, power (including in cognate fields of knowledge and regulation) can affect returns to different players on the same asset, not to mention the distribution of net rewards between them. In short, rather than being stable or somehow fixed, the subject–agent–logic relationship is considerably more fluid, changeable, and power-dependent than our economic or sociological understanding of money and securities markets and transactions might allow (Maurer 1999). Nor, despite idealized intuitions nourished, say, by axiomatic beliefs such as the efficient markets hypothesis, can one discount the costs of information and the presence of investor classes, distinguished by their access to information and the capacity to act on it.

Speaking generally, monetary relationships are liable to be framed horizontally (e.g. between sellers and buyers) or in rather simple vertical relationships (e.g. colonial states and tax-subjects). This split is famously reflected in Hart's metaphor of money as a two-sided coin representing the state and the market (Hart 1986). But currencies possess specific markings of time, place, space, power, and political agency (Gilbert 2005). Though there could be considerable room for play in regard to these attributes which can morph and multiply in circulation, currencies may also coexist or substitute for those with other marks of place, space, power, and agency, and have the potential to upend existing patterns of circulation, distribution, and accumulation. Money is implicated furthermore in making states and markets, and may be triangulated with them into something resembling three-dimensional shapes capable of remaining in unstable balance for prolonged periods. State- and empire-making projects are rarely free from disputes between different layers and conceptions of sovereignty, and among entities with competing sovereignty claims or flourishing in their interstices. The nature, use and circulation of monetary media can reflect these dynamics, as the enduring popularity of the Maria Theresa (MT) thalers for certain trades in the Red Sea region till nearly the Second World War illustrates (Kuroda 2007). Even in a former colony such as India—with extensive internal commerce, a network of commercial banks at least in the major cities, a long-established monetary system presided over by a central bank, and a relatively well-developed successor state commanding popular legitimacy—the orderly reform of money, treasury and remittance mechanisms, banking, and public debt inherited from the colonial patchwork of direct and indirect ruling arrangements, ranks as a significant milestone in state-making (Balachandran 1998). Here modernist conceptions of money formed part of the technology of state-building, they were equally a pedagogical project for putatively resistant subjects that bespoke a critique of the colonial capacity for it.

A possible pathway, hence, to moving beyond thin histories of universal money that embed a bias towards abstracting from its processes and effects, might well be to view money as a political project engaging a multiplicity of actors interacting with different motivations and aims, traversing different paths, and capable of producing a range of possible outcomes. Such actors might include states at different levels, merchants and commercial agents, employers, households differentiated by source of income, wealth, and social location, motivation, and so on. In thus attending to the processes and effects of a spreading universalizing money form, it may not only be possible to better address money's differential material effects. We may also thereby be able to explore the broader political and social contexts for monetary ideas and theories whose mutual relationships and interplays have not received the attention they deserve. Restoring money and ideas and theories about money to their respective time and place may thus enable us to attempt stories about money that do not prefigure its unfolding.

This chapter aims to situate dominant late-nineteenth and early-twentieth century sensibilities, claims, and practices about money in the contemporary political–economic contexts of colonialism and the worldwide expansion of accumulation. It accordingly focuses on their programmatic and pedagogical aspects. With the waning of British financial might in the interwar period, the latter began to be channeled through the League of Nations, and through the Bretton-Woods institutions following the waning of formal colonial power from the 1950s. Central banks were established in individual colonies or states as part of this project. But with the reinforcing effects of deregulation and the intensification of financial accumulation on a global scale exposing their inadequacies, an attempt was made in the 1990s to revive colonial-era currency boards. Such attempts proved thankfully short-lived. Meanwhile there has been greater appreciation, particularly since the 1997 East Asian financial crises, that the exponential growth of cross-border financial transactions might necessitate reinforcing some barriers while lowering others. The 2008 financial crisis, which continues to ramify financially, economically as well as politically, underscored such lessons and drew attention to domestic financial concerns. It remains to be seen in these backdrops how ideologies and technologies of "financial inclusion," from micro-finance to mobile moneys, unfold. These latter developments are not covered in this chapter. Hence it is useful to preface here that the professionalization and institutionalization of monetary economics and practices in the twentieth century, which trace back to a longer history of attempting to depoliticize money, their wider circulations through society, and their appropriations into diverse political projects, have all contributed to reinforcing money's ontic appeal even while fissuring its value-scapes in new ways. What they do make clear, however, is that the study of money, including its histories, from the inside, can be usefully complemented with perspectives from its boundaries. That is one of the principal motivations of this chapter.

MONEY ILLUSIONS

Interlaced assertions about the universality of money, the "unnaturalness" of intervention, or about money being above politics mirrored or reinforced political projects to evacuate politics from money and insulate its management from the pressures of expanding representational politics in the nineteenth and twentieth centuries. However, money had always been a subject of contestation, and the argument that it was beyond politics reprises an older argument locating it in the domain of universal natural laws and as such beyond human control. Dominant views about money in nineteenth-century Britain reflected this powerful belief in natural laws subsuming social relations. Joyce Appleby (1976) intriguingly traces this belief to the opposition of landlord and rentier interests, spearheaded by John Locke, to the "devaluationist" solution for a late seventeenth-century coinage crisis in England.

The immediate cause for this crisis was the 1690s appreciation of the silver shilling in relation to gold guineas whose price was not yet stabilized by mint intervention. Shillings disappeared from circulation because they could be more profitably exported to France as bullion, or circulated in mutilated form, their ends clipped to reflect their bullion value. At issue here was whether to reduce the silver content in the shilling as the markets were already doing, and as an expert report commissioned by the privy council recommended in 1695. Doing so would have acknowledged that the shilling's domestic purchasing power did not vest in its metallic content, and by implication that money could be an object of reasoned social intervention. But powerful court officials and "deflationist" rentier interests were against. Throwing his weight behind them, Locke argued that the "value of money was rooted in nature" (Appleby 1976: 45). Gold and silver were held in "unique esteem" and were hence "natural" money and the focus of mankind's desire for wealth. The value of goods was also measured and exchanged according to the "quantity of silver." As shillings were merely "silver in another guise," changing their metallic content would, in modern parlance, render them a "counterfeit signifier" (Goux 1990: 102).

As Appleby notes, Locke's intervention was illogical, failing among other things to account for the free circulation of mutilated shillings or to distinguish between the value of currency in domestic and external transactions. It also rested on "already old-fashioned" premises (Appleby 1976: 52) and disregarded a growing disposition in English commercial society to value money for its uses, i.e. as a transactional medium. According to Dalby Thomas, a "devaluationist," money was merely "a scale to weigh one thing against another." It could, according to another, even be "anything that a Government or Dominion set a mark and value on." Locke's views nevertheless gave cover to the eventual political decision to preserve the silver content of the shilling and refuse mutilated shillings as legal tender. The decision led as expected to severe deflation and transferred wealth from farmers, artisans, and merchants to landlords and bondholders, including through a curious exception permitting the use of clipped shillings at face value for paying taxes and subscribing to royal loans and encouraging landlords and rentiers to mop them up at a discount.

The battle lines and outcomes of the seventeenth-century English coinage controversy would become more familiar over the next two centuries. However, the latter remains of interest because money has never fully been dislodged from the domain of natural law where the 1690s controversy located it. Already in Platonist thought the idea of "legal tender" had introduced a "social standard of value . . . as a rational contrivance," allowing a "common measure of diverse realities," thus helping to produce an opposition between nature and law and mark the "passage from mythology to philosophy" (Goux 1990: 91–92). However, according to Appleby, the English coinage controversy proved a "turning point" (and perhaps equally a feint) in this philosophical tradition for revealing a latent rationale in the "Western concept of nature and the nature of God's created universe . . . for supplanting the laws of man by the laws of impersonal market forces" (Appleby 1976: 44). In short, in being subjected to natural laws, money became an exemplary medium for asserting their primacy for social relations.

By the late nineteenth century, as silver prices dropped, gold began increasingly to be claimed as a transcendental guarantee of value. It also began to embody conceptions of universal money—as Europe colonized new territories and the United States and Japan followed in short order, the gold standard became a lever for financial accumulation on a world scale, presumptions about gold's "stable" price and the system's "automaticity" and capacity for self-correction reinforcing associations with natural law and establishing the market as a force of nature. Besides serving as a vector for naturalizing conceptions of universal money, not unlike other liberal universalist ideas including as a tautology, gold also configured its teleological arc.

At the same time controversies over metallic values and standards had made money too important to ignore for economists such as Alfred Marshall, a founding father of orthodox neoclassical economics, who had begun paying more attention to its short-term real effects while also growing concerned at the monetary consequences of rival European powers accumulating a war chest (Walker 1896). Support for silver and bimetallism revived or intensified monetary controversies fuelled by the 1880s slump particularly in agricultural prices, and set the stage for a spate of national enquiry commissions and international conferences. In the United States they also inspired Frank Baum's memorable 1900 children's classic *The Wonderful Wizard of Oz* (Ritter 1999). Marshall was himself a supporter of bimetallism, and even gold standard Britain witnessed a vigorous campaign against gold and in favor of bimetallism that could only be defeated by administering an irreversible shock to silver prices through closing Indian mints to free silver coinage in 1893 (Green 1988; 1990). The Indian rupee had until then been on silver, and the colony was a large importer of the metal and a mainstay of the silver market. India's abandonment of silver predictably intensified the slump in silver prices and put paid to sporadic attempts since the 1870s to stabilize them through international cooperation. Within the next few years much of the industrial world and large colonies such as India had adopted the gold standard, yet almost immediately afterwards the South African war and the 1907 financial crisis revived concerns about global liquidity (De Cecco 1975; Burke 2002).

In short, by the early twentieth century, a notion of monetary standards as overtly political projects and emerging conceptions of money as a policy variable jostled with more entrenched ideas of universal money, the enchanting of gold which briefly became a stable basis of Western currencies as a universal medium, and the natural laws supposedly governing money. While there was no shortage of debate, and no lack of incoherence and inconsistency among gold advocates, by the late nineteenth century these ideas had recombined into a potent ideological and political mix reaching into new areas to generate or restructure economic, monetary, and financial relationships for worldwide accumulation. Rival financial powers kept a wary eye on outflows and competed to expand the use of their respective gold-based national currencies, yet also colluded to spread the use of gold-backed money, with the US dollar and the Japanese yen following rapidly in the footsteps of the British pound (Conant 1909; Rosenberg 2003; Metzler 2006). Many national and colonial elites collaborated or were complicit in this spread, which however also encountered resistance, crises, retreats, and collapse.

Considerably more disjointed than what simple, naturalizing tautologies about universalizing money convey, the historical evidence affords a possibility to probe the seeming timelessness of ideas about the universality of money, and speculate as to their constitution. Even in commerce or in realms overlapping with trade and exchange, money was merely one form of giving expression to value. Distinguishing currency from money perhaps offers an interesting perspective on the latter's emergence as a universal and singular measure for expressing value. A distinction between money and currency is powerfully intuited in the literature, perhaps nowhere more so than in studies that distinguish qualitative and quantitative values particularly in the presence of multiple currencies (Weiss 2005). As discussed further below, scholars have emphasized the importance of studying "encounters" between different currency and value regimes and attending to the terms on which commensurability is achieved or represented (Guyer 1995; Gregory 1996). But the distinction between currency and money is rarely sustained because at some point the former is collapsed conceptually, albeit often inconsistently, into the latter. The resulting "erasure" of money's "institutional genesis" promotes a view of currencies as relative forms of a "general equivalent" and reinforces the standpoint of power and privilege (Goux 1990: 94–95) implicit in the erasure. Never as singular as the claims made for it, money is also open to interpretations in ways that reveal fissures even in spaces of its modern everyday use (Zelizer 1994). The switch from currency to money can nevertheless encode a subtle translation by which modern ontologies and meanings associated with money colonize the worlds of currencies and historically reconfigure them. "Social inquiry" is complicit in this translation and reconfiguration, to which may also be traced folk theories where currencies discharging limited functions represented a stage in the evolution of money as a fully functional universal medium, and thereafter its local expression; or to paraphrase Marx, in assuming that in "quantitative" and other respects, currency gave limited expression to money's "boundless" qualitative form (Marx 1867: 150). It may therefore be instructive, and help deepen our understanding of money in the nineteenth and twentieth centuries, to attempt to apprehend currencies on their own terms and the terms of their translation into the universal form of money.

In the nineteenth century the dialectical affirmation of universalism as an abstract concept and of money as its expression in the sphere of exchange, could ironically be performed in the reverse and, to paraphrase Michael O'Malley (1994b) on freedom and identity, as a "historical movement" from an "essentialized" universal to an "idealized" universalism. In the parallel instance of money, the former meant building on the historically established use of precious metals, particularly gold, as a concrete universal medium. In many places silver found greater acceptance than gold. While both metals were valued and accepted or acquired for many reasons, not solely for their use as currency, silver had more diversified uses than gold. Whether this "naturally" made gold rather than silver the universal, late nineteenth-century money form as Kuroda (2009) appears to imply, or such a perception of "nature" reflected anxieties about accumulation and modern state-making in the West given the greater difficulty imperial states faced in controlling the more decentralized silver market, would seem moot. In the end the interruption that even gold's "non-monetary" uses represented for its role as a universal standard, or their potential for checking the expansion of trade and accumulation, would open up perspectives for envisaging "money" as an abstract and universal medium while at the same time loosening its link with precious metals. In his 1913 monograph on Indian currency John Maynard Keynes, Marshall's student who started his professional career as a civil servant at the India Office, sought to make just such a case in his monograph defending the currency system his former colleagues had put in place for the colony since the 1890s, and upbraiding its critics (Keynes 1971). In emphasizing the desirability of loosening the tie between gold and money, Keynes made the outcome and its effects appear symmetrical between Britain and India. But the political and cultural legacies of colonial rule made them unavoidably asymmetrical, even somewhat coercive (De Cecco 1975). These asymmetries intensified and became more visible and unmistakeable during and after the First World War because of credit-fueled monetary expansion in several countries including Britain, they also grew more complicated and convoluted thanks to the differential effects of this expansion on the main protagonists in the interwar international monetary system (Brown 1929; Balachandran 1996). One upshot, nevertheless, was the severance of domestic convertibility obligations between currencies and gold during the interwar years. From the late 1960s, a relentless decade-long expansion of foreign claims on the United States similarly brought the external convertibility of the US dollar, which had anchored the post-1945 gold-exchange standard, to a gradual close.

The idea of universal money was not new, it was well enough historicized by the nineteenth century to draw from the wellsprings of Hellenic thought where, according to Goux's interpretation of the philosophical influences on Marx's reflections on money, universal money was sacralized in "solidarity with the deity," with money and God being "universal equivalents" respectively of commodities and subjects, with the "same value of unification and transcendence" (Goux 1990: 91). Consider here the parallels with the Hegelian idea of the state, the universal spirit, and divine providence (Dodd 2014: 51). Nor was any new financial innovation needed to normalize the idea, only a suitable political and economic climate. On the contrary, in addition to gold and silver, token currency, deposit certificates or other transferable claims such as bills, the monetization of public and private debt—none of these were new or nineteenth century. Yet, at the same time, again as Africanist critiques of 1960s ideas of a "currency revolution" powerfully show, neither precious metals nor abstract conceptions of universal money swept away everything before them to clear the decks for accumulation on a world scale (Guyer 1995). Precious metals were not equally valued everywhere. As so many historical and anthropological studies show, and as partly elaborated in the next section, local value norms and money forms—multiple currencies, transaction-specific currencies, currencies differing in ritual status or use, etc.—were widespread and resisted permanent banishment until well into the twentieth century. Their imaginative potential endures strongly to this day.

Hence, despite the tautology and the technologies, the idea of abstract, universal money and its practical realization needed a lot of work. Much of it is continuous and ongoing. There is also the often-unspoken issue of whose universal claims, subjectivities, and agency abstract conceptions of money and their concrete representations embodied and affirmed. Unlike the common belief and assumptions inherent also in their critiques, of Europe or the West as the abode of the universal spirit in the nineteenth century, this could be a matter of conflict even within the West. Such conflicts were evoked not only in the conventional "battle of the standards" that raged through Europe and the United States for nearly three decades following Germany's adoption of the gold standard in 1871, and in the economic, financial, and moral debates over the virtues of gold, silver, monometallic standards, or bimetallism during this period. In Reconstruction-era United States, for example, the basis for claims and counter-claims about the rights of African-Americans to freedom and civic-political citizenship, i.e. "intrinsic" qualities *versus* legal fiat, also resonated through claims and counter-claims about the proper form of money, i.e. gold *versus* greenbacks. White Southerners rejected as "counterfeit" both greenbacks, which promised liberated slaves "market freedom," and the latter's "coining" as free citizens (O'Malley 1994a). As with freedom and rights (see also Holt 1991), so with money, projects to democratize the idea of the "universal" subject or object provoked fears and anxieties over shifting values, unstable standards, and "counterfeit" claim(ant)s. Negotiations to stabilize standards and relative values were framed around such fears and anxieties. Even though not all protagonists based their arguments on natural law or regarded money as beyond political contestation, such negotiations nevertheless reinforced the ideas of money as an absolute and universal medium.

Technical disquisitions about money and the organized practices of government associated with them emerged in this cognitive shadow and arguably helped advance it. They helped reinforce taboos around speaking politically about money, and to reproduce them through histories of modern monetary thought and sociologies of knowledge and expertise. The disposition to view money as being beyond politics tends also to be sustained by contextually fluid meanings of what actually constitutes "politics" in relation to money. Hence the divorce between money and politics was and remains uneven, asymmetric, and never total. For instance, money never ceased to be deployed for political projects as the example most recently of the euro illustrates. The political perspectives implicit in Keynes's 1913 monograph became operative policy in India over the next three decades (Balachandran 1996), with Keynes himself taking the lead, six years later in 1919 at the height of Britain's financial crisis after the First World War, to elaborate the policy implications of his essay on the rupee and the political advantages of presenting them in similar discursive frames (Balachandran 1993). The French opposition to the sterling standard in the late 1920s and to the dollar's global role in the mid-1960s present other illuminating exceptions that prove the rule, not least as few thought the French opposition was anything but political (Balachandran 2008). The use of money to political ends, however, appears to have done little to disturb the pragmatic disposition towards viewing its management, and hence money's intrinsic nature, if not beyond politics, at least as being guided by shared norms, principles, or interests. One reason for this could be that orthodox technical and technocratic arguments about money, markets, monetary policy, the latter's effectiveness and so on, share more than a passing kinship with the normative beliefs of practical bankers. Not coincidentally, they also render them palatable to governments dependent on popular support but reliant on bankers to manage, market, or hold their loans, and generally preserve a stable monetary and fiscal environment. Many heterodox discourses share the main orthodox premises while differing in their prescriptions. Presumptions about the universal and universalizing features of money and its seamless spread do not require a large imaginative or intellectual leap against this backdrop.

COLONIAL CURRENCIES AND PERSPECTIVES

In treading lightly around power, theories and associated histories of money dislocate it from broader processes including broader economic processes. In doing so, they stylize our understanding of how currencies function, and gloss over their pathways and trajectories of use and circulation. In this narrow, stylized view, after money has somehow made an appearance, attention is quickly shifted to the spread of "modern" currency issued by a "modern" state. "Modern" here usually denotes currencies issued by states, especially states that have survived, as in rapid steps the telos of money and statehood are braided and mutually naturalized through the figure of the sovereign of whose power, currency—its issue, circulation, value, availability, and so on—represents a symbol, test, and measure. In this world there is one currency, issued or authorized by the state which, once established, expands to fulfil all the roles that money is supposed to play. Historically, grand projects like the nation-state have supplied the dreamscapes and legitimacy for instituting single currencies in societies characterized by a plurality of money forms, value scales, and practices. Money and language, as Nigel Dodd notes, evoke frequent comparisons (Dodd 2014: 35). This comparison is usually made in the abstract, for example of both money and language as "semiotic intermediaries ... in their respective domains of exchange" (Shell 2005: 85). But Rousseau's remark on the similarities between money and language as social bonds, interestingly in an idiom that also naturalized their singular forms (Dodd 2014: 31), speaks to language in its specific, or relative form. Yoked to sovereignty, stories about currency become a story about money and the state. Yoked to the territorial nation-state currency becomes, like the nation-state or its supposed proto-form, the colony, the singular local expression of a universal form (Helleiner 2003a).

Hence, not surprisingly, since especially the late nineteenth century, the introduction of new currencies has formed part of programs of "monetary reform." In countries and colonies across Africa, Asia, Latin America and the Caribbean, and the Pacific, monetary reform was in turn part of wider projects to "reform" state and society—i.e. plans to establish "modern" states, which included blueprints for rudimentary banks and financial institutions to facilitate the business of the state, and draw them into emerging international patterns of division of labor and specialization as producers and exporters of agricultural commodities and minerals. Overseas borrowing represented a dimension of such "governance reforms" in present-day parlance, with particularly profound consequences for monetary and banking institutions. Monetary and governance reform projects drew on external expertise and assistance—foreign advisers ("money doctors"), overseas banks, metropolitan governments or other foreign states, and since the 1920s, international organizations such as the League of Nations, and after the Second World War, the Bretton-Woods institutions (Balachandran 1996, 2008; Flandreau 2003; Rosenberg 2003; Clavin and Wessels 2004). They were technical fixes guaranteed to work; if they failed, it was usually because local political elites were either "corrupt" or had failed to educate the people about their advantages.

The likeness between money and language with respect to nation or state can extend to how they relate to their respective local forms and usages. In the "summer of 1916 or 1917" D.D. Kosambi, the renowned historian of ancient India and numismatist, recalled seeing "in the till of a single village shop in Goa," Portuguese and British Indian coins, Australian half-crowns, English shillings, American cents, "in a word the small change of almost all the world." They circulated as coins "equivalent to the nearest Indian coin in appearance and weight" and relieved wartime currency shortages. The "unification" of the rupee by the East India company in 1835 remained fraught and conditional for the better part of a century, with many indigenous rulers continuing to issue currencies affirming their own authority under the queen's overall sovereignty (Siddiqi 1981; Dreyell and Frykenberg 1982). Yet colonial officials as well as the emerging Indian intelligentsia tended to ignore them, and other indigenous currency practices, as inconsequential or residual. Not surprisingly Kosambi himself remarked, somewhat contradictorily, that the variety—which he attributed to Goan seafarers employed on Western merchant vessels—was "unusual for India," but not the "procedure," which he described as "typically Indian." Cowries, he recalled likewise, were in use as small change "in so important a centre as Poona [now Pune]" during the early years of the First World War (Kosambi 1981: 41). In 1901 their use seems, in fact, to have been widespread enough for Ugandan colonial officials to consider exporting cowries to India as a somewhat paradoxical outcome of their efforts to popularize Indian copper pice in their colony (Pallaver 2015: 484).

We know too little as yet about Indian currencies in the late nineteenth and early twentieth centuries. However, Kosambi's village shop was not untypical of the world of currencies until even half a century ago in many parts of the world (Hughes 1978; Swanepoel 2015). There is a rich body of scholarly research on local currencies and their interactions with currencies introduced by various colonial or other trading powers in the nineteenth and twentieth centuries, and the accompanying changes to trade, labor relations, and taxation (see Pallaver 2015 for an introductory survey). Much of this literature deals with colonial societies, a context relevant to this essay's focus on continuities between nineteenth- and twentieth-century colonial projects and other projects to reorder the world's money.

Currencies circulated in contexts (cultural, material, political, social, ritual) so dense and complex that no single work can unpack them. Besides, generalizations can be risky or seem banal given differences in contexts, perspectives, and methods between individual studies. A few points nevertheless seem clear. The idea of money and market exchange replacing barter is at best of conceptual expository value in undergraduate economics textbooks; and while Jane Guyer's challenge to work with multiplicity to reconsider "questions of equivalence, difference, and commensuration" (Guyer 2004: 20–21) remains relevant, historians studying multiple currencies today are less likely than before to frame them through simple structural binaries. Most societies used multiple currencies, their relative importance varying according to their contexts of use, such as ritual (i.e. the ritual preference, though not unvarying, for one currency to others at a point in time); the nature of transactions (e.g. ceremonial or gift transactions); the types of goods bought or sold; the nature of the trade (distance, value, volume, e.g. wholesale *versus* retail, and size and social contexts for retail transactions), and who mainly participated; payment of wages, payments to government departments (e.g. taxes, customs payments); nature of the function performed (e.g. medium of exchange, store of value, or unit of account); and so on. Multiplicity could reflect practical necessities such as for subsidiary coinage. Even any seeming decline in multiplicity may be very gradual or interrupted—cowries as we saw above could make a comeback during periods of currency shortages or crises, as also they did in the interwar depression (Johnson 1970: 352). Certain temporal and spatial features such as seasonality in currency demand or trading linkages may generate a multiplicity of paired, sequential interfaces partaking of the character of "complementary currency circuits" (Kuroda 2008), or overlapping "circulatory loops" (Mwangi 2001). Multiple currencies and currency circuits may have no stable anchor, and firms and merchants may keep accounts in imaginary moneys bearing no necessary relationship with government-issued currency (Kuroda 2008).

The idea of a "currency revolution" in which "modern" state money suppressed and replaced "primitive" customary currencies commands few adherents today. Despite its many seeming "infirmities" to the modern eye, multiple currencies did not everywhere yield, or yield easily or equally, to currencies issued by the territorial sovereign. Instead the latter might simply become one currency among several, existing alongside them, and serving some uses or fulfilling parallel functions such as a unit of account (Eagleton mimeo; Eagleton 2019 forthcoming). To the extent currencies served a "special purpose," sovereign territorial money was as likely as the other currencies, if not more, to serve as "special purpose money" (Swanepoel 2015). Currency preferences could also vary according to gender, and the acceptability of sovereign territorial money conditioned by their bearing for household or marketplace relations.

Until a generation ago, currency was a problem of administration in the colonies, with states, colonial officials, and settler interests central to its histories (Kaminsky 1980; Nelson 1987; Maxon 1989). While administrative concerns are naturally enough not absent, recent studies devote more attention to how colonial currency projects worked or failed—the colonial writ with regard to currency sometimes failed to extend even to its own employees—and to resistance, adaptations, negotiations and compromises through which they unfolded (Mwangi 2001; Pallaver 2015; Swanepoel 2015; Eagleton mimeo). Projects to introduce unique, sovereign territorial currencies in plural currency settings could hence be complex and prolonged, necessitating several intermediary stages and negotiations each step of the way with different affected groups and interests who were not merely passive or reactive, but who could also drive the process.

Despite some notable recent advances (Pallaver 2015; Eagleton mimeo) our knowledge, for want of a better term, of colonial "currency transitions" (Swanepoel 2015), remains patchy. The existing literature nevertheless highlights some interesting puzzles that seem to justify further speculation with reference to the material, discursive, and political realization of the project of universal money.

The idea of money is bound up with the idea of spreading market relations. As evinced by liberal, colonial, and neoliberal projects to reconfigure them internally and externally, markets are not alike or boundless. As the example most recently of the euro illustrates, currency is also a means to reconfigure markets. By realigning credit and affecting relative financing costs, currency "unification" could hold implications for the scale and nature of competitive businesses. The relative decline of Indian merchant houses in external trade had been underway before the East India Company's introduction of a uniform silver rupee in 1835, which, along with the abolition in the same year of some tolls on internal trade, is regarded as an important milestone in unifying the Indian market in India (Siddiqi 1981). As noted above, rupee unification was rather more prolonged than one may conclude from quantitative indicators. Nevertheless, a unified rupee, together with the creation of something like a uniform remittance system by the middle of the nineteenth century, is argued to have facilitated the expansion of European trading houses into the interior and led to a relative decline in native bill broking and banking. This is in interesting contrast to China where a decentralized monetary system characterized by privately managed assaying and competing "money shops" is said to have helped restrict the participation of European firms in trade with the interior (Ray 1995: 486).

Though the project of unifying currency and markets often went hand in hand, and the resulting hierarchical ordering of both currencies and markets is widely acknowledged, they continue to be studied as parallel structures with some links, rather than as interlaced relationships with conceptual kinships warranting connected historical inquiry. In the nature of things neither money nor markets can be completely universal or unified. Breaks, ruptures, and discontinuities remain (or as with financial markets, explored for arbitrage), as we also know from the continuous redrawing and displacement of boundaries with respect to norms, laws, institutions, their related knowledge, epistemes, and so on, under the sign of the "global." It could be useful for histories of money to trace and explain these displacements in their specific contexts, and the boundaries and landscapes they make. Where are the new breaches and boundaries, why or how did they form, what keeps them there, how stable are they, how do they affect incumbents and new entrants, who gains, who loses, what adaptations have agents to make, how costly and what are their consequences, what becomes of the norms, laws, practices, institutions, and knowledge or skills that are displaced—such questions, though somewhat adjacent to cultural historians' and anthropologists' preoccupations with currency, might still be usefully addressed to currency and other similar projects making outsize global or universal claims. Historical answers to them could depend, among other factors, on the level of detail of the study, the sources used—for example records of rival colonial powers and indigenous or incumbent merchant groups versus those of the colonial state and colonial settler or commercial interests records—and its temporal and spatial frame.

There are interesting echoes of such questions in recent historical studies of colonial currencies. The two main illustrations cited here share common features, including their colonial East African contexts, use of multiple currencies among them another colonial currency namely the Indian rupee, and colonial efforts to standardize currency and subsidiary coinage. They also, however, offer some complementary emphases. Pallaver's study (2015) of colonial Uganda's official adoption of the Indian rupee in 1895 focusses on users of existing and new currencies and currency interfaces between rulers and subjects. Thanks to Indian merchants, the rupee had for several decades been absorbed into fluid geographies of circulation and scales of value (Mwangi 2001). Its official status further pluralized currencies and associated regimes of value, cowries for instance retaining a role as the only legitimate currency for paying market taxes, as unit of account for bride wealth, and for use in marriage ceremonies (Pallaver 2015: 487–90): they and other "independent 'non-cash' currencies" were "islands of economic liberty" from colonial rule (Mwangi 2001: 777). Decimal cowrie accounting conventions also modified fractional rupee coinage. Originally divided into sixty-four pice, the Indian rupee in Uganda was divided despite settler opposition into a hundred cents, each cent worth ten shells, and a cowrie worth a tenth of a cent. Thus, the new system ended up "mirroring" the cowrie system, and cowries continued to circulate in the absence of suitable low-denomination substitutes (Pallaver 2015: 497–98).

Another layer of negotiations, and a further set of questions, latent in this Ugandan story is elaborated in Eagleton's pioneering account of the rupee's introduction in Zanzibar (Eagleton mimeo). Despite the rupee's circulation in pre-colonial Uganda, its adoption as official currency instead of the smaller denomination Egyptian coinage, as local officials had proposed, carried the risk of orienting Uganda's trade towards the Indian Ocean at the expense of more established ties with the north and the Sudan (Pallaver 2015: 480–81). Subsequent discussions over subsidiary coinage reveal tensions among Indian commercial interests who wanted to persist with the pice (perhaps because they profited from importing, transporting, and exchanging them for cowries), British settler interests who preferred the sovereign and direct commercial ties with the mother country, and the colonial government which, in decimalizing the rupee, effectively stabilized the cowrie–cent conversion rate even if it meant prolonging the former's use (Pallaver 2015: 494–6).

In East Africa, the Indian rupee may have intertwined and advanced the colonial project and Indian commercial interests (Mwangi 2001). But Indian merchants in the region were not everywhere, nor had they always been, in favor of the rupee's circulation. Despite Zanzibar's close historical association with Indian trade and serving as a bridgehead for its penetration of East Africa, the Indian rupee did not make an appearance there until the 1860s (Eagleton mimeo). The standard legal tender until the late-1860s was the MT thaler, which circulated alongside non-legal tender such as French five-franc pieces and Spanish dollars whose fluctuating values in relation to the MT thaler was a profitable mainstay of the "shroffing" (i.e. money-changing) business dominated by Indian merchants. The latter had consequently no interest either in fixed rates of conversion between these currencies or in promoting a new currency. It was only when the American civil war disrupted monetary remittances to Zanzibar and the associated trades that they acquiesced in stable conversion rates, and shortly afterwards to the introduction of the silver Indian rupee whose use, initially boosted by its possibly accidental overvaluation *vis-à-vis* the MT thaler and the British sovereign, expanded on the back of the post-1871 fall in silver prices. With Indian trade also expanding rapidly, by 1878 the Indian rupee had taken over as Zanzibar's main currency and begun to spread its presence along the coast (Eagleton mimeo).

One of the arguments in favor of making the rupee the official currency in East Africa was that its trade with India would act as an automatic currency stabilizer. As already noted, white settlers with direct commercial ties to Britain were unhappy with this arrangement. They got their chance when the rupee's appreciation after the First World War *vis-à-vis* the floating sterling inflicted exchange losses on settlers and raised ominous doubts about the solidity of pre-war colonial and racial hierarchies, particularly in East Africa (Maxon 1989; Mwangi 2001). Unlike at the time of its first introduction in Zanzibar, the Indian rupee was a token currency for the larger part of its career as East Africa's official currency. On the surface, Zanzibar, Uganda, and East Africa's currency "transition" of nearly five decades, from partially convertible local commodity currencies to the token but convertible Indian rupee, and eventually to a currency linked directly to the pound sterling, may seem to trace a story of monetary "progress." But it is a story driven by contending interests attempting to protect or displace entrenched positions in the face of challenges—the American civil war, fall in silver prices, the wartime and post-war depreciation of the pound sterling—that were largely in themselves open-ended or indeterminate in nature and impact. What this history nevertheless discloses is a conflict over rents between different layers of intermediation. Such conflicts may be seen during the course of the Indian rupee's introduction in Zanzibar, between the island's moneychangers and its European trading interests (also see Eagleton 2019 forthcoming). We may suspect a similar conflict in the wake of the post-war instability of the pound sterling between British settler interests wishing to remit funds home and Bombay-based intermediaries through whom they may have been obliged to transact their remittance business.

In a conventional, neoclassical view such rents represent barriers to efficiency—wasteful transaction costs causing uncertainty, restricting markets, reducing scales, and raising prices. But eliminating intermediary layers may not arguably reduce as much as redistribute rents, channeling them upwards through reshaped geographies of intermediation that substitute vertical alignments and singular conceptions of value for more horizontal or layered arrangements open to plural normative, value, and distributive registers. Or put simply, rather than eliminating intermediary layers, one consequence of monetary "transitions" may be to interpose or substitute new layers and transfer rents from small, local intermediaries to large Western or other "modern" banks and agency houses, which besides being more amenable to political and bureaucratic regulation, were less likely to draw colonial or successor states into complex cultural negotiations with indigenous agents and institutions. An apt albeit inexact analogy is suggested by the recent history of *hawala* trades through which for many decades East African and Asian laboring migrants in West Asia remitted their earnings home. *Hawala* trades had long survived attempts at uncoordinated interdiction by individual states in the region aspiring to control their external transactions. But with *hawala* networks forced to fold up or go underground as a consequence of the US-led, UN-coordinated campaign to regulate cross-border remittances in the aftermath of September 2001, a large part of this remittance business passed into the hands of mainly Western corporate entities. Despite the latter incorporating some aspects of *hawala* business models (such as employing nonspecialized retail agents), there were no palpable cost or efficiency gains, only presumably a renegotiation of margins and redistribution of revenues. (However, new technologies to which these changes unfolded may yet qualify this generalization while making such comparisons moot.) We may hypothesize similar processes in late nineteenth- and early twentieth-century projects for reorganizing currency and exchange arrangements, i.e. the substitution of "modern" Western intermediaries for local brokerage institutions and informal hedging mechanisms that indigenous players in multiple currency markets could, in particular, employ to their relative advantage. Hence normative pronouncements about efficiency, or even legality, as evinced for instance in debates in late nineteenth-century India over legitimate "speculation" *versus* illegal "gambling" in raw jute futures (Birla 2008) may, in fact, reflect business competition or conflicts over commissions and rents. In the case of currencies and money, such conflicts may entail competition between rival upstream or downstream businesses embedded in different geographies of commerce and profit. Conventional neoclassical accounts of monetary or banking "transitions" acknowledge their "disintermediating" effects. But the vocabulary of "disintermediation" may gloss over indigenous competitors as agile and adaptable competitors in liberal narratives of monetary progress, while perhaps reconfiguring them as subordinate borrowers or lending agents of Western banks.

CONCLUSION (AND REPRISE OF A PROLOGUE)

Despite a large body of work challenging the underlying premise, the story of money unfolds as a story of progress itself. Money has also at various times served, and continues oftentimes to serve, as an ideological and political Trojan for the supposed primacy of "natural laws" acting independently of human agency, when not immune to it. Of course, economic policy-makers know differently; the enormous investments societies make to "manage" money could hardly otherwise be justified. Yet money retains a quite unique capacity to tap into anxieties both about "progress" and "natural laws," and to mobilize them, often in combination, to blunt transformative agendas, not least with respect to itself. The enduring power of monetary policy, and the subordination of other potential means of intervention in a modern economy including fiscal policies (with the possible exception of tax-cuts) to the former's symbiotic relationship with debt markets, speaks also to money's transformation into a dissolving myth to which historical and cultural accounts are no less susceptible.

It is not altogether surprising, therefore, that except perhaps perversely through neglect, money has for the greater part eluded decentering with respect to many of its supposed relationships. When it comes to money, agency tends to be centralized by assumption, and structures tend to be unitary: for instance, money's idealized circuits invariably originate and come to rest in the metropole, be they imperial, colonial, national, or global. This chapter has drawn on a rich body of anthropological and historical work, most of it interestingly about Africa, to attempt a more contextual and granular story of money, and of nineteenth- and twentieth-century ideas about it. Even a selective reading suggests that colonies and other conventionally marginal locations for accounts of modern moneys provide illuminating standpoints for thinking about them.

Money commands rent, though we may not think that is its whole point. The spread of money and related forms of debt was spurred by states and entrepreneurs cooperating to expand their circulation and competing among themselves to appropriate their returns, further in doing so evincing contestations over value and accumulation. Collisions between European accumulation paths and colonial value relationships can help uncover nexuses between accumulation and the spread of modern moneys, as well as the ideational and discursive shifts that occurred around ideas about money in the nineteenth and twentieth centuries. The idea of money as a form of debt is not new. But its growing nineteenth-century ubiquity demanded splitting money from other forms of debt in ways that naturalized it as a bearer of value. To this may also be traced the conjoint origins of modern theories of money and theories of finance, and the endogenous categories and conceptual and institutional structures needed to enable capital to move freely between different markets and types of debt.

Retracing ideas about money thus involves, at one level, retracing contestations over wider notions of debt, risk, categories of debtors and creditors—e.g. states disposing of varying degrees of power, banks, other agents including "vernacular" intermediaries, "retail" lenders, borrowers, savers, other users of money—and their respective rights and liabilities. Such contestations were power-laden and inseparable from conflicts over accumulation even in colonial-type settings where they might be masked by postulations of economies in static equilibrium (homeostasis).

This homeostasis was sustained by currency board-type arrangements, supplemented at times by seasonal issues of fiduciary currency, and in the accumulation of colonial balances in the metropole. This seeming dualism might gloss conflicts, actual or potential, over margins and profits from colonial commerce. Hence while the homeostasis may have been a cause for lament, indigenous commercial and entrepreneurial agency could not also be permitted to destabilize it, howsoever briefly, particularly if it posed a risk to colonial commerce. (This is an important reason why major world crises such as wars and depressions have been so crucial to colonial economic and political histories.) Control over colonial "liquidity" was key to managing such conflicts. They were consequently intrinsic to ideas and discourses about money, its forms, lives and meanings, and projects to "reform" money without ceding colonial-style control over break-out pathways from the homeostasis.

CHAPTER THREE

Money, Ritual, and Religion

Reason, Race, and the Re-Enchantment of the World

BILL MAURER

Examining the relationship between money and religion in the Age of Empire, one feels as Michel Foucault (1978) must have done when, in attempting to understand the repression of sexuality in the Victorian era he found everywhere a profusion of discourse on the subject. It was not that the Victorians could not bear sex; it was that they could not stop talking about it. So, too, with money and religion—or, to be more precise, the separation of the two into distinct domains and the assertion, common to nineteenth-century social theory, that the value of money had usurped the values of the religious life, and that industrialization had ushered in a progressive march toward secularization.

The consensus of nineteenth-century social theorists on the relationship between religion and money was straightforward. The characteristic elements of nineteenth-century political economy—first, industrial-style agriculture based on slave labor in some parts of the world and indenture in others, then growing industrialization and international trade, and the rise by the end of the century of a consumer market—elevated the drive to seek pecuniary gain over all else. Money was ascendant. Religion, sidelined. "Confined more and more to Sunday and then to Sunday morning, religion became for many more a social affair than a moving experience," wrote historian Samuel P. Hays of the period between 1885 and the First World War (Hays 1957: 72). Spurred on by the Protestant work ethic, the foundations of which were laid in the period after the Reformation and given new political life in the Enlightenment revolutions' proclamations of liberty, equality and property, capitalist calculation infused social life. Objectification, rationalization, bureaucratization, instrumental rationality, scientific reason—and, Karl Marx would add, the wage labor system—all served, together, to remake civilization. As Max Weber famously declared the world was thereby disenchanted. "[T]he ultimate and most sublime values," he wrote, "have retreated from public life" (Weber 2009 [1919]: 155).

EMANCIPATION FROM RELIGION OR SUBORDINATION TO THE MARKET AND THE SECULAR STATE

In this light we can consider Marx's reflections on Jewish emancipation—which had been taking place throughout the world, from the Ottoman Empire in 1839 to England in 1858, and would continue into the twentieth century. Challenging the very idea that Jews could be politically emancipated as Jews, rather than as the generic human atoms of liberal theory, stripped of all identity other than their status as civic persons, Marx wrote: "Because you can be emancipated politically without renouncing Judaism completely and incontrovertibly, *political emancipation* itself is not *human* emancipation" (Marx 1844). Human emancipation, true freedom, would entail freedom from the state and civil society as Marx saw them coming into being after the Enlightenment, which presupposed the relations of private property. Political emancipation of the Jew as Jew would simply extend to Jews these relations—allowing them to be as subordinate as anyone else to capitalism, private property and the state. Satirizing while echoing virulent European anti-Semitism, Marx chastised those who believed the political emancipation of a religious minority would change the inequality that the proponents of emancipation had sought to abolish. He believed, rather, it would merely extend new, capitalist forms of inequality to the Jews themselves. Equating the Jew to the avaricious capitalist, Marx prefigured his later calls for a workers' revolution:

> What is the secular basis of Judaism? *Practical* need, *self-interest*. What is the worldly religion of the Jew? *Huckstering*. What is his worldly God? *Money*. Very well then! Emancipation from *huckstering* and *money*, consequently from practical, real Judaism, would be the self-emancipation of our time.
> —Marx 1844

In other words, true emancipation would only come from the emancipation of the workers—Jew and Gentile alike—from money. The Jew therefore could not be truly emancipated without this broader, human emancipation from capitalism, the self-interested, amoral market relations Marx saw as dominating all else.

Emile Durkheim, the father of sociology and of the social scientific study of religion, similarly viewed the era in terms of the decline of religion in the face of the amoral market:

> [W]e are going through a stage of transition and moral mediocrity. The great things of the past which filled our fathers with enthusiasm do not excite the same ardour in us, either because they have come into common usage to such an extent that we are unconscious of them, or else because they no longer answer to our actual aspirations; but as yet there is nothing to replace them.
> —Durkheim 1912: 427

Except if it lay in science, and if society could be brought into line with science itself as a site for that ardor. Insofar as religious thought is a system of sorting and classifying nature, existence, and the social order, Durkheim argued, "scientific thought is only a more perfect form of religious thought" (Durkheim 1912: 429). "Thus," he wrote, "it seems natural that the second should progressively retire before the first, as this becomes better fitted to perform the task" (Durkheim 1912: 429). He continued:

> And there is no doubt that this regression has taken place in the course of history. Having left religion, science tends to substitute itself for this latter in all that which concerns the cognitive and intellectual functions. Christianity has already definitely consecrated this substitution in the order of material things.

Thus even Durkheim's plea to his contemporaries to acknowledge that religion rests on people's real experiences and contains truths, far from being an argument for its transcendence, instead was meant to prove its social character, and thus to make a case for the notion of society itself as the site for our moral development. This had not yet happened, however, owing to the disruption of capitalism: there had not yet been the rise of a social feeling to take the place of the religious one. The result was anomie. Durkheim was not arguing for the return of religion, but rather for the rise of a science that would understand and guide society, which he understood to be an integrated, functional whole capable of serving individual and collective well-being.

The consolidation of capitalism, the rise of self-interest above all other values, the march of reason and one must add the incredible impact of the work of Charles Darwin on science and society: the age of empire, from 1820–1920, was also a vastly expanded world. European colonization and conquest of much of the planet by the nineteenth century's close meant that learned discussions of both religion and money would incorporate examples from the "civilized" and "barbarous" lands alike. Take Georg Simmel's attempt to deduce a concept of religion "in that which is common alike to the religion of Christians and South Sea islanders, to Buddhism and Mexican idolatry" (Simmel 1905: 359). Or William Stanley Jevons' account of a French opera singer in the Solomon Islands who received in payment "three pigs, twenty-three turkeys, forty-four chickens, five thousand cocoa-nuts, besides considerable quantities of bananas, lemons, and oranges" (Jevons 1896: 1). Darwin's evolutionary theory and its social Darwinist offspring attempted to place such diversity in hierarchical trees and sometimes distinct lineages, propelling both a quest for origins of all manner of social formations and phenomena from marriage to money, as well as scientific racism and a justification for colonial domination.

All of these world-making events and processes were taking place alongside the global move toward religious disestablishment—the withdrawal of state funds from religious institutions and organizations in the name of the liberal ideal of the separation of church and state. Although associated with the revolutions of the late eighteenth century, the idea of the separation of church and state was formalized earliest and perhaps most effectively in the New World. For example, while in France the term *laïcité* did not even appear until the early 1870s' debate over the secularization of schools (Ford 2005: 6); in Mexico, the Ley Lerdo was passed in 1859, mandating the forced sale of Church properties (mainly realized during the later regime of Porfirio Díaz at the turn of the century [Hamnett 1999: 162–3]). After the New York City political organization Tammany Hall in 1861 successfully secured municipal funds for Catholic schools serving largely Irish immigrants (Golway 2014), thirty-four states passed laws forbidding the use of public money for religious institutions, and an unsuccessful attempt was made to amend the United States Constitution to forbid the use of public funds for parochial schools (Green 2010). The political cartoonist Thomas Nast depicted Catholic cardinals as crocodiles on the Ganges River preparing to feast on hapless schoolchildren (Figure 3.1). Disestablishment and other efforts to diminish the role of religious institutions in political life add further weight to the consensus of scholarly opinion that religion was on the wane, pushed aside by the forces of money and the market aided by the secular state.

Outside the West, too, and often in response to European colonial expansion and war, religious reform was taking place in ways that served an emerging secular modernity. In the Ottoman Empire, intellectuals squared Western-style, interest-bearing credit and banking with Islam in the Mejelle, the Ottoman civil code. In Meiji Japan, Shintoism was brought into the state apparatus and for a time was financially supported by it. It was also partially secularized, its practices folded into nation-state building and formally separated from Buddhism (Hardacre 1989: 27–8). The Meiji seal was struck on the coinage and affixed to

FIGURE 3.1: Thomas Nast, "The American River Ganges," *Harper's Weekly*, September 1871. Public domain, Bill Maurer.

Shinto temples, too—affirming a tight linkage between money and the new nationalist rituals (Figure 3.2).

In India, numerous movements in Hinduism sought to integrate its varied traditions with monotheism while reformers decried the role of money in terms that would be familiar to European nineteenth-century social theorists. The Hindu reformer Dayananda Saraswati (1824–83) railed against religious leaders' extraction of massive sums of money from worshippers to build lavish temples (Pruthi 2004: 34). In his own commentary on money, Rabindranath Tagore (1861–1941) almost seems to echo Marx on the self-expanding nature of the capitalist desire for profit:

> The greed of gain has no time or limit to its capaciousness. Its one object is to produce and consume. It has pity neither for beautiful nature nor for living human beings. It is ruthlessly ready without a moment's hesitation to crush beauty and life out of them, molding them into money.
> —Tagore 1917 [2011]: 35

As European powers expanded across the globe, ethnologists discovering "primitive" forms of money slotted them into an evolutionary scheme in which

FIGURE 3.2: One-rin coin, Meiji Emperor Year 16, 1883, Japan. Courtesy of Tom Boellstorff.

common property gave way to private property and the rise of money co-occurred with a fall from grace. Thus, W.H.R. Rivers, in his account of Melanesian society, argued that the presence of money indicated the "disappearance of communism" (Rivers 1914: 385).

Money and markets were the acid eroding traditional forms of moral authority, solidarity and communion. Such was the consensus among learned scientists and political reformers, at any rate.

PROSPERITY AND FAITH

And yet religion was *everywhere* in this increasingly calculative, rationalizing world. Often it was actually fused with, not opposed to, rising interest in the meaning of money and its growing role in social life. It was a time of religious revival, albeit often in popular or even what our learned scholars may have considered profane form, not least because revival was thoroughly saturated, obsessed even, with money.

Take two influential religious movements that became worldwide in scope: Methodism, which flourished in the nineteenth century and melded with religious movements as varied as those of former American slaves and metaphysical thinkers, and Mormonism. Although John Wesley was writing in the eighteenth century, Methodism took off during the mid- to late nineteenth century, especially among the working classes in the US and England and then among American slaves and colonial subjects around the world. Wesley's (1744) Sermon 50, "The Use of Money," exhorts the faithful to "gain all you can," "save all you can" and "give all you can," for "[y]ou see the nature and extent of truly Christian prudence so far as it relates to the use of that great talent, money" (Wesley 1744). Money is here a moral force, if used wisely.

Where Wesley invoked the Parable of the Talents (Matthew 25: 14–30), the Church of Jesus Christ of Latter Day Saints invoked the Parable of the Pearl of Great Price (Matthew 13: 45–46) in its eponymous foundational text. Its other core text, the Book of Mormon, also weaves a tale of Nephite society's fall from grace in terms of the transformation of common property into the pursuit of individual gain, which occurred alongside the development of standard weights and measures. These, in turn standardized money, and led both to commercial success as well as bribery, political corruption, and the society's downfall (Welch 1999: 45)—a cautionary tale in line with other nineteenth-century concerns over the demoralizing force of money. Yet at the same time (and likely also because of disestablishment more generally) the Mormons famously instituted tithing. The sacred books of this new faith were given to Joseph Smith in the form of tablets made of precious metal. They thus had to be hidden for fear that they would awaken covetous thoughts of melting them into ingots (Welch 1999: 45). We will return to this close association of money and precious metal, for it dovetails with other associations having to do with religious belief, natural law, and the emerging racial ideologies of the age.

Nineteenth and early twentieth-century religious belief and practice melded faith and finance, money and morality, despite the Weberian assertion of growing secularization. "The era after the Civil War, often known as the Gilded Age, witnessed a flood of religious ideals that bathed the period with hearty individualism and bold pragmatism. Self-mastery became an art and occupation, as people sought to consolidate the era's advances with improvements to their own lives" (Bowler 2013: 12).

Bowler writes that, in particular, the technological and scientific advances of the day helped popularize the idea of "invisible causal forces" (Bowler 2013: 12) that could be manipulated and harnessed with the right methods, attitude and action. Religious movements that adopted this into their practice included Christian Science, Pentecostalism, the New Thought movement, Adventism, the Swedenborgians, homeopathy and various other metaphysical currents. Other religious leaders adapted Wesley's notion of sanctification—the idea that by receiving God's grace the faithful could attain blessings in this life instead of the next—and rendered it a "calculable moment" (Bowler 2013: 17). It was a small step from this calculable moment to the belief in faith healing and the prosperity gospel. If Weber's Calvinists took their material success as a sign of their membership in the elect, adherents to the new prosperity religions sought actively to harness the causal force of grace to make them wealthy, such wealth indicating not election so much as a "victory over sin" in this world (Bowler 2013: 17). And if for John Wesley and Joseph Smith, money could be rechanneled to make religion—either in the sense of seeking gain to offer gifts with greater than material return, or in the sense of simply building a religious empire, founded itself on tablets of gold, through the institution of tithing—for the new prosperity gospel, religion could be harnessed to make money as a sign and realization of spiritual triumph.

BUILT ON A ROCK

In England at the beginning of the nineteenth century the hymnist James Montgomery could decry colonial conquest and love of gold in one breath, linking both to the ruin of nations. Montezuma, Cortez and Pizarro all brought about their "country's ruin by avenging gold—"

> That gold for which unpitied Indians fell,
> That gold, at once the snare and scourge of hell,
> Thenceforth by righteous Heaven was doom'd to shed
> Unmingled curses on the spoiler's head
>
> —in Montgomery 1861: 23

But gold got increasingly sanctified in the nineteenth century, and did so in a manner that linked it to imperial conquest, white racial hegemony and literary naturalism.

Where Montgomery feared the lust for gold would lead to ruin, the Latter Day Saints' gold tablets capture a growing ambivalence: gold may lead men to greed, yet the gold tablets suture the relationship between God's word and the precious metal. In the aftermath of the American Civil War, the debate over the nature of money as commodity or alternately as promise took on a decidedly religious cast. Thomas Nast once again provocatively captured the mood with his political cartoons excoriating the US Congress for instituting money by fiat—and the religious reference to the first words of God in Genesis should not be forgotten—rather than rooting it in precious metal (Figure 3.3). Promissory notes were seemingly as worthless as insubstantial paper, and the work of governments in creating them was akin to the work of a human artist (and in Nast's view, a bad one at that), not the divine one.

Hard money proponents in the nineteenth century thus sidelined John Locke and other Enlightenment figures' assumptions that gold had become money by common consent and instead asserted its moral superiority. Thus, US Secretary of Treasury Hugh McCulloch stated in 1865:

FIGURE 3.3: Thomas Nast, "Milk Tickets for Babies in Place of Milk," in *Robinson Crusoe's Money*, 1876. Public domain, Bill Maurer.

> By common consent of all nations, gold and silver are the only true measure of value. They are the necessary regulators of trade. I have myself no more doubt that these metals were prepared by the Almighty for this very purpose, than I have that iron and coal were prepared for the purposes in which they are being used.
>
> —quoted in Ritter 1999: 35

Senator George Hoar from Massachusetts said in a speech before Congress, "A sound currency is to the affairs of this life what a pure religion and a sound system of morals are to the affairs of the spiritual life" (quoted in Ritter 1999: 172). An 1897 textbook relates, "Sound money must mean money that under all conditions, unaided, will be able to establish, by the force of its own virtue, its own supremacy in the markets of the world. [. . .] [T]herefore *sound* money consists *only* of gold" (quoted in O'Malley 2012: 152, O'Malley's italics removed, original italics retained).

After the American Civil War, thus, the sound money position had hardened even further, to exclude silver in favor of gold as the true and eternal source of value. The US had financed the war by issuing "greenbacks," paper currency backed only by the promise of the American government to honor them. After the war, different interests—farmers *versus* financiers, rural Midwest *versus* urban East, Democrat *versus* Republican—consolidated themselves over the money question, and whether the resumption of a specie standard would only benefit creditors, leading to a further concentration of wealth. The Democrat William Jennings Bryan passionately advocated for a bimetallic standard, backing the money by silver and gold, while his critics saw in bimetallism a sure road to inflation and national decay. Bryan framed his argument in regional, class and populist terms. But he did so in a religious register. Bryan concluded his speech before the Democratic National Convention in 1896—the speech which virtually secured him his party's nomination as its candidate for president—with the following:

> Having behind us the producing masses of this nation and the world, supported by the commercial interests, the laboring interests, and the toilers everywhere, we will answer their demand for a gold standard by saying to them: "You shall not press down upon the brow of labor this crown of thorns; you shall not crucify mankind upon a cross of gold."
>
> —Bryan, in Cherny 1996: 28

He then stretched his arms out "as if on a cross" and stood before a crowd stunned into silence for several seconds before leaving the podium (Cherny 1996: 11).

He would go on to lose the election to William McKinley, who took up the gold standard together with, not incidental to, American imperial expansion.

Historian Gretchen Ritter summarizes, "Silver was the money of radicals and atheists. [. . .] Silver would group the United States with impoverished, pagan nations such as China. Good morals required good money, and the only true money was gold" (Ritter 1999: 172).

MONEY IN THE MAKING OF IMPERIAL SUBJECTS

Again, McKinley's imperial program was not incidental to the ascendance of gold. Ritter notes that gold standard proponents would frequently castigate their opponents in explicitly racist terms, calling them "'peons,' 'coolies,' and 'rancheros'" (Ritter 1999: 171). They associated gold with civilization and progress, as well as what they considered the God-given right to colonialism through manifest destiny. As President William McKinley's campaign posters proclaimed, "The American flag has not been planted on foreign soil to acquire more territory but for humanity's sake." Gold—and imperialism—meant divinely ordained progress, global expansion in the name of moral uplift. The poster also included propagandistic representations of the fortunes of the populace under his sound money policies: idle factories versus active ones belching smoke, "a run to the bank" rather than "a run on the bank" (Figure 3.4).

FIGURE 3.4: "The Administration's Promises Have Been Kept," 1900. Wikimedia Commons.

The debate between greenbackers and goldbugs, and the later debate over a bimetallic standard and a gold standard, circled around the question of whether money was or could ever be "real" *versus* a mere "representation" and if the latter, a representation of what. Yet gold or silver are simultaneously real—they are what they are, prior to any representation—and also representation insofar as their constitution as money renders them representatives of some kind of true or abstract value. Walter Benn Michaels identified nineteenth-century American literary naturalism in part as "the need to end representation, and the desire to represent" (Benn Michaels 1987: 26). His discussion of anxieties over the distinction between realism and representation in literature spills over into the American monetary debate and links anxieties over whether gold is a transcendent thing or a thing that represents something else to the analogous debate in nineteenth-century psychology over the nature of human perception as well as the status of "man" as a beast with a soul. And the nature of literature, too: does it represent a social reality? Or does it stand alone, timeless, eternal?

This debate over the real and the represented was also central to Christian eschatology not limited to the Age of Empires with which I am concerned here over the nature of Christ: man, god, both, representation of god? In the period at hand, however, the conundrum found expression in a host of new religions that obviated the question altogether: Unitarianism, for example.

It also found expression in the reception of both money and Gospel by colonized peoples. If nineteenth-century Euroamericans were disputing "the nagging discrepancy between face value and substantial value" both around the status of "Jesus, the coinlike wafer-God-man" and money (Foster 1999: 216–17), some of their new colonial subjects simply did not care. This was not a meaningful distinction for them. First, their experience of both the Christian God and western-style money was one of violent imposition. Being compelled by force in many instances to play the religion and money game of imperial powers the fetishistic hold and paradoxical ambiguities of transcendence and representation surely had less hold over their imaginations. And being animated by other games: for Melanesians, for instance, their own concerns over the direction of flow of value and the creation and dissolution of relationships made the "true" value of abstract money less compelling a problem (Foster 1999, Strathern 1975).

The constellation of hard money, white supremacy, imperialism and natural law was made quite explicit in the American context during the Civil War and after (and arguably, even to this day). Lincoln's "bitter enemy," Ohio Congressman Clement Vallandigham, referred to the former's "greenback abolition," which historian Pat O'Malley interprets as "an ethical system which sought to abolish nature itself by declaring rag paper into money and making negroes the equal of whites" (O'Malley 2012: 88). O'Malley tracks the alignment between nineteenth-century conceptions of "specie" and "species," between support of hard money and state-enforced racial inequality. "Gold bugs tended toward racist ideas because they wanted to stop the promiscuous circulation of goods and peoples and meanings, the negotiation of identities" (O'Malley 2012: 135). He also notes that both gold bugs and silverites believed in natural law. Even our bimetallist populist William Jennings Bryan did not escape the pull of this configuration of race and money. "Bryan's passion for democracy," historian Michael Kazin writes, "always cooled at the color line" (Kazin 2006: 278).

Nineteenth-century naturalism expressed anxieties over the relationship between words and things, representations and reality, in religion, money and law. It is no wonder perhaps that in the colonial enterprise, Euroamerican powers sought to engage in a linguistic project of renomination, not just remonetization. In colonial South Africa, the anthropologists Jean and John Comaroff relate, missionaries sought to put "a lasting imprint of Christian Europe" in indigenous languages. Dutch and English loan words gave form to the "emerging colonial universe," with new terms for church, believer, wage labor, school and of course money itself (Comaroff and Comaroff 1991: 218–19).

The colonial enterprise further sought to inculcate spiritual and market values, often together in the same instance. At the same time, however, the values of the market were potentially "corrupting" (Comaroff and Comaroff 1997: 8). Wage labor had to be instituted therefore as a form of discipline, labor as virtue:

> In the liberal humanist worldview of the missionaries, such pursuits involved the conversion of value from lower to higher species, requiring universal, standardized, fungible currencies—like money and the word—all of which were ultimately redeemable in the form of grace and eternal life. Viewed thus, conversion and civilization were two sides of the same coin, two related means of 'trading up,' of accumulating merit and honoring the Glory of God. This vision was not without its contradictions. Apart from all else, it flirted openly with Mammon.
>
> —Comaroff and Comaroff 1997: 8

Note that conversion "from lower to higher species" embodies within it the same racial logic as metallism.

AS IT WAS IN THE BEGINNING

It was during this Age of Empire that the orthodox origin story for money infused political economy and the emerging distinct discipline of economics. Jevons' Parisian opera singer story is meant to self-evidently explain the necessity of money in a world where barter simply will not do owing to the problem of the double coincidence of wants: it is rare that you will have available to trade what I need at the precise time and place when I happen to have available what you need. The nineteenth century saw the consolidation of the particular vision of human nature laid out by Adam Smith in 1776 in which is it our propensity to truck, barter, and exchange that defines us. Institutionalized in evolutionary theories of the origins of money, from barter to gold to banknotes backed by gold, and welded to theories of racial superiority and progress embedded in religious conversion and imperial practice, the barter origin story for money became common sense. It both bolstered the belief in gold's natural or god-given transcendence, as well as a justification for colonial expansion in the name of our intrinsic nature to trade. Capitalism and manifest destiny, together, made this intrinsic nature self-expansionary, limitless even.

During the close of our period, however, alternative theories of the origin of money began to gather steam. These placed money's beginnings in the time of the rise of organized ancient states. With new archaeological discoveries in the Near East, a growing ethnographic archive, and changing political economic circumstances in the core capitalist countries, chartalist and credit theory proponents of money's origins challenged the orthodoxy. A. Mitchell Innes in 1914 put forward a credit theory of money opposed to commodity theories of money and also to the barter origin story. He did so by considering the practices whereby debts would be settled not with tokens but through tallies, recording devices like clay tablets or tally sticks. Innes also went after gold and silver: "Credit and debt have nothing and never had had anything to do with gold and silver," he wrote (Innes 1914: 32). Rather:

> the value of a credit depends not on the existing of any gold or silver or other property behind it, but solely on the 'solvency' of the debtor, and that depends solely on whether, when the debt becomes due, he in his turn has sufficient credits on others to set off against his debts.
> —Innes 1914: 32

Innes locates the value of money in the quality of human interrelationships rather than in some transcendent commodity or exchange of use values presumed in the barter situation. "What we have to prove is not a strange general agreement to accept gold and silver, but a general sense of the sanctity of an obligation" (Innes 1914: 30). All over the world, he observed, "debts and credits are equally familiar to all, and the breaking of the pledged word, or the refusal to carry out an obligation is held equally disgraceful" (Innes 1914: 30).

In examining the more formalized credit systems in the ancient states, he found a thorough intertwining of religious and political authority. The sanctity of obligations to divinely ordained rulers rendered the debts incurred by subjects to be of a quasi-spiritual quality, to be settled with tribute offerings.

As sites of the collection and recording of tribute, temples also became the locus of commercial transactions. "The relation between religion and finance is significant," he wrote (Innes 1914: 36).

> It is in the temples of Babylonia that most if not all of the commercial documents have been found. The temple of Jerusalem was in part a financial or banking institution, so also was the temple of Apollo at Delphi. The fairs of Europe were held in front of the churches, and were called by the names of the Saints, on or around whose festival they were held. In Amsterdam the Bourse was established in front of or, in bad weather, in one of the churches.
> —Innes 1914: 36–7

Placing religion at the center of the origin of money is far removed from the earlier nineteenth-century social theorists' counterposing of the two phenomena. Denying the co-constitution of money and religion permitted those earlier theorists to argue that money and religion are opposites, that money taints faith or belief. Yet the fusing of faith and finance in the new religions of the Age of Empire and in the process of colonization and conversion perhaps lend further weight to Innes' argument that money is tightly welded to the state and the sanctity of human obligation—it is just that colonial powers were seeking to shift the locus of those obligations, from traditional authorities and local relations to their own rulers and gods.

ACKNOWLEDGMENTS

I would like to thank Tom Boellstorff, Taylor C. Nelms and the editors of this volume for their comments on earlier drafts of this chapter.

CHAPTER FOUR

Money and the Everyday

Paper Money, Community, and Nationalism in the Antebellum US

MICHAEL O'MALLEY

In 1837, Tennessee Senator Thomas Hart "Bullion" Benton introduced a bill to ban the use of "shinplasters" in the District of Columbia. Before the Civil War, Americans could print their own money, which worked in commerce so long as people accepted it. In hard times especially—there was a financial crisis in 1837—shopkeepers, merchants, saloons, restaurants; businesses of all kinds and even private individuals all printed small denomination paper notes, typically for amounts less than a dollar, which they gave as change. These "fractional notes" notes were nicknamed "shinplasters," a term examined in detail below. Benton called them "filthy," and "putrid," and "trash:" he wanted to eliminate all such paper money and establish a money based purely on specie, on gold or silver. Benton's bill would have made it "unlawful for every individual" to pass shinplasters in the District of Columbia.

The idea of a pure specie money had, and still has, a powerful hold on the imagination of a vocal minority of American politicians. "Specie" means "gold or silver." "Specie money" can mean only gold and silver coins themselves, or it can mean paper notes redeemable in gold or silver at the bank. But if banks print more money than they have in their vaults, not all paper in circulation can be redeemed for gold. This is called "fractional reserve lending," and it is central to capitalism itself. Along with specie money, at various points Americans had experimented with purely legal tender paper money, backed only by the labor of the people who issued it. Benjamin Franklin had argued for paper currency as early as 1723 (Franklin 1969: 1:24). The American Revolution was financed with legal tender paper money.

Hard money partisans like Benton dreamed of removing paper money from circulation altogether. Benton and his ally, President Andrew Jackson, collaborated to eliminate the Second United States Bank, which since 1816 had aimed to establish a standard, universally accepted and reliable paper currency, backed by gold and silver. Jackson claimed, in his speech vetoing the bank's recharter, that a pure specie economy, with no central bank, would remove "artificial distinctions" and allow "natural and just" differences between men to flourish. But forms of paper money multiplied after the Second US Bank collapsed. Benton wanted to see the "filthy shinplasters" gone from circulation in the nation's capital, replaced by specie money, and so he proposed simply banning its use.

In a seemingly bizarre objection to Benton's shinplaster bill, Kentucky Senator Henry Clay pointed out that "the consequence of this would be that if a negro were sent to market to purchase food, and offered [shinplasters] in payment, he was placed on the same footing with whites, and made subject to the same punishment." In other words, Clay warns, the bill treats white and black citizens as equal actors in the marketplace.

Clay's objection shows us several things: first, it suggests that African Americans regularly "offered shinplasters in payment." Second, that they did so as servants, when they were "sent to purchase food." That is, they did so as surrogates for white people's needs and desires. Third, Clay suggests that if it were illegal for white people to use shinplaster notes, and then it would also be illegal for black people, and the law would thus be treating them the same, something Clay apparently sees as objectionable.

Benton's answer was even more strange. "In reference to negroes," he insisted, "no acts of congress were ever understood to apply to them." That is, the law he proposes, banning shinplasters, would only apply to white people— he appears to be proposing a law which, though it does not say so, will be understood not to apply to African Americans, who will, he seems to suggest, still be able to use "shinplasters" as before. Benton thus seemed to be endorsing a bill which would grant African Americans special permission to pass shinplaster notes when whites could not. Clearly, Benton imagines two economies in place here: a white man's economy in which shinplasters are forbidden, and an alternative economy in which their use is confined to African Americans.

Clay echoed this sense of a separate, alternative economy in his attack on the measure, which he labeled "a bill of pains and penalties against the poor people, the negroes and beggar girls" of the District.[1] Shinplaster money circulated in the communities of the poor. "Attack the banks", Clay continued, but "do not attack the negroes and little children, whose necessities may drive them to spend their little all" in shinplasters: "Spare! Oh spare! The little game, the poor, the weak, the helpless, the unwary, the women and children and market people. They *must* take money in some shape; they are compelled to dispose of their few commodities; they are obliged to carry home something from the sale of their little adventures." "They have no remedy," he insisted, "but to take and pass this money. Attack more noble game."[2] Shinplasters were the special money, then, of the poor. Clay thought they should be allowed.

The phenomenon of shinplaster currency demonstrated how in everyday life in the United States, "multiple economies" prevailed. The point is hard for modern readers to grasp, but will become more clear below: because orthodox economics insisted on "specie" money, an actual medium of exchange was often scarce; there often was simply no money around. Shinplasters allowed marginal individuals—poor people, negroes, and beggar girls, in Clay's words—to participate in economic exchange. But not just marginal individuals—as numismatic historian Richard Doty wrote, shinplaster notes issued from "professions including 'butcher, grocer, singing master, restaurant owner, hotelier, dry goods merchant, printer and druggist'" (Doty 1998: 107). Small businesses of all kinds, local corporations, and even individuals issued shinplasters. They circulated freely in communities of people willing to accept them, and represented an alternative, unsanctioned model of economic exchange.

Shinplasters dramatized a number of tensions in American life, focused on unresolved questions about the nature of money, value and status in community. Shinplasters demonstrated the failure of standardization, and a determination to evade and thwart the goals of elites, who wanted a limited money form they could control. Shinplasters were almost a literal representation of the person who passed them: they amounted to an act of faith in the personhood of the bearer. By throwing the source of value itself into question, shinplasters undermined the social position of elites. Shinplasters further demonstrated the flimsiness of American nationalism. Americans consistently rejected a limited, sovereign national money in favor of a promiscuous mix of local money forms they generated themselves. They represented an alternative imaging of individualism, community and reciprocal obligation.

WHAT WERE SHINPLASTERS?

Understanding shinplasters and their role in everyday life requires understanding the remarkably chaotic money system of the United States before the Civil War. Although officially only gold and silver could be "real money," in everyday life people used a wide variety of orthodox and unorthodox forms of money. By the 1850s, for example, more than 9000 different kinds of paper money circulated in the US. There were notes issued by state and local banks, some of which were little more than legal counterfeits, others of which enjoyed substantial gold backing and good management. There were non-bank forms of paper money issued by insurance companies and other businesses. There were letters of credit issued by merchants and slaveholders, which could pass as money if signed over to other people. Most of these notes lost their value as they moved farther from their place of issue, and were discounted as they traveled. Complicating the situation, the US suffered from truly rampant counterfeiting, to the extent that at times nearly half the money in circulation was counterfeit. Merchants subscribed to weekly or bimonthly "Counterfeit Detectors," bound volumes that listed banknotes, described their appearance, and gave an assessment of their reliability. Every exchange involved not just the price of the goods, but the kind of money being proffered, and a sharp look at the apparent character of the person doing the spending.[3]

Complicating things even further, "a separate category of paper money—alternatively called shinplasters, scrip, bastard paper currency, private money, and unaccounted currency—was issued by merchants, businesses, and municipalities and operated on the fringe of the law" (Greenberg 2015). These shinplaster notes were deeply troubling to elites on multiple levels.

Given the slightest chance, *DeBow's Review* lamented, "the corporations of cities and towns, turnpike companies, bridge companies, rail-road companies, and individuals in all the private walks of life immediately commence the issue of notes for dollars and the fractional parts of dollars."[4] In Georgia alone, between 1810 and 1866, "more than fifteen hundred varieties of currency of this type circulated" (Schweikart 1987: 80). "Fabulous sums in shinplasters, from five cents to a dollar, were circulated by the people, so that to a considerable extent every man was a banker, and distributed his own notes," recalled traveling magician Antonio Blitz: "In this manner every State was crowded with all descriptions of worthless paper. Property and merchandise became subject to the influence it produced, creating an artificial value beyond belief" (Blitz 1872: 209). The *Chicago Tribune* lamented the flood of shinplasters and paper money sweeping over the western territories in 1858 and singled out Nebraska as the source. It called for the arrest of the "Nebrascals."[5] "If the butchers, bakers and grocers would only set themselves up in opposition to it," wrote "A Citizen" in 1848, "the accursed trash would soon be banished from the city." But they do not, he continued, and so the general public must continue to be "agents of the 'shinplaster' gentry."[6] Shinplasters, a tool of the lower classes, were a crisis for the upper classes.

The origins of the term "shinplaster" are somewhat obscure. If someone barked their shin in 1800 they might stop the bleeding with a "sticking plaster" or a "shinplaster" made of paper or cloth soaked in some home remedy. The Oxford English Dictionary describes the word as meaning, in the US, "a square piece of paper saturated with vinegar, etc., used as a plaster for sore legs." Calling low denomination notes "shinplasters" associated them with illness and dirt; with folk remedies and infirmity, with trash. And indeed critics invariably referred to shinplasters as dirty, greasy, rank, disease-bearing, filthy, trash. "A Nervous Man," writing from Washington DC in 1838, even asked how "those of us living in the southern cities" may "escape disease generated by these foul, loathsome things, with which every man woman and child is forced in *actual* contact?" He suggested public regulations requiring that all shinplaster notes be dipped daily in salt water, "saturated with chloride of lime."[7] They were "dirty" because, like "dirty money" itself, they passed promiscuously from one thing to another, crossing boundaries of class and race and gender, but also because they contaminated the middle class with the associations they picked up on their travels.

The "Autobiography of a Fip [five penny] Shinplaster," published in 1838, describes the career of a shinplaster, issued by "the corporation," as it passes variously through the hands of butchers, bakers, spinsters, beggars, tavern keepers, millers and merchants. Some preserve it and even iron it; others mix it with other money in a greasy wallet or crumple it in a pocket. "Passing back and forth between men and women who were wealthy and impoverished, wholesome and unhygienic, the shinplaster kept promiscuous company" (Gamble 2015: 42). Tattered and dirty, it passed into the hands of "Betty, the chambermaid" and then wound up torn and mostly forgotten: "I am one of a fated race," says the shinplaster.[8] Shinplasters were doubly dirty because they were the communal resort of the underclass, part of a separate, ill-fated "race."

The following quote from the *Baltimore Sun* in 1837 describes the process of "shinplaster banking" and shows something of why elites detested it. "This business of issuing individual [shinplaster] notes," wrote the editors, "is monopolized by:"

> that class of people which is engaged in small trade . . . . A small dealer in stay tape, and buckram, or the vendor of codfish and treakle, who is without means, and who should never be entrusted with them, is anxious to extend his trade and his capital—he cannot get credit, for the very good reason that he is not entitled to it, and he, of course, resorts to his wits to raise the wind.

The article expresses disdain for the small merchant—the "vendor of codfish and treakle"—who cannot get credit because he "is not entitled to it." Entitled by whom? The editors? Respectable upper-class people? Lacking the "entitlement" of class this man, against the better judgement of the *Sun,* "resorts to his wits" to raise money, rather then simply inheriting it.

"What is his first stop?" the editorial continues: "He proceeds to the office of a printer or engraver, gets a private note struck off, and sets up as a private banker."[9] Printing private notes, shinplasters, allows the vendor of codfish and treacle to raise money by circulating paper notes backed by his own reputation and ability. People would accept them to the degree that he had a good reputation and they planned to continue to do business with him. Indeed, Senator Robert Strange of North Carolina thought "shinplasters" were better than "corporation paper" because "there was no secrecy about them. They would not pass if the individual was in bad credit."[10] The vendor of codfish and treacle would trade on his own reputation. But the *Sun* saw no credit in the aspiring codfish merchant. Shinplasters allow him to evade the censure of the upper class, who are appalled to find that: "at last the valueless stuff [shinplaster notes], having shoved itself, like an imposter, through the ranks of good society, gains the credit and reputation of something valuable."

The *Sun,* like Senator Strange, quite rightly saw a confusion between the paper note and the person who had it printed: shinplasters were representations of individual people or individually owned businesses. As we shall see: they were an extension of the self. The Sun's editorial further imagines value is real, something which cannot be faked; not something derived from puffery or salesmanship: it tries to imagine value as a tangible, essential thing which the small vendor manifestly does not have. The *Sun* is irritated that shinplasters allow ordinary people to shove themselves, "like imposters," through the ranks of "good society" and gain a reputation as something valuable.

Having described the victim here as respectable people of "good society," the article then tries to claim the victims will be people who cannot read: "A poor negro slave, or a poor white woman who cannot read, is as likely to take an old state lottery ticket or an old bank corporation paper checque [sic] for currency as anything else." In this claim shinplasters are bad because they deceive the illiterate, who are described as women and negroes, as in the quote from Clay above. "But the evil does not end here," the editorial continues: the paper note "annoys the more enlightened classes of society. Few men pause to notice particularly a bank note before accepting it—and the consequence is, that spurious stuff falls into the hands of those who possess both integrity and the intelligence to guide them."[11]

So the problem is not just that the shinplaster note falls into the hands of the illiterate, in the communities of the impoverished: it's that it falls into the hands of people who can read but don't. In effect, this puts "men of integrity and intelligence" on the same footing as poor women and slaves, which was Henry Clay's objection in the exchange with Thomas Hart Benton that began this article. We can see this by looking at the confusion about subject in the sentence quoted above: "The spurious stuff falls into the hands of those who possess both integrity and the intelligence to guide them." Who is "them" in this sentence, and what is being guided? Is it the poor negroes and women who need guidance? Or is it the hands of the man of integrity and intelligence? Shinplasters recapitulated fundamental anxieties about the stability of social place and social class, and they called attention to the way daily commerce blurred these lines of distinction.

The *New York Morning Herald* raged against shinplasters regularly. It sent its intrepid reporters into the offices of shinplaster printers including the "North River Exchange Company" on Greenwich Street in Manhattan. They offered a description of the notes and the office. "The signatures look like those of common loafers," wrote the *Herald*, "and the miserable shanty where they keep their office looks like the headquarters of a loafer." The *Herald*, under James Gordon Bennett, was well known for its nativist, anti-Irish sentiment: calling the office a "shanty" associated it with the underclass of Catholic immigrants. "We would not give ten dollars for all we saw in the establishment," the article claimed. The reporter spoke to a clerk, and described him as "having the appearance of one of the rough scruff that run after our [fire] engines, and knock respectable people down on our sidewalks, upon the plea that they are serving the public."[12] In the 1830s, New York had only volunteer fire companies, notoriously manned by young men prone to enthusiasm in the pursuit of their duties. Fire companies stood somewhere between civic clubs and streets gangs. Like the *Baltimore Sun*, the *Herald* saw shinplasters as the emanations of shady and disreputable class of people who did not deserve credit, and like the *Sun* they felt themselves to be under siege, being "shoved" by the unworthy.

Shinplasters are clearly part of what historians have identified as anxiety about "circulation" and the unboundedness of commerce.[13] There was of course fraud involved in some shinplaster issues, and there were men who issued shinplasters they could never hope to redeem. But these same things happened in the orthodox economy as well: legitimate bankers regularly issued more paper notes than they could redeem. The "problem" of shinplasters further illuminates the complex relationship between money, community and nationalism. Shinplasters were a form of community exchange, virtually impossible to destroy. They represented an alternative to white nationalism, to elite dominance, and possibly to capitalist exchange itself. Shinplasters grew out of communitarian, subaltern experience. Attempts to eliminate them reflected a nationalist impulse to subject those communities to hierarchy and order.

MUTUAL DEBT AND COMMUNITY

We can find theoretical support for this argument in the work of anthropologist David Graeber. In *Debt, the First 5,000 Years*, Graeber draws on the anthropological literature on the gift to treat debt not as competition but as mutuality, as part of the fundamentally social nature of human life (Graeber 2011). In normal life all persons are in debt to parents, spouses, friends, neighbors: borrow the neighbor's lawnmower and you enter into his debt: help a neighbor with a childcare emergency and he or she enters your debt. Debt is part of the fabric of social life. Further, Graeber points out, neither historians nor economists have ever found an actual example of the fabled "barter" economy, in which people exclusively trade goods for other goods in place of money. Instead, in pre-modern societies people keep a complex sense of mutual indebtedness in their heads: A owes B for X who owes C for Y who owes A for Z. I ask your help in mending a fence with the expectation that in return your wife will help with the birth of my child: your daughter comes to help in our household in a crisis with the expectation that you can claim like help from our son in turn. To imagine escaping such debts, Graeber insists, is a form of sociopathy and in fact shunned. Imagine, for example, your mother calls and asks you for help moving furniture. What sort of person would reply "sorry mom, but my debt to you was repaid ten years ago?" Such a conversation *might* take place, but it would be a sign of things gone badly wrong.

For Graeber, recasting intersocial debt in monetary terms, and imagining it as something you could either escape from or use the law to compel someone to pay, was a profound moral transformation. "The criminalization of debt," he writes, "was the criminalization of the very basis of human society:"

> It cannot be overemphasized that in a small community, everyone normally was both lender and borrower. One can only imagine the tensions and temptations that must have existed in communities—and communities, much though they are based on love, in fact, because they are based on love, will always also be full of hatred, rivalry and passion—when it became clear that with sufficiently clever scheming, manipulation, and perhaps a bit of strategic bribery, they could arrange to have almost anyone they hated imprisoned or even hanged.
>
> —Graeber 2011: Kindle locations 7070–3

Casting exchange relations in these terms highlights the degree to which exchange itself begins in mutuality and reciprocity: the foundations of exchange are always social and communitarian rather than competitive and individualistic. Gift economies have a negative side: accepting a gift ensnares the receiver in a cycle of obligation, and gifts can be weapons of intimidation. But for Graeber seeking to "pay off one's debts" and escape the cycle of reciprocity then becomes a sign of profound and asocial alienation from the community.

Graeber further connects the rise of a standard money form, and the idea of escaping debt, to nationalist aggression. In standard economic accounts, money appears because barter is held to be too clumsy: you wish to buy cloth, but have only apples to trade, which the cloth merchant does not want. In pre-modern practice, says Graeber, the cloth merchant gives you the cloth knowing that he will claim the apples (or something else) at a later point. He keeps a mental accounting, and so do you. Neither historians or economists have ever found an example of a barter economy as imagined by economists: instead, they find people enmeshed in complex social relations of mutual indebtedness. "But the 'Myth of Barter' cannot go away," Graeber concludes, "because it is central to the entire discourse of economics" (Graeber 2011: Kindle locations 871–2). The myth of barter naturalizes money and makes it seem like an inevitability, like the invention of fire or the wheel: the story of barter legitimates money as a way of depersonalizing human relations. But it is crucial, Graeber insists, to remember "that money has no essence. It's not "really" anything; therefore, its nature has always been and presumably always will be a matter of political contention" (Graeber 2011: Kindle locations 7841-7842).

Graeber's specific historical arguments about money are subject to criticism and quibble, but the central point about money and exchange communities applies perfectly to shinplasters, which circulated in subaltern communities which shared a set of problems and values and which were often in extreme tension with nationalist goals. Shinplasters reflected the anxieties of the nation state, and in particular its inability to establish hegemonic control of the terms of exchange.

We can consider the example of T.W. Betton of Baltimore, MD, who manufactured shirts, collars, and cloth "stocks" for shirt making at his factory. In 1839 the *Baltimore Sun* published a short article denouncing Betton, under the heading "Vermin." The *Sun* compared him to "bugs and reptiles" for "attempting to crawl into the high prerogative of the general government—the regulation of the currency." Betton was printing shinplasters. The *Sun* included a facsimile of the notes in question, issued for the value of six and one quarter cents (Figure 4.1). The notes included a vignette of shirt stocks lying on "a pile

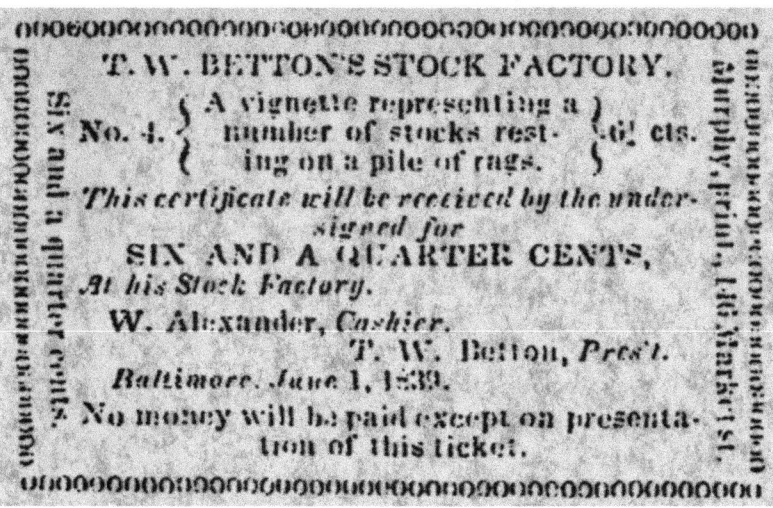

FIGURE 4.1: Reproduction of a Shinplaster Note, *Baltimore Sun*, June 13, 1839. Library of Congress Washington DC.

of rags [. . .] This certificate will be received by the undersigned for six and a quarter cents at his stock factory," it continued, with the name of "T.W. Betton., President."[14] The *Sun* sought to publicly shame Betton.

Betton responded with a letter the next day. The certificates in question, he explained, were "not intended as a tender for circulation," that is, as money; they were "merely for the convenience of myself and those who work for me." For more than four years, he continued, he had written these certificates by hand. "But with some three or four hundred females who work for me," he continued, each day brought the inconvenience of writing more than 100 of such tickets. He had gone to printing them, he continued, "as 'certificates of work' to be redeemed by me at the convenience of the giver and the holder."[15] Betton describes the shinplasters as a tool of convenience, not as an alternative money, though clearly they carry out much of the office of money.

The *Sun* was not persuaded. That same day they denounced Betton as "a Rag Baron" who "not content to make a handsome profit from the stocks made by poor women for a mere pittance, has assumed the office of a banker, and issued a flood of shinplasters, which he palms off on his workwomen." Paper money was often referred to as "rag money" and often compared to rags: but calling Betton a "Rag Baron" called attention to the fact that he made cloth and shirts—he worked in "the rag trade," as it would later be known. The *Sun* inadvertently pointed out that Betton's "rag money" was backed by actual "rags" turned to shirts. Like the shinplasters circulated by the vendor of codfish and treacle, cited above, they blur the line between the person represented and the object they represent. In doing so, they raised troubling questions about the nature of exchange, value, and money.

"They are not intended to be palmed upon the community at large," the *Sun* sneered, paraphrasing Betton, "but only upon some three or four hundred poor women." "A prison house should be his abode," the article continued, "and the lullaby that stills him to repose, be the tears of the widow and the cries for bread by the fatherless."[16] The Sun continued in this vein for some time, holding itself as the champion of the oppressed. But for the editors, the sin was not the fact that the women were poorly paid: it was that he paid them in shinplasters, in a tightly closed economy in which rags were turned into shirts and the labor of making shirts was converted back into rag money.

Betton had a fairly large factory for 1839, employing up to four hundred women. The women were paid in what the twentieth century might see as "company scrip," usable at the company store, but which in 1839 served as a different kind of negotiable local money. Why would Betton pay in tickets rather than money?

It has to do, again, with the chaotic money supply of 1839. Seth Rockman, speaking of Baltimore in *Scraping By*, notes that:

> Money posed the initial challenge to working families—not merely the lack of it, but rather the variety of currencies circulating with fluctuating values and redeemability ... Dozens of Baltimore banks, hotels, and merchants issued paper currency in amounts as small as 3c. According to working-class critics, many employers went to money markets every Saturday to purchase bills below face value in order to pay laborers at the end of the week ... Working people had to decide when and where to use their 'good' bills or coins and otherwise negotiated the value of questionable notes with landlords and storekeepers.
>
> —Rockman 2009: 174

Officially, the only real money was gold or silver. But "Gresham's law" prevailed: when people have two forms of money, they will spend the lesser and hoard the better. If Betton had gold or silver, he saved it for other transactions where it was specifically demanded. Why didn't he pay his employees in notes of a local bank? Well, for one thing, money was again often scarce, an idea which will sound both familiar (who doesn't wish they had more money?) and odd. We might not have as much money as we would like, but there is no shortage of paper notes or electronic bits and bytes. Money based closely on gold is in limited supply and the supply is not "elastic:" the gold is yet undiscovered in the earth or in vaults somewhere else or has gone to pay for seasonal demands elsewhere, or is on its way to England and France to pay creditors. You are working and thriving but people do not have money to pay you, even though they are also working and thriving. In such a circumstance money is literally, physically scarce, and when it appears, expensive to borrow. As a result, repeatedly, "the American population faced a profound shortage of cash during the antebellum and Civil War eras, and to fill the void merchants, nonbank institutions, and municipalities printed their own" (Greenberg 2015: 56).

E.P. Thompson long ago commented on the alternative economic strategies working class communities employed. He pointed, for example, to pocket watches as objects of exchange. "The timepiece was the poor man's bank, an investment of savings; it could, in bad times, be sold or put into hock." Not simply a timekeeper, a watch was a store of value and an instrument of exchange, was part of a complex of strategies that marked the subaltern economy, an economy in which mutuality was as strongly pronounced as it was in the interlocking corporate boardrooms of the Gilded Age (Thompson 1967: 70). Shinplasters, an unorthodox form of money, demonstrate the same kind of creative unorthodoxy. As numismatist Richard Doty noted, "Faced with an economy that constantly outstripped the orthodox money supply, Americans did as they had done before: they replied with an unorthodox one" (Doty 1998: 86–8). The *New York Times* claimed shinplasters were "a sort of rogue's resort when dimes, for good reasons, are not forthcoming. At some honest counters they were handed out in change for bills, but only to regular customers, who are sure to eat them all out during the week."[17] That is, lunch counters would offer shinplasters in change, knowing the notes would likely come back the next day. Shinplaster change, in fact, helped secure return business and form a community. Shinplasters served as an improvisatory money, but also as a sign of communal reciprocity. In that context, why should Betton try to find money to pay his workers, if he could simply issue his own shinplasters?

His employees might not be disadvantaged by this. They could redeem them for some other kinds of possibly more legitimate money, or they could spend them at local businesses whose owners knew *they* could redeem the shinplasters at Betton's pay window. The certificates *entitled the bearer* to six and a quarter cents. Anyone who held one could redeem it for other money at Betton's factory. So if one of his workers went to the butcher, she could offer one of Betton's shinplasters in payment. The butcher might accept, or he might not. He might accept it at a discount, crediting it as, say, a five cent note rather than a six and a quarter note, hoping that he could then take it to Betton's himself and claim the profit. Why would the woman take the ticket, rather than some other form of money? She might not have a choice in the matter, or, it is very possible that Betton's shinplasters, in local use, were *better* than other forms of money also circulating: less subject to discount, greeted with less skepticism by local merchants. Or the women might engage in their own arbitrage, taking Betton's certificates, using them in trade, and counting on getting other, better money in change which they could then use elsewhere.

By modern standards it seems an absurd situation, but it points out very clearly that exchanges were local and social; that there was a subaltern economy outside of elite regulation. "Ultimately, what was threatening" about this kind of "promiscuous economy," writes historian Robert Gamble, was the "ability to forge expansive commercial networks that were invisible, illegible, and impenetrable to authorities" (Gamble 2015: 42). It would be a mistake to imagine Betton as benign: he is trying to pay his workers in a form of money he simply made up and as a convenience to himself. And it would be a mistake to minimize the grinding poverty working-class Baltimore women experienced. But it would also be a mistake to miss the way shinplasters delineated a community of working women, for whom money's value came not from the essential properties of specie, or the authority of government, but from the social recognition of their labor by their peers. Betton took care to note that the paper tickets were symbols of actual labor performed—that is they represented tangible human labor, made portable, and his notes bore an image of shirts sitting on a pile of cloth, both made by the people who carried the notes. The *Sun* heard this argument, even quoting Betton to the effect that the tickets were "an evidence of labor performed by them." But it simply ignored it; and while claiming sympathy, the *Sun* clearly objected not to low wages *per se*, but to low wages paid in shinplasters. The *Sun's* opening salvo against Betton denounces him for "attempting to crawl into the high prerogative of the general government—the regulation of the currency." Shinplasters signal the failure of white, male nationalism and the regulatory authority of the state.

MONEY AND NATIONALISM

The failure of nationalism appeared wherever money changed hands. By 1838 the US Mint had four facilities issuing "official" American coins, and these coins formed the "real money" of the nation. But Americans never seemed to feel them sufficient, and in daily practice continued to use Spanish, French, Brazilian, and other Latin American coins in large number, in addition to the sundry mass of paper money described above. The undocumented immigrant coins made the native economy seem illegitimate, or indecent.

For example, in Thomas Satterwhite Noble's painting "The Price of Blood" (1868) we see a wealthy slaveowner sitting a table, clad like an oriental potentate in an ornate dressing gown and slippers (Figure 4.2). He is listening as the agreement to sell a slave is read aloud by the slave trader, dressed in plain black.

FIGURE 4.2: Thomas Satterwhite Noble, "The Price of Blood," 1868. Oil on canvas. Morris Museum of Art, Augusta, Georgia.

A mixed-race slave stands to the left, barefoot, in simple clothes: the slave, Noble wants us to recognize, is the trader's son.

For our purposes we can note the money itself: Satterthwaite wants us to see it. On the table there are stacks of seemingly identical gold coins, but also a scattering of other mixed coins which clearly have been differently valued. On the floor the slave master/father has placed a very mixed assortment of paper money: we can assume it includes banknotes and smaller sized shinplasters which have been rejected as worthless. Noble, an anti-slavery Kentuckian, wanted to highlight the grasping baseness of the transaction, its improperness. To do so he scattered the paper notes on the floor to demonstrate that all parties had waded through the mixed money available. The mixed coinage on the table, like his orientalist dressing gown, points to the mixed national economy in the same way that the mixed-race slave points to the failure of racial segregation. The slave master's decadent orientalism reinforces this point: illegitimate commercial and sexual intercourse, commercial and individual promiscuity, are related.

Out of necessity, foreign gold and silver coins remained legal tender until the Civil War. The situation embarrassed Americans and amused foreigners. "The circulating medium of Cuba," noted an English traveler in 1840, "consists exclusively of the precious metals, so that in passing between the island and the neighboring state of the North American Union the contrast is not a little striking, and is certainly all in favor of the doubloon." He concluded that the Cuban economy would be "quite a relief to the North American visitor who has been accustomed to handle noting in his own country in the shape of change, but the filthy rags to which they have given the agreeable name of 'shinplasters'" (Turnbull 1840: 87–8). In the US, wrote the English novelist and naval officer Frederick Marryat:

> Every man is now his own banker. Go to the theatres and places of public amusement, and, instead of change, you receive an I.O.U. from the treasury. At the hotels and oyster-cellars it is the same thing. Call for a glass of brandy and water, and the change is fifteen tickets, each 'good for one glass of brandy and water.' At an oyster-shop, eat a plate of oysters, and you have in return seven tickets, good for one plate of oysters each. It is the same everywhere. The barbers give you tickets, good for so many shaves; and were there beggars in the streets, I presume they would give you tickets in change, good for so much philanthropy. Dealers, in general, give out their own bank-notes, or as they are called here, *shin plasters*.[18]

The Scotsman James Lumsden toured the US as "a mercantile man" in 1843. He went to Baltimore where, as we have seen, respectable opinion deplored shinplasters. He described a large empty space which had been laid out for the suburban community of Canton, "but, alas! scarcely a single building of the anticipated city has yet made its appearance—a melancholy proof of the overissue of paper dollars and shin-plasters" (Lumsden 1844). Shinplasters embarrassed American nationalism in the eyes of the world—but their use continued.

When the nation state encountered shinplasters in the courts, they often found themselves confused. Many cities, as was the case of Washington DC that began this article, passed laws making the issue of small denomination notes illegal. In multiple instances persons were arrested for stealing shinplasters, and courts were unable to decide if a crime had actually occurred. If the notes were illegal, could they be stolen? And shinplasters were such resolutely local entities: "even judges who prosecuted the use of notes they knew to be illegal found their tasks difficult, for shinplasters' immediate exchange value vanished when taken out of their local market context." In Delaware County, Pennsylvania, in 1838, for instance, "A man was arraigned for stealing a pocket book containing two fifty cent notes. He was convicted of stealing the book, and a verdict of not guilty was rendered as to the notes, it being decided that as they were issued in violation of law, it was not an offence against the law to take and carry them away" (Greenberg 2015: 69).

Moreover, if they were of so little value, were they effectively *de minimus* and no crime worthy of notice had been committed? One Batavia, New York man was arrested for stealing a two-dollar Rochester, New York shinplaster. The judge declared that the prisoner stole "nothing," so he "was discharged." Historian Joshua Greenberg concludes: "such cases demonstrate the murky legal standing of shinplasters in American society, especially in the midst of a financial downturn. Demand prompted the creation of the notes, and there was little desire to prevent them from circulating, as they served an indispensable service to the local community who invested them with value" (Greenberg 2015: 69).

This last phrase points to the key fact: those who passed and received shinplasters invested them with value according to their own criteria. The *Sun* saw Betton's notes as signs of fraud and imposture, but we might just as easily see them as signs of mutuality, trust, and community; part of a network of unofficial exchange and reciprocity. Shinplasters frequently served as mobile advertisements but also as markers of shared interest and fellowship. The Library of Congress, for example, has a ten-cent shinplaster issued by a tobacconist, Pearl & Obrieght, at N.10 Cedar St. in New York (Figure 4.3). The bill, labeled "tobacco currency," bears a portrait of George Washington and promises equivalence to "one package" of tobacco.[19]

The shinplaster note has an interesting historic resonance. In colonial Virginia, "tobacco notes" had served commonly as money. A government official would inspect a tobacco crop and then issue notes certifying its quality and

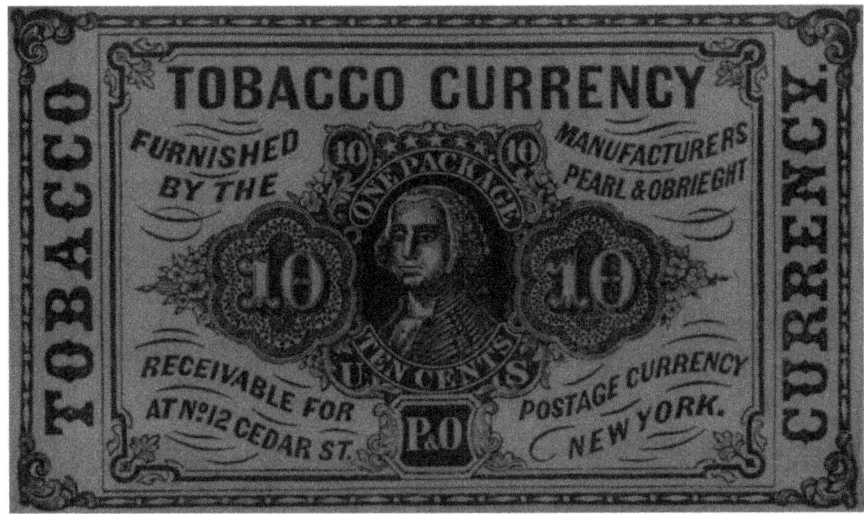

FIGURE 4.3: Commercial Shinplaster Currency, 1863. Library of Congress Washington DC.

weight. These "tobacco notes" would then circulate as money. Pearl & Obrieght's tobacco note continued this tradition, except that no third party—no external authority—certified the existence of the tobacco. The notes circulated in what we might see, again following Graeber, as communities of trust and reciprocity. Any regular customer of Pearl & Obrieght would know the notes worked at the tobacconist: moreover, the passage of a Pearl & Obrieght note to another person marked the existence of a community of customers who had formed a set of exchange relations they found useful. Shinplasters were saturated with the values of the local economies where they passed. The *Western Reserve Chronicle*, an Ohio newspaper, noted in 1862 that "Some of the shinplasters in Western New York are made payable at Utica next July, in strawberries, *if the crop does not fail*." Clearly, the shinplaster circulated among those willing to have faith in the local strawberry crop and the labor required to produce it.[20] The *Baltimore Sun* disdainfully reproduced the shinplaster note of the "Vauxhall Drinking Institution," which offered regular tipplers notes in change (Figure 4.4).

"It is certainly a good currency for 'loafers and suckers'," sniffed the *Sun*, "as it promises to pay in that which is to them more valuable than specie, more desirable than silver and gold."[21] The *Sun* is mocking these patrons, but again it points out how shinplasters represented both subaltern communities and alternative systems of value. People who shopped at the same tobacconist; people who had faith in their neighbor's strawberry crop; people who had chosen to value their meeting at the Vauxhall tavern.

MONEY AND THE EVERYDAY

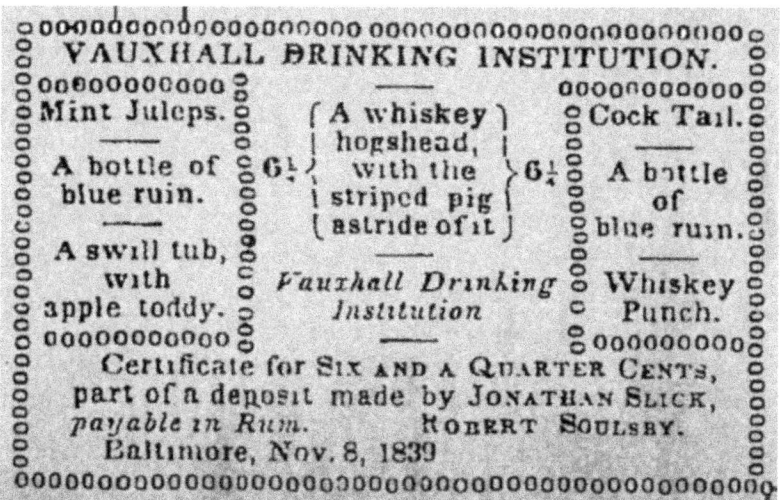

FIGURE 4.4: Reproduction of Shinplaster Note, *Baltimore Sun*, November 21, 1839. Library of Congress Washington DC.

We see this even more clearly in the astonishing account of William Wells Brown, who escaped slavery in the 1830s and later made a career as an author and anti-slavery lecturer in the US and England. Brown traveled to Monroe, Michigan, on Lake Erie, and on his arrival asked a local barber if he could work in the man's shop. The man turned him down, and Brown resolved to start his own. He managed to acquire space in a building and set up a few chairs and a sign styling himself "Fashionable Hair-dresser from New York, Emperor of the West" (Wells Brown 1852: 99).

In this story we must recall that Brown is an escaped slave, subject to capture and return, without friends or family. Monroe is a town of about 1700 people, but with considerable traffic from Lake Erie. Brown continues:

> At this time, any person who could raise a small amount of money was permitted to establish a bank, and allowed to issue notes for four times the sum raised. This being the case, many persons borrowed money merely long enough to exhibit to the bank inspectors, and the borrowed money was returned, and the bank left without a dollar in its vaults, if, indeed, it had a vault about its premises.

These were often called "wildcat" banks. "Banks were started all over the Western States," Brown says, "and the country flooded with worthless paper." The worthless paper included "notes from 6 to 75 cents in value; these were called 'Shinplasters'" (Wells Brown 1852: 99–100).

"Some weeks after I had commenced business on my 'own hook'," Brown continued, one of his customers told him, "Emperor, you seem to be doing a thriving business. You should do as other business men, issue your shinplasters." Brown recalled, "from that moment I began to think seriously of becoming a banker" (Wells Brown 1852: 100–101).

He went to a printer, chose some designs, and a day later received a stack of paper money totaling twenty dollars: "after being duly signed [they] were ready for circulation. Through the assistance of my customers, and a good deal of exertion on my own part, my bills were soon in circulation; and nearly all the money received in return for my notes was spent in fitting up and decorating my shop" (Wells Brown 1852: 101). We should note here that passing these bills requires considerable exertion of Brown's part along with the help of men who are willing to speak for him: it requires a social reputation. But by printing his own money, Brown creates the cash needed to outfit his shop. He circulates the money by means of personal persuasion: his local reputation as a hairdresser, his charm. We can possibly assume—although Brown does not specifically say—that the community he worked in was largely African American.

But Brown soon discovers the disadvantages of shinplasters. "One day," Brown recalled, "as I was sitting at my table, stropping some new razors I had just got with the avails of my 'shinplasters'," a stranger entered and said, "Emperor, you will oblige me if you will give me some other money for these notes of yours" (Wells Brwon 1852: 102). This was a process called "redemption:" the paper money was "redeemed" for something held to be more reliable or valuable. The same process would happen with legitimate banks. Any bank would dread the moment when a "carpetbagger" might show up with a valise full of its paper money, and demand gold or silver in return, because no bank ever had enough specie in its vaults to redeem all the paper it issued.[22]

Brown does what anyone of his day would do: "I immediately cashed the notes with the most worthless of the Wild Cat money that I had on hand, but which was a lawful tender." Like anyone doing business in the 1830s, Brown has a cash drawer full of mixed money, of different types from different banks or non-banks, all of different degrees of stability or value. He quickly pays off the stranger with the worst of what he has on hand. But almost instantly another stranger appears, with a handful of Brown's shinplasters, and asks for cash. "These were cashed, and soon a third came with his roll of notes. I paid these with an air of triumph, although I had but half a dollar left" (Wells Brown 1852: 102). He begins to think he has perhaps survived this crisis, when he sees a fourth man crossing the street, with a handful of his shinplasters. "I instantaneously shut the door, and looking out of the window, said, 'I have closed business for the day: come to-morrow and I will see you'." Across the street he sees the rival barber, grinning and clapping his hands. The rival had sent men to redeem Brown's shinplasters and thereby bankrupt him. "I was completely 'done Brown' for the day," says the "Emperor" (Wells Brown 1852: 103).

Here we see shinplasters as the poor man's source of personal credit. Brown convinces a community of people who know him to accept his paper money. They accept it because they know Brown and esteem his skill and enterprise. The merchant selling razors will accept Brown's shinplasters, knowing that his customers will accept them in turn. And Brown himself must accept the notes: if you received one of Brown's notes in change, you could use it to get a haircut. Or you could ask him to "redeem" the note. Brown thrives among people who agree to help him thrive, but also thrives at their mercy and forbearance. As Graeber describes, the circle of mutuality and trust that Brown initiates is broken by the rival barber's demand for "real money."

According to Brown's account he snuck out the back door of his shuttered shop and went to see a friend for advice. "He laughed heartily, and then said, 'You must act as all bankers do in this part of the country. . . . When your notes are brought to you, you must redeem them, and then send them out and get other money for them; and, with the latter, you can keep cashing your own shinplasters.'" "I immediately commenced putting in circulation the notes which I had just redeemed," Brown wrote, "and my efforts were crowned with so much success, that before I slept that night my 'shinplasters' were again in circulation, and my bank once more on a sound basis" (Wells Brown 1852: 103–104).

Likely Brown exaggerated to some extent, but he also accurately described how shinplasters worked in practice. In this story shinplasters act in a purely self-referential way: there is no "referee" or standard of value, no external authority certifying them. There is only what they will pass for. Shinplasters symbolized labor and character, themselves variable; shinplasters did not symbolize political authority or the "natural" value of gold. Brown's paper notes embodied his charisma and drive and potential: they also represented actual labor he would perform. They were advertisements for himself, extensions of himself, but they only worked in a community of people who knew Brown or knew of him. And they were dangerously subversive because in this account they allowed Brown—a runaway slave, a man with almost nothing—to show up and build a business. Brown never mentions race in this story: but in his telling, in a country deeply committed to white supremacy, shinplasters render that political regime of white supremacy, and its goal of economically containing black people, irrelevant.

SHINPLASTERS AND THE AMBITIONS OF THE SUBALTERN

Shinplasters offended elites because they amounted to a demand for consideration, an evasion of evaluative norms. They complicated judgements about worth and merit. In a pure specie economy someone either has the money or they do not: who they are, how they act, what they look like mostly does not matter. In a shinplaster economy that same person effectively says, "Well, I don't have that, but I do have this—will you take it?" Instead of a purely rational calculation, depersonalized by the standard money form, the shinplaster *personalizes* exchange. Again, this echoes Graeber's argument about money, that money was a way of breaking the interdependent mutuality of human societies. "The story of capitalism," Graeber writes, was "the story of how an economy of credit was converted into an economy of interest; of the gradual transformation of moral networks by the intrusion of the impersonal—and often vindictive—power of the state" (Graeber 2011: Kindle locations 7028–30). Taking Brown's shinplasters meant acknowledging Brown's ambition and ability, his potential and his claim on your humanity.

If respectable authorities detested shinplasters because they allowed subaltern groups to evade control, they also saw them as something that might be contained in the subaltern classes, or help to contain the subaltern classes. As in the debate that opened this article, shinplasters are often imagined as part of an alternative economy in which things forbidden or constrained in the legitimate economy might take place.

Over time the term's meaning began to shift. Originally "shinplaster" referred to small denomination, private notes issued by individuals and businesses. Gradually, the term came to encompass all sorts of paper money of suspect value. "By the 1850s, the term "shinplaster" was used to define any bad paper money that lacked confidence" (Greenberg 2015: 74). The Civil War heightened the problem of the mixed economy. Both the Union and the Confederacy financed their wars by issuing paper money. The North issued the famous "greenbacks," legal tender notes which the law compelled you to accept for all payments. The Federal government issued small denomination "fractional currency." These low value notes were often called "shinplasters" even though they enjoyed the backing of the federal government. In 1863 the Union also agreed, in the face of considerable public hostility, to allow African Americans to serve in the US army. Opponents of Lincoln frequently conflated actual legal paper money of the Civil War with "negro soldiers." Both represented an attempt to create value out of nothing, or to evade what were imagined as natural constraints on value. In that respect, shinplasters and paper money generally came to be synonymous with the project of racial equality.

One Ohio newspaper editor, complaining about the draft, wrote, "The old idea was that the militia could be drafted to defend the state, not invade foreign countries . . . what the idea is now we do not know, since the nigger has become white and paper shinplasters are a legal tender" (Robinson 2012: 45). Black men in uniform, "become white," were equivalent to paper money. "For finance, issue greenbacks; for war, blackbacks," one New York newspaper complained, sarcastically.²³ Southern humorist George Bagby claimed, "a free nigger is a monstrosity, a paradox, a hand without muscle, an amputated leg, a glass eye-ball, and a shinplaster—uncurrent at that" (Bagby 1885: 174). Comparing freed slaves to valueless shinplasters reiterated the sense in which shinplasters marked a separate community of exchange.

Shinplasters frequently appear in minstrel shows, in which white men dressed in blackface and parodied black Americans. Minstrel shows were far and away the most popular form of entertainment in the antebellum US. They embodied white supremacy and scorn for the subaltern, but they also contained more complicated feelings of identification and desire, and they regularly highlighted the tension between the real thing (black people) and the representation (white people in blackface makeup). In this sense, minstrel shows recapitulated the tension inherent in money itself, the ambiguity about the difference between the representation (the shinplaster, the dollar, the coin) and the thing it represented. Not surprisingly, shinplasters, and paper money, recur in minstrel performance, and particularly in minstrel performance during the Civil War.

In 1863 Hoolley's Minstrel troupe published some of the songs they performed during the Civil War. In "Sambo's Opinion" a character describes how, "I see in de papers, de oder day, To make de army bigger, Dat Congress dey had made a law, To go and draft de nigger." The song then links African American soldiers to worthless paper money and shinplasters:

> Dere is no silver now-a-days,
> And money dat has flew
> Except lots of postage-stamps,
> And greenbacks cut in two:
> Shinplasters now are all de rage,
> Most all are good for noffin;
> I s'pects dey'll ask percentage,
> By-and-by, on sojer-buttons.²⁴

In this song a white man in blackface sings about values gone topsy-turvy: negroes in uniform and shinplasters signify a renegotiation of value and social position; the soldier's buttons might pass for money. In a famous argument for enlisting black men in the Union Army, Frederick Douglass had insisted, "once let the black man get upon his person the brass letter, 'U.S.', let him get an eagle on his button, and a musket on his shoulder and bullets in his pocket, there is no power on earth that can deny that he has earned the right to citizenship."²⁵ "Sambo" wondered if "sojer buttons" would become money: Douglass insisted that "an eagle on his button" would allow the African American men to circulate as equal citizens. In both cases value comes from public service and acceptance of that service's value, not from any essential property. We can see here again why shinplasters outraged orthodox opinion. They rendered not just monetary but social values, identities, up for renegotiation.

As Michael Germana notes, "shinplasters were used in antebellum minstrel performance to comment, with tongue in cheek irony, upon the artifice of the form itself and to mock the aspirations of those characters ... who sought recognition for their humanity. In minstrel shows, he writes, "shinplasters" "stands in for 'nigger'" (Germana 2009: 35). In the eyes of Lincoln's critics, the subaltern economy had now become the general economy. "Shin-plasters sure were bad enough," another song argued:

> That is when Rebels used them;
> And well the Nigger-worshippers,
> In consequence abused them,
> But now to cap the climax, of
> Our manifold disasters,
> We've had to come to one and two
> And three cent *sticking plasters*.

That is, low denomination shinplasters and paper money, once the province of "nigger worshippers" have now become the norm. The song continues:

> What next I wonder? Nigger troops
> Or some such abomination;
> As Niggers being our equals in
> The states and in the nation.[26]

This song sees African American soldiers, "an abomination," as the next logical step after the issue of "cheap" fractional paper currency. If shinplasters personalized exchange and allowed subaltern people to create their own credit, then where did the negotiations stop?

The Civil War ended the issue of shinplasters and paper money generally. The Union initially taxed their issue and then made them illegal. Despite debates over the nature of money, and whether it had to be based in specie, the federal government acquired a monopoly in the issue of money and, to a large extent, on the regulation of value which it has maintained to this day.

Shinplasters show us an alternative economic world, in which the underclass—women, people of color, the poor—devised their own instruments of exchange. They worked because people in similar straits agreed to accept them. Shinplasters and paper notes signified a community of poor and "disreputable" people working for their own survival and betterment. They represented a challenge to orthodox systems of valuation: a challenge by their very existence, but also a personal challenge, a call for recognition of the passer's community and humanity. Each shinplaster note carried a claim about the value, the labor, the ambition and potential, of its issuer. In that sense they represented the pull of the social. Orthodox economics imagined a world which depersonalized exchange, in which the possession of "real money" answered all questions about the character of the possessor. Shinplasters forced the personal, and the social, into a world which was trying to calculate them away.

THE PERSISTENCE OF SHINPLASTERS

Our modern money form is an odd combination of the desire for standards and the persistence of community. At the time of writing the US dollar remains the standard currency of international exchange, the "unit of account" against which other currencies are compared and valued. The dollar's hegemony marks the ascendance of the Unites States in the decades after the Second World War, and the power of a liberal world order which American military power policed. At the same time, the dollar no longer has any connection to gold: the source of its value is the military might and the gross national product of the US. In other words, the dollar might be seen as the extension of shinplaster currency: a self printed money form deriving its value from general acknowledgment of the worthiness of the community and people it represents. Advocates of the gold standard often insist that dollars are "founded on nothing," but community is real, and the labor and creativity of individuals are real, and in fact might be the source of all value. The history of shinplasters reminds of the degree to which value is derived in community with each other.[27]

CHAPTER FIVE

Money, Art, and Representation

"T'was only a balloon"—Seeing and Satire in the Cultural History of Money

NICKY MARSH

At the end of 2011 Virgin Money was launched as a new provider of financial services in the UK. Bearing the strapline, "Virgin Money, 40 years of better now in a bank," the advert accompanying its launch placed the Virgin brand's association with transport at its heart, from the futurism of "Virgin Galactic" speeding through starry space to the nostalgia image of the Virgin hot-air balloon gently climbing over the English countryside. This balloon, condensed as a red bubble, went on to dominate the visual identity of Virgin Money (previously Virgin Direct) and appeared on its High Street shop hoardings and its credit cards, and formed the basis of its single visual logo. The profound irony of the rock's absorption by a bubble—Virgin Money had bought the profitable sectors of the former building society, Northern Rock, from the government after a bail-out following the first bank run in the UK in 150 years—seemed to provide its own unwittingly wry commentary on both the abstract, speculative nature of contemporary finance and the failure of the UK Government to respond to the dangers that these were now conclusively demonstrated as possessing.

Yet Virgin Money's use of the bubble and the balloon as visual identifiers for credit was actually in keeping with the iconographic register of the financial services industry, especially in terms of its representation of personal credit and especially after the moment of crisis. Credit cards have obviously been associated with literal and metaphorical flight since their origin in the 1950s—both the actual luxury of international travel and the imaginary luxury of being able to escape the financial constraints of one's immediate time and space—and the hot-air balloon has been repeatedly evoked in this context. It is no surprise, then, that the aftermath of the financial crisis saw financial institutions hurrying to repair the positive associations of that which David Harvey was more critically diagnosing at the time as capital's faltering spatial and temporal "fix" in ways that were, appropriately, both fantastic and entirely literal (Choonara 2009: 335). The crisis had yet to reach its peak when Barclaycard launched its "Waterslide" campaign in 2008 (to be supplemented by a rollercoaster in 2010),[1] a strategy that was quickly emulated in 2009 as American Express and Lloyds TSB both launched campaigns that promoted flight and escape; the strapline of the former was "Come Fly with Me," and the visuals included pictures of brightly colored planes or space rockets urging potential customers to "Be a Traveller not a Tourist,"[2] and the latter was "For the Journey," and the visuals included not only hot-air balloons but trains, planes and bicycles.[3] It was not only personal credit that imagined itself in such terms at this moment: an analysis of financial adverts shown during the crash noted that in their self-representations financial institutions are "shown to exist above, outside, or across and beyond the cityscape" and their employees are subject to an "'architectural inflation' where the consulting partners are shown walking and talking casually on a platform or floor that towers above the towers" (De Cock 2009: 16).

In some ways the task of this chapter is a beguilingly simple one: it is to explain how and why the bubble, easily assumed to be one of credit's most satirically critical metaphors, had turned, by the start of the twenty-first century, into one of its most ubiquitous self-promotional icons. Of course, as I've already noted, the reasons that the bubble and the balloon are associated with credit are not hard to see: the mixture of fragility and flight that they suggest combine the reach that credit's spatial and temporal fix provides with an amplified sense of money's enduring imaginary reality, as it is that which is at once both entirely real (a physical token of exchange) and exponentially abstract (an idea sustained through a collective act of belief). The chapter explores this familiar tension between money's real and imagined status by elaborating the changing significance of the parallels between cultural representations of the bubble and theoretical representations of the function of credit money. In this reading the bubble indicates not only temporary escape but the illusion of control that money requires: these recurring images represent not the ephemerality of air but the presence of air that has been captured—that has been tethered and directed, improbably divided from itself by the flimsiest of skins. I read this illusion, and the paradoxical and fragile agency it suggests, as an example of the contradictory nature of modern rationality suggested by Slavoj Žižek—a rationality in which it is the fantasy of seeing beyond the illusion, of seeing the real relations of money or unveiling the hegemonic operation of ideology, that becomes the paradoxical source of their authority. It is the tightening of this paradox, in which it is not seeing money but seeing *beyond* it that becomes impossible, that this visual and literary history of the bubble as a metaphor for money directs us toward understanding. The history that the chapter suggests—starting with Jonathan Swift's originary critical "bubble" satires of the 1720s, moving to the ambivalently gothic accounts of Edgar Allan Poe's monetary satires in the 1830s and, finally, to the adulatory tone of Frank Baum's moneyed *Wizard of Oz* in 1900—is a history of the changing relationship between money and satire, a history in which credit's erosion of the distinction between the real and the not real comes to encompass, if never completely, the very possibility of its satirical representation. It is the critical history of our contemporary ability to accept credit money as entirely real, while simultaneously knowing that it cannot be, that we can see in this narrative.

SWIFT'S SATIRE: "THE SOUTH SEA PROJECT, 1721"

The complex relations that have sustained both state and private credit since the Financial Revolution have been frequently captured through comparisons with air. Some of the most compelling images of paper money—Joseph Addison's allegorical nightmare from 1711 in which the Bank of England's bags "filled with Mony" are "blown up with Air", the "waggon-way through the air" conjured by Adam Smith in 1776's *The Wealth of Nations*, the figures who sit amongst the clouds to print money in Hogarth's *Some of the Principal Inhabitants of ye Moon* from 1788 (Figure 5.1), the flatulent financial "surplus" emitted by the Secretary to the Treasury George Rose in William Dent's satirical *Public credit, or, the state idol* in 1797 (Figure 5.2)—all represent the credit of the Financial Revolution as a form of expelled air (Addison 1854: 22; Smith 1982: 42).

Such images of money as air represent the formative illusion of money, as that which is self-evidently both there and not there, in predictably dualistic ways. Paper money's power to create "good pastures and corn-fields" is born, in Smith's terms, upon "Daedalian wings" and these leave the economy open to the political dangers—of inflation, corruption and crisis—that credit money's shift of "the seat of power away from the country and into the city" in the early eighteenth century represented (Dick 2013: 5). This identification of wealth with credit money, rather than with land, had ontological as well as political implications: Joseph Vogl finds paper money's disturbance of the Newtonian natural order being represented in its metaphorical "windy emptiness," as credit

Some of the Principal Inhabitants of yͤ MOON, as they Were Perfectly Discover'd by a Telescope brought to yͤ Greatest Perfection since yͤ last Eclipse; Exactly Engraved from the Objects, whereby yͤ Curious may Guess at their Religion. Manners. &c.

FIGURE 5.1: William Hogarth, "Some of the Principal Inhabitants of ye Moon," 1788. © Trustees of the British Museum. Reproduced with permission.

money replaced an economic system that had assumed a natural solid equilibrium existed between signifier and signified, between paper signs and the materiality of land, between the government and the law with discourses which "focused less on acts of exchange and the balancing powers of the market," than on an ephemerality that was, like air itself, at the whim of "irritating factors of uncertainty, potential outlooks, and future expectations" (Vogl 2014: 52).

Vogl's account of money's illusory properties, its disturbance of a "natural solid equilibrium," finds a different vocabulary in Slavoj Žižek's account of money as paradigmatic of ideology itself, as a fantasy which *is*, rather than *conceals*, our reality. Money is a "double illusion" for Žižek because it "consists in overlooking the illusion which is structuring our real, effective relationship

FIGURE 5.2: William Dent, "Public Credit or the State Idol," 1791. © Trustees of the British Museum. Reproduced with permission.

to reality. And this overlooked, unconscious illusion is what may be called the ideological fantasy. [. . .] it is not just a question of seeing things as they 'really are', of throwing away the distorting spectacles of ideology; the main point is to see how the reality itself cannot reproduce itself without this so-called ideological mystification" (Žižek 1989: 21). The importance of Žižek's insight into the constitutive contradiction of money has been made apparent in the work of critics who have historicized how this belief functions. Ole Berg, for example, has carefully reconciled Žižek's recognition of this "real fetish" of money with established monetary theories in order to trace the operation of the belief in the impossible to obtain "real" that produces value for fiat currency: differentiating between the belief in the integrity of the state that supports state credit, the belief in the value of financial reserves that supports the private credit of the financial system and the "inherently unstable" and "self-propelling" desire for credit itself that supports the "post-credit money" of the contemporary (Berg 2014: 239). Yet, as Ian Baucom has also drawn on Žižek to suggest, this belief in credit money is better read as evidence of the abstract nature of modern rational agency than an irrational faith-like suspension of credulity. Baucom finds in Žižek's account of the "absolute freedom" of the enlightenment, "the exchange between the particular and the universal Will" in which "the subject gets nothing in exchange for everything," a causal analogy with the logic of fiat money. What Žižek understood, Baucom suggests, is that as the subject becomes modern, an "anonymous, interchangeable bearer of a universal will-to-freedom," that relates to itself as "an abstract representative of the universal," then it also comes to understand "the abstract value form typical of finance capital" and hence "abstract reason and Exchange alley" actually "predicate one another" by serving as "mutual conditions of possibility within that overarching speculative revolution which organizes abstract reason as a method for generating conceptual general equivalents and licenses a finance capital that has learned to profit from the trade in abstract values" (Baucom 2005: 55–6).

I want to begin by reading the eighteenth century representations of credit that deploy the bubble as suggesting not simply the ontological anxieties suggested by credit money's "windy metaphors," as fiat money inverts what is assumed to be the natural physical order of specie money, but the possibility of an agency arising from within this situation of radical uncertainty: the bubble offers the possibility that the most ephemeral but necessary of the elements has been captured and given direction. The very term bubble was associated primarily with deception rather than with mania in the eighteenth and nineteenth centuries, suggesting fraud rather than the herd behavior that produces an unsustainable rise in commodity prices familiar from its use today. The first dictionary of financial terms and advice, Thomas Mortimer's *A New and Complete Dictionary of Trade and Commerce*, describes the bubble as the means by "which the public are tricked and deceived" and suggests that the word functions both as a noun for the deceived (Mortimer urges that "proprietors" should be asked to "make a right judgment of the state of their affairs" in order to prevent the "public being made a 'bubble of'") and a verb for the practices of deception themselves (which Mortimer describes as "stock bubbling," which he notes has been brought to a "kind of science") (Mortimer 1776: 412). This sense of a deception that has been elevated to a "science" reinforces the sense that the metaphor of the air captured in the bubble or balloon might differ from that escaping from Addison's open bags, from Hogarth's clouds or even from George Rose's grotesque bottom. The air in the bubble is, in Steven Connor's much more elegant terms, "air limned, embodied, given a shape, given surface tension," and it is precisely this sense of tension, and the possibility of control that it suggests, that informed the satirist's use of the bubble as a metaphor that could register the peculiar new powers, as well as obvious dangers, of the credit economy (Connor 2008). I want to read the bubble, then, as an example of an intellectual culture that responded to the futural speculative mobility of money by seeking what J.G.A. Pocock so influentially described as "the stabilisation of this pathological condition," a culture that understood that if all one owned was "promises" then "not merely the functioning but the intelligibility of society depended upon the success of a program of reification," upon the quixotic act of rendering real that which is self-evidently not (Pocock 1979: 16).

This reading of the bubble as marking a necessarily impossible form of agency accords with the innovative intellectual history suggested by Peter Sloterdijk, for whom the bubble endures as a visual metaphor for a paradoxical form of lapsarian subjectivity. For Sloterdijk we blow bubbles in order to withstand our existential nakedness: the "raising" of human consciousness, he suggests, the asserting of the self in place of God, "turned man into the idiot of the cosmos" who has willingly embraced "exile and expatriated himself from his immemorial security" and is only able to afterwards exist through "self-blown bubbles of illusions" (Sloterdijk 2011: 23). Sloterdijk describes this as a "sphereological drama of development" in which the "mental resettlement shock" that occurs "when the first bubble bursts" is assuaged by the building of new bubbles which offer a way of negotiating the unbearable solipsism of modernity. Sloterdijk's examples range infamously widely but he uses a coin to demonstrate the commercial world-making logic of the bubble, providing a reading of the coin minted by the future Caeser Augustus in 38 BC, which includes his own profile alongside that of his adoptive son in an attempt to establish a dynasty against Mark Anthony. For Sloterdijk the coin represents the success of the pairing, and the effective ending of the Republic that they brought about, and hence "a monetary empire with omnipresent impartial money. Money is the third person in the Roman trinity—[. . .] father and son are united by the spirit of what is *valid*; the circular form of the coin draws the joined two together into the ideal form. As long as the coin was in circulation, one could indeed obtain everything with it" (Sloterdijk 2011, 180).

We can see something of this ambivalence, the bubble as a phenomenon that can embody money's capacity to break and re-make a series of worlds, written into the very structure of its first association with credit money in the modern age: Jonathan Swift's poem "The South Sea Project, 1721" (McLeod 2015: 34). The South Sea Company was a private company that was chartered in 1719 in response to fears about the political powers that the Bank of England's monopoly over "permanently funded national debt" gave it: the scheme encouraged creditors to "exchange their investments in government securities for South Sea stock" but the presence of these government securities led investors to incorrectly assume that the stock itself was backed by the government bonds and gave rise to a speculative mania that ended with a financial crisis in 1721 (Poovey 2008: 112). Swift, "the first prominent practitioner of the modern prank," wrote the poem in 1721, the year after he had begun work on *Gulliver's Travels*, and it similarly showcases the satirical political power of his fully-realised and inverted near-worlds.

The poem is an extended formal conceit—it becomes the bubble, in other words—as although the word itself is saved until the very end, it is preceded by a series of images that perform the cycle of the bubble, its swelling and bursting, in ways that are represented as simultaneously uncannily unnatural and productive. So the "pond'rous metal" of the "shilling," for example: "seems to swim | It rises in both bulk and height, | Behold it swelling like a sop; | The liquid medium cheats your sight, | Behold it mounted to the top!" and the "fishes | rising from the main | Can soar with moisten'd wings on high; | The moisture dried, they sink again, | and dip their fins again to fly." Swift combines this elemental sense of distortion, as the physical properties of land, sea and air are all repeatedly inverted, with his political anger at the "Directors" who had caused, and profited, from this collapse. He is clear that the bubble represents not simply the belief that money can be created from nothing—"put on what spectacles you please, | Your guinea's but a guinea still" he writes—but the specific power of the Directors is to create and ride the distorting effects of these creations—"Directors, thrown into the sea, | Recover strength and vigour there; | But may be tamed another way, | Suspended for a while in air." Hence when the bubble appears, as both a first and a furious finale—"The nation then too late will find, | Computing all their cost and trouble, | Directors' promises but wind, | South Sea, at best, a mighty bubble"—it is as a metaphor that encapsulates not an inevitable bust predicated upon an irrational boom but a more radical sense that the bubble of credit has been able to fraudulently remake the very fabric of the world from which the poem itself is formed (Swift 2013). Swift's reference to the superficial irrelevance of credit money's apparent illusion ("put on what spectacles you please, | Your guinea's but a guinea still") is in contrast to Žižek's claim about the impossibility of "throwing away the distorting spectacles of ideology" and appears as a neat, albeit teleological, marker of the contrast between the meanings that he and Swift assign to credit money's improbability. Swift, the self-identified "'rational surgeon' of mass delusion," uses the form of the poem to match, rather than simply to deflate, this power and in the process he demonstrates his own possession of an abstract reason that can confirm the existence of the real beyond the faulted hyperbolic promise of its exponentially unlikely increase (Mcleod 2015: 33).

The ability of the bubble to function as a metaphor that can both embody, and yet also satirically remove itself from, money's reforming of the natural world itself continues to be evident as the image of the hot-air balloon began to supplement, or sometimes even supersede, it as a visual metaphor for credit money, at the turn of the eighteenth century. In some ways the social reception of the hot-air balloon in this moment served to amplify the ambivalences suggested by the metaphorical associations between money and the bubble. Whereas figures such as Montgolfier were able to confidently assign a global expansiveness to the balloon that shared credit money's vocabulary, "one day men would travel the skies as fearlessly as they now sailed the seas. What would make that happen was trade and commerce [. . .] 'the life-blood of an ordered world'," others, including Sir Joseph Banks and Thomas Jefferson, regarded the balloon's apparent ephemerality with a familiar suspicion, deeming them mere "windbags" and "playthings with little scientific use" (Brant 2011: 75).

It was no surprise, then, that only three years after the Montgolfier's first took to the air that Francis Jukes' 1785 satirical "Stock Exchange" replaces the bubble with the hot-air balloon in its satirical representation of state credit (Figure 5.3). The cartoon represents the national debt as an over-sized gold orb

FIGURE 5.3: Francis Jukes, "Stock Exchange," 1785. © Trustees of the British Museum. Reproduced with permission.

that sits grandly on top of the Stock Exchange. The striking visual simplicity of the piece is belied by its full title—"The English Balloon, or National Debt in the year 1782, with a full View of the Stock Exchange, and its supporters the Financiers Bulls, Bears, Brokers, Lame Ducks, and others, and a proportionate Ball of Gold, the specific size of all the Money we have to pay it with supposing that to be Twenty Millions of Pounds sterling, the Gold, and Silver Trees entwined with Serpents, & upheld by Dragons, for the pleasure of Pluto & all his Bosom Friends"—and it is the platonic perfection of the two golden balloons that is at the center of the discrepancy. These balloons dominate and distort the image, appearing almost like a planet and its moon that has made a stately descent into London, and they paradoxically render the City's actual buildings mere facades as everything else becomes a fantasy in the face of their hyper-real grandeur. The title tells us that these ponderous orbs are balloons that measure the absence, rather than the presence, of the wealth necessary to repay the national debt, and they reveal that this is a fantasy of wealth creation that is as chimerical, and as dangerously tempting, as the Edenically serpent-entwined "Gold and Silver Trees" that surround them. Jukes uses the balloon, just as Swift had the bubble, to both acknowledge, and satirically deride, credit money's ability to create the real in its own image.

POE'S PRANKS: "THE GOLD BUG" AND "THE UNPARALLELED ADVENTURE OF ONE HANS PFAALL"

The hot-air balloon continued to function as a ubiquitous symbol for credit money in the early nineteenth century, although the sense of monstrous deception that characterizes Swift and Juke's representations begins to wane as the sense of wonder and horror that accompanied credit money's ability to re-shape the very meaning of the real begins to diminish. Images such as James Gillray's 1802 "William Pitt" ("The national parachute,—or—John Bull conducted to plenty and emancipation") (Figure 5.4), or Isaac Robert Cruikshank's 1821 "The Air Balloon or the Ascension of Drury," for example, represented the dialectical relationship between the ascension of credit and the decline of debt in fairly literal ways, pointing to the mendacity of political involvement in the creation of money rather than its capacity for an ontological transformation of the world. Slightly later images, including George Cruikshank's 1811 "The Land of Promise!!!" (Figure 5.5), Thomas Howell Jones' 1825 "The Reign of Humbug!!" (Figure 5.6) and Edward Williams Clay's 1837 "The Times" (Figure 5.7), go further, providing the moment of crisis with a more detailed, even realist, historical narrative.

These latter cartoons contained remarkably comparable panoramic structures: in each the long horizontal foreground suggests the chaotic

FIGURE 5.4: "The national parachute," 1802. © Trustees of the British Museum. Reproduced with permission.

destruction of money in the moment of crisis, as moneylenders and campaigning politicians are surrounded by the detritus of worthless bonds, bankrupt companies and, most pointedly, the bubbles of empty political speeches, while the background suggests the near-future that the crises will soon bring about—depicting images of the rural unemployed, shuttered buildings and stilled ships. In each cartoon the balloon's ascension intervenes in this indexical frame, its treacherous ascension extends the eye beyond the spatial and temporal horizons of the condensed narrative image and suggests both an escape from, and an endless extension of, the moment of crisis.

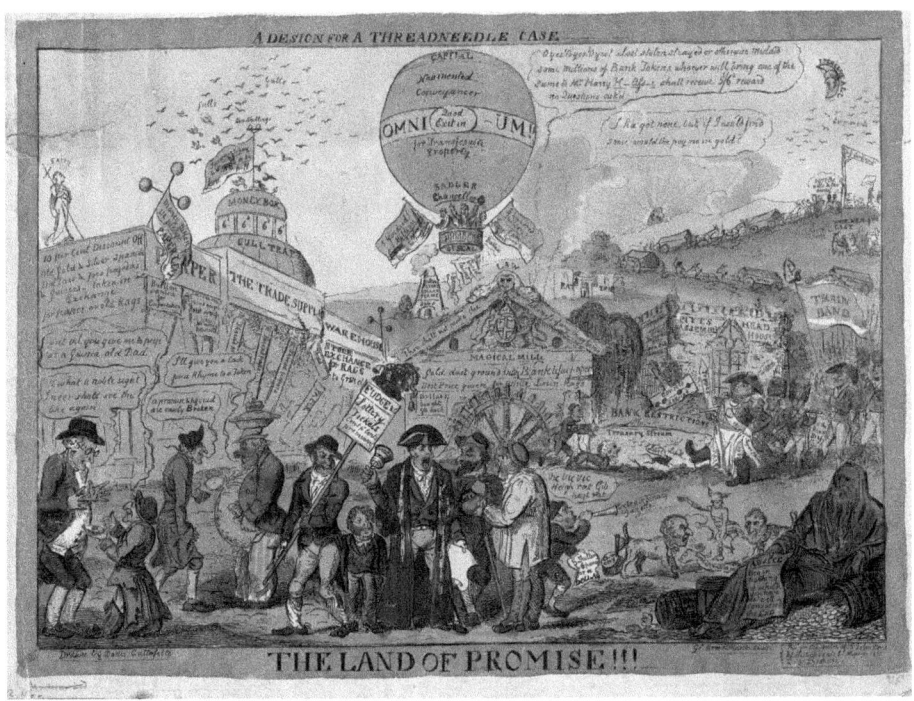

FIGURE 5.5: George Cruikshank, "The Land of Promise!!!," 1811. © Trustees of the British Museum. Reproduced with permission.

FIGURE 5.6: Thomas Howell Jones, "The Reign of Humbug!!," 1825. © Trustees of the British Museum.

MONEY, ART, AND REPRESENTATION 109

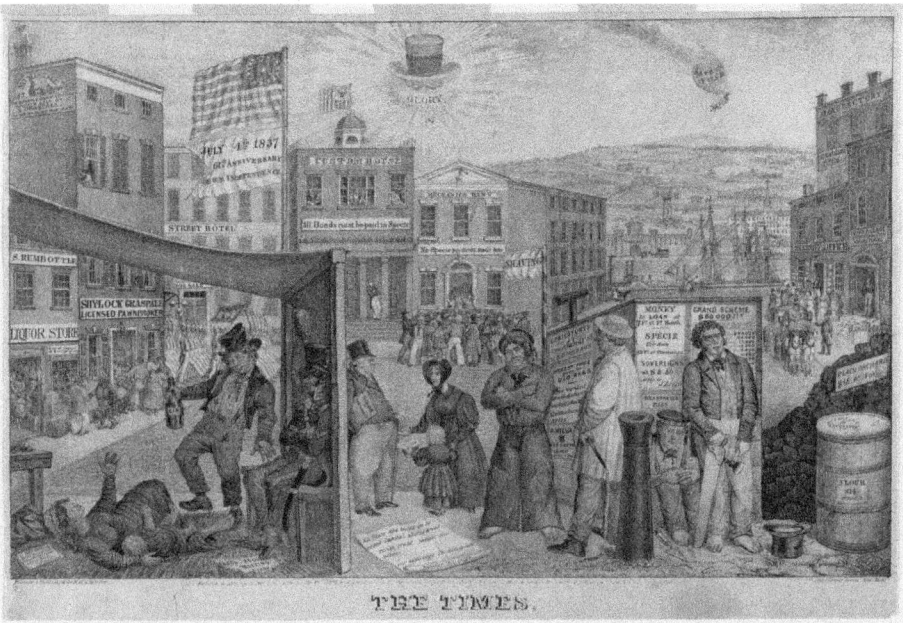

FIGURE 5.7: Edward Williams Clay and Henry R. Robinson, "The Times," 1837. Retrieved from the Library of Congress: https://www.loc.gov/item/2008661304/ (accessed August 11, 2016).

The last of these images, published in New York in July 1837, indicates that the monetary metaphor of the hot-air balloon, like the effects of the contraction in credit that it depicted in this image, traversed the Atlantic with more ease than the balloon itself was able to at this point (it was, appropriately, only in the late twentieth century that Richard Branson, the proprietor of the Virgin company, made this journey). The descriptive, even realist, register of Clay's cartoon, as it attempts to detail both the causes and the effects of this credit crisis, also opens us to the subtly different meanings that money and the hot-air balloon, and the connections between the two, accrued in nineteenth-century America. The hot-air balloon was received with particular alacrity in the still young nation because, as Richard Holmes has suggested, the fantasy of an uninterrupted Continental or transatlantic flight was beguiling, proffering the possibility that one could "celebrate the land as one vast, rolling entity" in ways that promised to "both discover" the new nation and "knit it together." Yet this was also a vision, Holmes notes, that was compromised by its own instant commodification, such flights were regarded as "moneyspinners," as the successful selling of the story was regarded as important as the flight itself (Holmes 2013: 99). Hence the arrival of the hot-air balloon, Will May suggests, "drifted uneasily" in America "between final frontier and town-fair diversion.

In moving back and forth between the aeronautic sublime to a provincial entertainment, the balloon also became a symbol for the epic turned farcical, for deflation, distraction, and the inconsequential. It promised escape and aerial perspectives, but its wonder was no longer unprecedented" (May 2015: 9).

Credit money experienced its own comparable, but distinct, grounding—the loss of an unprecedented wonder—in American culture of the nineteenth century as the primary debates around its meaning were characterized, not by the dangerously illusory lure of the magic shilling that "seems to swim" for Swift, but by the deep geographical and racial differences that came to shape the political territory of the nineteenth century. On the one hand credit money was, as Jason Goodwin's popular history of the greenback attests, entirely central to the self-identity of the post-Revolutionary independent American economy (Goodwin 2003). Yet, on the other, the relative sparseness of America's financial institutions also meant that its credit money had to be created not by the complex system of private banks that operated in London, but by "public institutions" that were "directly shaped by political interests and objectives," interests that had extraordinarily far-reaching effects, played out in terms of geography, class, and race (Konings 2014, 52). Credit money was thus both accepted as entirely necessary for the economy and yet also deeply contested in America in the nineteenth century—from Andrew Jackson's refusal to recharter the Second Bank of the United States and the subsequent "free banking era" of the 1830s in which credit money could be issued by very small private institutions, to Abraham Lincoln's issuing of the ill-fated state fiat greenback currency in the 1860s, to the bimetal debates that made William Jennings Bryan one of America's most famous political orators, if never President, in the 1890s.

Hence although the bubble and the balloon continued to symbolize the fraught and deceptive nature of credit money in nineteenth-century America, the nature of these deceptions were themselves of a qualitatively different nature from those of the British Financial Revolution of the century before, as credit money became both more quotidian and more explicitly politically, often electorally and institutionally, contested. America's satirical tradition provides something of a visual shortcut for narrating this shift as a number of cartoons from *Puck* from the 1890s suggest something of the ways in which the grand world-altering proportions of the balloon and the bubble apparent at the end of the eighteenth century—that produced their own satirical counter-real—became drastically reduced by the end of the nineteenth. Far from disrupting the very horizon of the visual image the balloon has become a plaything within it, represented as a child's fairground balloon in the cartoons of Charles Jay Taylor and Louis Dalrymple, for example, an icon that suggested not only the fraudulent emptiness of political promises about new kinds of money but one that ridiculed the simplicity of those who continued to believe in them (Figs. 5.8 and 5.9).[4]

MONEY, ART, AND REPRESENTATION 111

FIGURE 5.8: Charles Jay Taylor, "Coxey's Paternalism," 1894. Retrieved from the Library of Congress: https://www.loc.gov/item/2012648716/ (accessed August 11, 2016).

FIGURE 5.9: Louis Dalrymple, "The 'advance-agent of prosperity' on the road," 1896. Retrieved from the Library of Congress: https://www.loc.gov/item/2012648544/ (accessed August 11, 2016).

This shift, a politically skeptical acceptance of the inevitability of credit money, was marked in literary culture by texts that suggested a very different attitude to the question of satire itself and nowhere are the complexities of this difference more fully explored than in the work of Edgar Allan Poe. Poe had an intimate but aloof relationship to both the politics and economics of the money debates of the 1830s: a diffidence that was necessitated by his financial reliance on the goodwill of politicians (he longed for a federal position of the kind held by Nathaniel Hawthorne and Herman Melville) as well as of the commercial tastes of the literary marketplace. His "exposure" to the "shifting political commitments of paper-money men and gold bugs," and to a "cultural regime of deception that was at once indulged in and denied," Heinz Tschachler has argued, made Poe reluctant to commit to either a political or monetary position and he often "counterbalanced" his disdainful sense of both with "images of mere chance [. . .] or futility" (Tschachler 2013: 126). This ambivalence was replicated in his relationship to literary commercialism, and Terence Whalen has detailed the ways in which Poe both defined literary quality through commercial success and entirely rejected this "apparent philistinism and instead argue[d] that popularity should be taken as evidence of a book's demerit" (Whalen 1994: 35).

The 1834 short story "The Gold Bug" offers a compelling insight into the ways in which Poe's ambivalence toward the paper/gold debates produced a skeptical undoing of the rational/irrational dyad through which they were frequently read, in ways that point, instead, to the specific embeddedness of both in deeply held notions of American racial and class superiority. The story relates how William Legrande, of an "ancient Huguenot family" but reduced "to want" by "a series of misfortunes," discovers Captain Kidd's long-buried and forgotten treasure that allows him to be "reinstate[d]" in his "family possessions" (Poe 2001: 75). It is initially presented through the familiar racially-coded superstitious codes of the gothic: the disenfranchised Legrande is bitten by a "gold bug" when he discovers a rare golden-colored beetle and his subsequent belief in this species (read as code for specie by Marc Shell) is initially presented by the narrator, via Legrande's manumitted but loyal black servant, Jupiter, as a form of irrationality, that seemed to accord with the desire for specie currency in an already contracting economy.[5] The tale's narrative resolution, assumed by Legrande himself, undercuts this by revealing that his discovery derived from neither luck nor irrational faith but from honed and hyper-rational cryptographic skills that have solved riddles "of an abstruseness ten thousand times greater [. . .] it may well be doubted whether human ingenuity can construct an enigma of the kind which human ingenuity may not, by proper application, resolve" (Poe 2001: 92). Yet the apparent rational triumph of a fiat currency is compromised by Poe in the language of the denouement, which also unpicks the self-evident nature of the relationship between rationality and vision. Whereas the narrator holds to his belief in an empirical rationality, assisting Legrande in his hunt for the treasure only in an attempt to "convince the visionary, by ocular demonstration, of the fallacy of the opinions he entertained," Legrande reveals that this "visionary" status actually shares more with Jupiter's superstitions than the narrative arc initially allows for. His inspiration for translating the obscure parchment marks into legible code, for example, is associated with the presence of a kind of "gold bug" in his mind—an idea that "seemed to glimmer, faintly, within the most remote and secret chambers of my intellect, a glow-worm-like conception [. . .] do you know that Jupiter's silly words, about the bug being of solid gold, had a remarkable effect on my fancy?"—and he acknowledges that the series of "accidents and coincidences" that his quest relied upon were "so very extraordinary." In the final paragraph this resistance to rationality is connected to the submerged malevolence of the gothic as Legrande evokes the hierarchical implications of his possession of what were "silly words" in Jupiter's mouth. The narrator wonders aloud at the presence of the two skeletons that they find accompanying the treasure, and Legrande's response provides the story with its final words—"[Kidd] must have had assistance in the labor. But, the worst of this labor concluded, he may have thought it expedient to remove all participants in his secret. Perhaps a couple of blows with a mattock were sufficient, while his coadjutors were busy in the pit; perhaps it required a dozen—who shall tell?" The barely veiled threat to his own assistants' lives that the question leaves open provides a final reminder of the more ominous history of inherited privilege that Legrande's now "reinstated" familial position suggests (Poe 2001: 98).

The publication of his "hoax" story, "The Unparalleled Adventures of Hans Pfall," the following year further develops Poe's ambivalent relationship to the apparent rationality of the belief that sustains paper money. The story is told in three parts and the account of credit money that each offers suggests Poe's simultaneous critique, and complicity, with his analysis of credit. The first part of the story describes the arrival in the center of Rotterdam of a "queer, heterogeneous, but apparently solid substance, so oddly shaped, so whimsically put together," which is revealed to be a "balloon manufactured entirely of dirty newspapers" driven by an "odd little gentleman" who is "dressed in a loose surtout of sky-blue satin, with tight breeches to match, fastened with silver buckles at the knees" (Poe 2001: 3). The second, lengthiest, part of the narrative is the message that this curious guest delivers to the town's leaders, the Burgomaster, President and Vice President of the States' College of Astronomers. This relates the story of the "humble artisan" Hans Pfall "who, with three others, disappeared from Rotterdam about five years ago." Pfall, we are led to understand, left because he could not escape his debt and was "besieged" by his creditors "from morning till night" to the point where he considers suicide but, instead, happens upon a book that describes the science of balloon flight and allows him to plan a different kind of escape (Poe 2001: 5). This plan is swiftly enacted and Pfall flies—in a manner Poe details, with an abrupt change of register, via a fantastically detailed verisimilitude—to the moon, where he "tumbled headlong into the very heart of a fantastical-looking city, and into the middle of a vast crowd of ugly little people" (Poe 2001: 27). This third section of the narrative explains that Pfall has sent one of these people back to earth to plea for his "reward" because he is "pining" to return to home and announces that "this, then, is the object of the present paper. Its bearer, an inhabitant of the moon, whom I have prevailed upon, and properly instructed, to be my messenger to the earth, will await your Excellencies' pleasure, and return to me the pardon in question" (Poe 2001: 28). This concluding part of the narrative details the "rumours and speculations" that deflate the fantasy, these include the observation that "certain wags in Rotterdam have certain especial antipathies to certain burgomasters and astronomers," that "an odd little dwarf" had recently gone missing, that the newspapers from which the balloon was made were actually printed in Rotterdam, and that Pfall was seen, "no longer than two or three days ago," keeping company with the "three idle gentleman styled his creditors" (Poe 2001: 28).

On first reading the story offers itself as a critique of the ephemerality of credit that seems to recall the anxieties of the Financial Revolution. The narrative begins in "the Exchange in the well-conditioned city of Rotterdam," a city led by the burgomaster "Mynheer SuperbusVon Underduk," and thus offers itself as a fantastically corrupted—a rotter's—version of Amsterdam, the site of the first financial bubble of the modern world (Poe 2001: 1). Pfall's flight is initially presented by Poe as a flight from debt, and a failed attempt to financial absolution, which is enabled only by a paradoxical increase in debt: he borrows "in small sums, under various pretences, and without paying any attention to future means of repayment, no inconsiderable quantity of ready money" that allows him to purchase the raw materials to construct his balloon and when it comes to the difficult task of launching the balloon he redoubles his debts to his creditors, persuading them to assist him with "promises of payment of all scores in full, as soon as I could bring the present business to a termination" (Poe 2001: 5, 7). So, in the most obvious of senses, Poe's hot-air balloon flight presents a familiar critique of the emptily self-fulfilling nature of credit money. The money that launches Pfall to the moon, his strategy of escaping debts by increasing them, corresponds with Joseph Vogl's description of credit money as an "endless proliferation of a nondischargeable debt" that disrupted the hitherto "mechanical assumptions of the economy" (Vogl 2015: 56). Indeed, Poe is clear from the start that the story remakes the world, that it relates "phenomena" that are "so completely unexpected—so entirely novel—so utterly at variance with preconceived opinions—as to leave no doubt in my mind that long ere this all Europe is in an uproar, all physics in a ferment" (Poe 2001: 1).

Yet the revelation of the story's internal hoax, the realization that the quasi-scientific description of the balloon's flight that forms its middle section is the real trick, allows Poe to critique not the wonder of credit money's ability to remake the world but the acts of political deception that conceal themselves behind this apparent magic. The financialized world of Rotterdam is a harmonious one—"credit was good, employment was never wanting, and on all hands there was no lack of either money or good-will"—and Pfall alone fails to thrive because his occupation is anachronistically literal: he is a mender of bellows and as the people of Rotterdam become modern, keeping up with "the march of intellect and the spirit of the age," they found that "if a fire wanted fanning, it could be readily fanned with a newspaper" to the point where his livelihood becomes redundant, "as the government grew weaker, I have no doubt that leather and iron acquired durability in proportion, for, in a very short time, there was not a pair of bellows in all of Rotterdam that ever stood in need of a stitch" (Poe 2001: 3). Credit and the hot air of empty political promises promulgated by newspapers are conflated and satirically presented: it is the lampooning of this belief in authority that Hans Pfall's second career, as a satirist describing a believable balloon flight, proves that he has mastered. Hence at the story's end, when the reader learns that Pfall is still in credit (he sits in a "tippling house" with his ostensible creditors and all have "money in their pockets, from a trip beyond the sea") we realize the hoax was intended not to restore Pfall's credit but to mock the credulousness of the townspeople and the mendacity of those who lead them: in this second layer of the story, in other words, we realize that the satire is mocking both those who believe in the political promises that were so frequently attached to credit in America and, much more ambivalently, the eighteenth-century satirical tradition that insisted on a reality outside of them (Poe 2001: 29).

This latter ambivalence is formalized because the story's narrative commitment to its own internal hoax, which continues into the third part of the story, means that it embodies as well as satirizes these acts of deception. As Mario Castagnaro has suggested, the story may be written in the satirical "vein of Jonathan Swift" but its "technical and scientific detail" suggests a "shift in hoaxing away from literary satire toward a more contemporary understanding of the term that invokes the idea of intentional deception" (Castagnaro 2012: 258). The afterlife of the story further highlights the contradictions that Poe's ambivalent relationship to satire, the simultaneity of his intention to deceive and his desire to critique deception, that this "half plausible, half bantering" narrative form produced (cited in Parrinder 2014: 14). Poe's plans for developing the story into a lucrative popular series, for example, were dashed only weeks after its first publication when it was overshadowed by the publication of Richard Adam Locke's moon hoax, inspired, like Poe's story, by the publication of John Herschel's *A Treatise on Astronomy*, but producing a more fully realized description of the discovery of a civilization on the moon from it. Poe was furious by what he considered plagiarism but his patiently waited-for retaliatory publication, in *The Sun*, of a fabricated account of the first transatlantic flight, was ironically pyric as although the hoax was successful (reprinted by the New York *Sunday Times* and read by some 50,000 people before being denounced) it increased the circulation of the newspaper whereas demand for Poe's work, from publishers grown wary of him, decreased in its aftermath (Sova 2007). So Poe's critical account of credit is compromised in complex ways: "The Goldbug" undercuts the privileged rationality of credit money by recalling the persistence of the power relations that sustain the value of both paper and gold, whereas the erosion of the critical distance that this subtle satire requires in the "Unparalleled Adventures of Hans Pfall" reveals Poe's own complicity with these power relations.

BAUM'S HUMBUG AND *THE WIZARD OF OZ*

By the closing decade of the century we can see a sanguine re-writing of the thwarted adventures of Hans Pfall that also re-writes the role of credit money in America in surprisingly radical ways. The narrative frame of Frank L. Baum's *The Wizard of Oz* comes surprisingly close to that of both Poe's "Hans Pfall" and, lying obviously behind it, Swift's *Gulliver's Travels*. Baum's balloonist shares much with the fate of these earlier satirical protagonists: he is a prankster who concludes his imaginary journey beyond the known world by arriving in a "strange and beautiful looking country" populated by small "strange people, who, seeing me come from the clouds, thought I was a great Wizard" and "promised to do anything I wanted them to." Like Pfall and Gulliver, the Wizard accepts the role of outsized leader in this new world of small people only to eventually yearn for his home and work with his people to build a craft that can return him there. Yet, of course, it is the formal differences between the three satires that are the most telling in regard of how their authors approached the satirical meaning of credit money. Swift offers Gulliver as the hero of a fully-realized, recognizable satire: his diminutive Lilliputians mock the aggrandizing cruelty of contemporary Whig politicians just as his Bubble poem names and mocks the mendacity of the South Sea Directors. Poe's critique is, however, comparatively opaque, caught somewhere between hoax and satire, it is never entirely clear whether he is mocking, or failingly attempting to emulate, the practices of political deception and inherited privilege that he associates with the production of credit money. The situation for Baum is very different again: the Wizard's hoax is not only successful but celebrated and this is never more true than at the moment of its apparent unveiling where it becomes clear that he understands, to return to Žižek's words, that "throwing away the distorting spectacles of ideology" is an act that affirms, rather than denudes, ideology's ability to construct the real. It is what this tells us about Baum's relationship to the formative, structural illusion of the new forms of credit money that were appearing at the turn of the century that I want to conclude by exploring.

The Wizard of Oz, of course, has played a key role in America's money debates. It was identified as an allegory for bimetallism in 1964 by Henry Littlefield who suggested that the quest at the story's heart was a version of the march to Washington in 1894 by Jacob Coxey (mocked in the cartoons of Charles Jay Taylor) and that the Tin Man represents Eastern workers, the Scarecrow the Midwestern farmers, and Dorothy, who walks with silver shoes on a golden road to reach the Emerald City, is Baum's bimetallic "Miss Everyone [. . .] the innocent agent of Baum's ironic view of the silver issue" (Littlefield 1964: 53). This is a reading that has never gone away and responses have been subsequently divided between economic historians who develop it, qualifying the allegorical connections between story and the bimetallism debate in order to quantify the nature of Baum's loyalty to the populist pro-silver movement and cultural historians who assert a biographical reading that identifies Baum with the Republican party and a new capitalist "positive approach to economics" that departed from "earlier laissez-faire ideas of scarcity and self-denial in favor of more appealing notions of supply and prosperity" (Leach 1993: 254).

Yet these critical approaches, like the false division between them, are oddly neglectful of both what is actually happening with money in *The Wizard of Oz* and the history in which populism and consumerism were united through their shared advocacy of consumerism at the start of the twentieth century (Konings 2014). It is the credit that enabled this consumerism, the "time" or "installment" credit of the 1910s, that I want to suggest is being imagined in the *The Wizard of Oz*, a prediction that can be added to the long list of other things, including a robot man, an artificial heart and limbs, a monitoring system, that Alison Lurie has suggested that Baum's novel imagines (Lurie 2000).

One of the first things that Dorothy notices upon her arrival in the Emerald City is the presence of a bustling commercial economy in which "green pennies" are being exchanged for "green lemonade" (Baum 2000, 63). This is a monetary economy that is clearly linked to the wizard: when he finally appears to his guests it as a head on a round dais and he resembles nothing less than a coin (Figure 5.10). When he eventually responds to Dorothy's petition he does so by bluntly refusing the implicit reciprocity that inheres in the logic of the gift that clearly circulates in Oz beyond the Emerald City: "'Well,' said the Head, 'I will give you my answer. You have no right to expect me to send you back to Kansas unless you do something for me in return. In this country everyone must pay for everything he gets.'" (Baum 2000: 68).

When Dorothy and her friends reluctantly do as the wizard demands, killing the wicked witch and returning for their payment, the head fails to fulfil its promise. It is revealed to be made only of paper and conceals a "little old man" with a "wrinkled face, who seemed to be as surprised as they were" (Baum 2000: 96). The old man is immediately denounced as a "humbug," a word which implied not only the trickster tradition of the hoax but also, as Marc

FIGURE 5.10: *The Wizard of Oz*, first published 1900.

Shell's reading of "The GoldBug" pointed out, as an ironical inversion of "goldbug" (Shell 1982). Yet although Baum's wizard can clearly be placed in this satirical tradition that surrounded paper money, he is entirely free of the suspicions that it had imprinted on American popular culture. The Emerald City is a place of peace and plenty that actually contrasts against the more divided and violent Oz—"it certainly is a beautiful place, abounding in jewels and precious metals, and every good thing that is needed to make one happy. I have been good to the people and they have liked me," and Baum celebrates the wizard's humbug status with palpable delight: "'exactly so!', declared the little man, rubbing his hands together as if it pleased him. 'I am a humbug.'" (Baum 2000: 97).

The heightened pleasures of the Emerald City, as some critics have pointed out, correspond more closely to those of the White City of the 1893 World's Fair in Chicago than to a metonymically nationalistic Washington DC that readings of the wizard through the greenback have faltered upon.[6] Baum wrote *The Wizard of Oz* while living in Chicago and he was known to have been a frequent visitor to the Fair. His description of the wizard as "a man who goes up in a balloon on circus day, so as to draw a crowd of people" identifies the wizard with the idea of the fair and, indeed, a balloonist at the Fair drifted from it, carrying a small child, in ways that echo Oz's own trip (McQuade 2007). The connection also makes sense in terms of Baum's biography. Both Baum and

William Wallace Denslow, his close collaborator and the illustrator of the first edition, were frequent visitors to the Fair, Denslow reputedly visited it every day and his illustrations of it were published in the Chicago *Herald*. Baum's own commercial ambitions were also explicitly influenced by the Fair, his letters contain the rather hubristic admission that he had designed "Baum's Bazaar", the shop that he had opened in Kansas in the 1890s, that had failed because he had both misjudged the appetite of his community for consumer goods and then given too much credit to try and sustain it, in "the same style as the 'Fair' in Chicago (on a much smaller scale)" (Baum 2000: 176).

The Fair itself is, of course, widely associated with the emergence of this economy: historians have traced explicit connections between the Fair and the development of the glass windows of the department store, that Baum (who published *The Art of Decorating Dry Goods Windows and Interiors; A Complete Manual of Window Trimming, Designed as an Educator in All the Details of the Art, According to the Best Accepted Methods, and Treating Fully Every Important Subject* in the same year as *The Wizard of Oz)* was so active in developing. Yet, crucially, exhibits from the 1893 Fair were *not* for sale: they were intended to narrate a privileged version of a nationalistic history and anthropologists have subsequently theorized the world's fairs as a version of potlatch, a ritualistic display of goods that serve to demonstrate cultural power rather than the pleasure of consumption (Rydall 1993). Indeed, in his diary of 1893, Denslow sensed the destruction of wealth that the potlatch display hints at, when he noted that his "first thoughts" on seeing the "miles of ground covered with tremendous and artistic buildings" were "what a magnificent ruin they must make when all is finished" (Baum 2000: 176).

Yet money *was* made *in* the Fair, if not *by* the Fair and some of this money, at least, suggested the future development of credit money that Baum so desperately needed and, his failed shop suggests, had tried and failed to realize. In a rather bizarre side note to the history of the Fair, it appears that the real versions of the green pennies which bought the green soda that Dorothy noted on her entry into the Emerald City grew to become a dominant source of credit money in America. The entrepreneur who held the soda and candy concessions inside the Fair, Aaron Nusbaum, used the $150,000 he made to purchase, along with his brother-in-law Julius Rosenberg, half of the "fledgling mail order company Sears, Roebuck" in 1895 (Ascoli 2006: 25). The Sears catalogue, of course, burgeoned in the period between the World Fair and the publication of Baum's novella and made the consumer revolution of the 1890s available to rural workers in a way in which Baum's own Kansas shop never could.[7] Sears consolidated these successes in the twentieth century by leading the revolution in domestic credit, hence whereas its 1910 catalogue "delivered a stern lecture on the folly of installment selling," warning its customers that buying on credit could only increase the price of their goods, the policy was abandoned within the year, so deluged was it by requests for "time credit" that it feared losing custom: where Sears led others followed and in the years immediately following the First World War "credit plans sprouted like mushrooms" (Calder 1999: 200). That Sears and Baum shared, by the turn of the century, a frame of reference for consumer culture is indicated best by the front image from the 1900 Sears catalogue, which depicts a green-frocked woman positioned between a rural landscape and an enormous balloon-like floating globe.

The history of air as a metaphor for credit money is, then, one in which the balloon exponentially expands until it fills the very critical distance which it was originally launched to highlight: the changes in the status of satire that we can see occurring from Swift to Poe to Baum, as the former's "radical surgeon" becomes the latter's hand-rubbingly gleeful showman imagining the burgeoning of a domestic credit that is yet to appear, is entirely commensurate with the changes that have occurred in credit money as the apparent threats to the Newtonian order that it once represented have been absorbed to the point of celebration: with credit we can all escape space and time. But, of course, the idea that credit money has entirely filled the space for resistance is itself part of its own narrative, that we need to always be wary of. And it is the critique of this history that I want my final reading from nineteenth-century American literature to note.

When Emily Dickinson was writing poetry in the early 1860s stories of balloon flights were a commonplace and she frequently deploys the image to suggest the liminal state of ecstatic liberation that her writing so frequently demands but is seldom able to sustain in the face of the quotidian world. In poems such as "You've Seen Balloons Set—Haven't You," for example, the balloon's ascension is fantastic, akin to the world-altering properties of Swift's bubble, its "liquid feet go softly out | Upon a Sea of Blonde | They spurn the Air, as t'were too mean for creatures so renowned" (Dickinson 2016: 276). Yet the peculiar literalism of Dickinson's balloon in this poem, the contraction of the hyperbolic promise of its "liquid feet," can be explicitly linked to its corrosively over-determined use as a monetary signifier and we can read Dickinson's poem as resisting the collapse of the satirical potential of the balloon, and thus the dominance of the credit economy and literature's complicity with it, that the narrative from Swift to Poe to Baum suggests.

Dickinson's chosen newspaper, *The Springfield Daily Republican*, carried regular accounts of balloon flights in the early 1860s and the military ascensions of figures such as Thadeus Lowe are recorded alongside the domestic ascensions of those aeronauts not selected for his Union Army Balloon Corps. It is a description of one of the latter from July 1862 that offers a surprisingly close parallel with Dickinson's poem "You've Seen Balloons Set." The story of this "Exciting Balloon Ascension," sandwiched neatly between reports from the war's frontlines and reports from the markets, relates how the "Star Spangled

Banner" balloon "ascended from Boston Common" only to be "blown seaward, where it descended, and the aeronauts were dragged through air and water at a fearful rate."[8] The accounts are comparable: the "Star Spangled Banner," which gets its line caught as it moves from the wooded Boston Common to the coast, becomes the "Gilded creature" that "Trips frantic in a tree" and "Tears open her imperial veins and tumbles in the sea." Yet it is in the shared bathos of the contracted conclusions to both that the parallel becomes so telling. The newspaper story undercuts the drama of the rescue of the men and the loss of the balloon, which subsequently "shot upwards to the clouds," with the flat reckoning that consistently completed such journalistic descriptions of balloon flights: the vehicle had "held 50,000 feet of gas and cost $1200." The radical possibilities of Dickinson's balloon are similarly undercut by the abrupt reference to the "clerks in counting-rooms" who simply, devastatingly, negate its possibilities with their observation that "T'was only a balloon."

CHAPTER SIX

Money and Its Interpretation

The Century of Mobility and Acceleration and Its Money

LEOPOLDO WAIZBORT

MOBILITY AND ACCELERATION AS EXPERIENCE

Mobility and acceleration are experiences and phenomena that defined the nineteenth century, not just in Europe but across the planet (Osterhammel 2011; Bayly 2013):[1] experiences of people and groups, both singular and collective; phenomena in the areas of culture, politics, economics, science, technology, society, and even the psyche (or soul, as some prefer). From the outset, then, we can perhaps formulate the following problem: to what extent and how is an inquiry into money—money and its interpretations—correlated with mobility and acceleration? Is such a correlation indeed possible?

In the sphere of money and finances, the nineteenth century consummated a world system as the outcome of a process of rationalization, efficiency, and optimization. The emergence of national currencies in Europe, correlated with the formation and integration of national markets, along with the polyform processes of industrialization and urbanization, increasingly demanded a standardized and, as far as possible, stable system. Undoubtedly this posed a political and an economic challenge, met in diverse but generally similar ways, backed by two forces that complemented each other: the nation states and the banks.

The growing control of the circulation of precious metals—silver and gold—enabled the management of their inflationary and deflationary effects, while the introduction of the gold standard, initially by Britain—the dominant imperial power of the nineteenth century—at the start of the 1820s, would generate a situation and a debate that would last the entire century, instilling a singular dynamic to the economic life of nations and peoples. The idea was that as well as lending currencies stability and security, the gold standard would also allow a consequent stability of prices, and a common ground for trading between nations. Integration, therefore, was paired with the nation. The fact that Britain—imperial center, industrial center, and global financial center—adopted this form created a real and symbolic imposition on other countries to follow suit. The practicality of adopting a common standard, one that at the same time would permit the operation and regulation of sets of exchanges, also indicated the hierarchies between the parties involved, since not all the world's nations adopted it and, in not doing so, effectively signaled their subordinate role in the dynamics of prestige, wealth, and political and economic power. So while the nineteenth century did not consummate the gold standard, a system that would be dismantled with the First World War, it did allow its gradual and uninterrupted diffusion, backed by the large central banks, combining diverse forms of control with political and economic power. The international relations between the major European nations and their banks were to some extent consolidated as a result, thereby guaranteeing free trade, the flagship of the liberalism characteristic of the century.

The counterpart to free trade, liberalism, and the gold standard as monetary ballast were the banks and international financial system, which enabled the flow of capital between firms and nations. Investments spread to every corner of the world, negotiated primarily in the City of London. While flows of international trade commodities—hugely facilitated by the new merchant ships, no longer made of timber or reliant on the whim of the winds—were two-way, capital mostly flowed in the form of investments from center to periphery, configuring the final phase of imperialism at the end of the century. Hence the planet was already divided into creditor and debtor nations, modelling a new ascendancy of this modality of hierarchy and inequality between peoples.

It is no coincidence that the formula "the Age of Imperialism" has been used so much that it has become synonymous with a situation characteristic of the end of the nineteenth century in particular. The developments and improvements to the British state machine—at administrative, fiscal, and military levels—were soon followed in varying degrees by other nations wishing to assume a leading role on the international scene.

The double revolution enabled the transition—complex, tense, very often incomplete—from feudal to class-based society. In social terms, this transformation, which would be realized at very different paces and intensities over the course of the century, entirely transformed the life of people and nations. The industrial revolution unleashed an unprecedented dynamization of economic life, yet the process expanded very slowly among the various territories. England's precedence had assured it a privileged position throughout the eighteenth century. At the end of the following century, a kind of "second" industrial revolution potentialized the transformative energies: between the 1870s and 1890s, a series of innovations—the phonograph, lamp, and automobile, cinematography, radio transmission, the telegraph, the machine gun—backed by the growing use of electricity, a marriage of science and industry, electrified the period.

The nineteenth century was the century of industrialization in which the mode of industrial production spread and took hold, imposing a new division of labor, a factory organization marked by mechanization, machinery, and the rise of big industry, all of which had huge consequences in terms of social differentiation, stratification, and morphology. At a regional level, industrialization was clearly unequal in its intensity and its modalities, and evolved gradually over the course of the century from the large-scale cotton industry in the early decades to the chemical industries at the end, for example, matched by the shift from isolated industries to the great conglomerates.

For some considerable time now, capitalism has been the default term to describe, or at least name, the multicausal and proteiform process assumed by the economic dynamic in the Modern Era, and in an ever faster and clearer form after the double revolution. Not free of controversies—controversies that traverse the nineteenth century and enter our own present—an "economic order" that is not only economic, but also political, social, and cultural, defined the decisive features of the nineteenth century (though not this period alone, given that the process is continuous). The economic movement accelerated, the dynamics of trade intensified, production became industrialized, agriculture mechanized, new institutions created, the legal order reconfigured, the social structure altered, and new modalities of subjectification took over bodies and minds. Although the differences between long, medium and short term views are irresolvable, each imposing its own specific mode of description and understanding, delineating distinct images of dynamics and processes, outcomes and situations, the nineteenth century stands out as a moment of self-consciousness (to which Marx's work testifies decisively) in which capitalism appears not just as a descriptive procedure, but equally as a set of descriptions vying with each other to comprehend a complex historical change—a change in which capital and labor, industry and mechanization, mentalities and conceptions are interwoven in a concrete historical formation, varied but at the same time susceptible to and demanding analysis and comprehension. The nineteenth century thus displays an especially dynamic stage of the capitalist process with some of its characteristic features, beginning with the accentuated division of labor concentrated in the sphere of market production, combined with private companies coming to occupy the place of agents par excellence, and the search for profit as the primary objective. To use a particular jargon, a mode of production related to relations of production, but in symbiosis with new modes of circulation of produced goods and new modes of consumption (including, for instance, the creation of "department stores" in the United States). A mass of wage-earning workers, free to sell their labor, within a labor system regulated by a specially tailored institutional and legal framework, enabling an unprecedented increase in the productivity of human work. Spreading around the world in uneven and combined development, nineteenth-century capitalism found in the monetary and financial markets—capable of speeding up the mobility of capital through transfers, methods of payment and the centralization of operations and banks—the means for its optimization: in other words, its dynamization, acceleration, and mobility. In the famous and perhaps unsurpassable formulation of the feats of the bourgeoisie in the 1848 Manifesto, *Alles Ständische und Stehende verdampft*: "All that is solid melts into air" (Marx and Engels 1848 [1982]: 29).

The so-called "Second Industrial Revolution," which exploited the possibilities created by electrification (the dynamo, electric motor, generation of electricity), enabling a levering of large, medium, and small industries within an unparalleled symbiosis of industry and science, with technology definitively taking on the role of a productive force. Companies also became larger and more anonymous, the employed masses were made up of both industrial workers and employees in the service sectors, both of whom populated the ever-expanding cities. Concentration was a phenomenon marking the era, the flipside of which was the global expansion of products and investments.

The city, always the place of the market and trading, a center for meeting and making deals, a hub of interdependences, saw a huge growth over the century. The nineteenth century was also a century of urbanization, which intensified like never before. The great cities, the metropolises, emerged as centers driving economic life as poles and machines of acceleration and circulation, in a process that spanned from the early traffic of pedestrians and carts to automobiles, trams, bicycles, trains, and eventually the "underground." Where there were walls, these were taken down. Where there was darkness, gas lighting arrived, followed by electric. Improvements to infrastructure, the housing market and property speculation, mortgages, urban planning, new forms of urban life, marked by the existence, in the same concentrated space, of distinct social sectors often in conflict—all of these aspects made the city "modern." Modern, moreover, in its strong relation with industrialization, which demanded new spatial arrangements. And modern too in its relation to its surroundings, in the increasingly pronounced difference between city and countryside, the large cities and small towns, as well as the relations established between the major cities, ever stronger networks of political, economic, and cultural interdependencies, often marked by migratory processes of different scales and origins nearby and afar. Modern as well in its strong relation to innovations and new industrial and urban technologies for public or private use.

These ever larger and more modern cities also became the centers of the nation states and national economies and, as a result, typically the hubs of interstate processes and the global economy. Commerce and communication were based in the large cities from where they radiated to the four corners of the world. Providing services thus became one of the central modalities of the cities, without which they would be unable to keep pace with the intensification and concentration of activities.

From early on, the train, railway, and station appeared as marks and symbols of the process of the nineteenth century, marking, occupying, and cutting across the city, connecting spaces, altering perceptions of time and space, transporting people and merchandise, creating jobs, stimulating migrations, and demanding innovations to machinery and buildings.

However, ships—now made of iron and motor-powered—were the great explorers of the major world trade routes, transporting people and products, enabling the flux of economic exchanges in an imperial regime and consolidating the wealth and poverty of nations. Local and regional markets and commercial centers overflowed their borders, reaching other markets and centers by land and sea.

Networks were created, ever larger, ever more intense: ceaseless and accelerating flows of people, goods, information, and also moneys. The communication networks expanded at an unparalleled rate and by the end of the century telegraph cables were connecting the continents. Wireless telegraphy also flourished during the same period. As the new century began, radiotelegraphy became the leading communications technology. Even so, letters continued to circulate, now more than ever: the ample development of postal services over the century and increases in literacy rates meant that letters were no longer a class privilege. Newspapers also multiplied, both in the number of titles and the amount of copies printed. Business and private life converged in these new and renewed forms of communication.

Human beings moved about like never before. Merchandise likewise. Even languages, beliefs and religions, and artistic styles circulated more widely than ever, transforming culture into a global phenomenon. This diffusion allowed for an unprecedented broadening of horizons. The world became bigger and more diverse for a large portion of its inhabitants, albeit not everyone: numerous asymmetries in wealth and social hierarchy remained and, moreover, many became more pronounced with the processes of "westernization," imperialism, urbanization, and industrialization. Concurrently, as Bayly argued, "over a relatively short span of 140 years [1780–1914], the variety of social, economic, and ideological systems across the world was significantly curtailed and [. . .] a much greater uniformity become apparent. At the same time, and paradoxically, most human societies demonstrated a much greater complexity within these limits" (Bayly 2013: 478).

The complement to such mobility was acceleration. The quickening pace of transformation was especially a feature of the final years of the century; up to then, in global terms, the capacity for adjustment and adaptation to changes, which were constant, was considerable. The temporal structures transformed and with them the human experience of acceleration, which became apparent everywhere—in the pace of work and industry, in the circulation of goods, in the transmission of information, in everyday life, in the new machinery, in the circulation of money, in the proliferation and omnipresence of clocks, and the establishment of timetables, beginning with working hours. The train and telegraph were the heralds par excellence of the acceleration of time and space—what some call their mechanization, others their industrialization. By detaching themselves from the natural world and the rhythm of nature, human beings, goods, and information acquired a quickened mobility, aboard wires, ships and trains, automobiles and trams, and even airplanes with the turn of the twentieth century. Historical experience itself sped up, something new was experienced, a world that between someone being born and dying was no longer the same, unlike the past (see Koselleck 2000: 150–76, 195–202; Koselleck 2010: 130–50).

Many authors have already underlined how energy was one of the themes of the century. From steam to coal, gas, petroleum, and electricity, the nineteenth century was the era of energy—which, not coincidentally, became a polyvalent concept, spreading even into theories of language, psychology, and other areas of the humanities. A metaphor of the century. Osterhammel proposes the idea of an "intensification of efficiency" as one of the characteristic features of the nineteenth century, manifest in work productivity, in the military domain and in the control of state apparatuses over national populations (Osterhammel 2011). As indicated earlier, this became manifest in the sphere of monetary economics too.

These are just some of the most decisive traits and characteristics of the transformation of the world over the nineteenth century, which appeared in discontinuous form in time and space, but presented here in more simplified form. Despite the enormous variety of situations and collective experiences found worldwide, Bayly stresses the uniformization that took place, not only in terms of major institutions and large-scale processes (the state, city, capitalism, global economics), but also in the day-to-day life of people, who began to live by the clock, dress in similar ways, and behave in a more standardized fashion. This same process, again unequal and combined, has been interpreted in a variety of forms ever since.

At the same time, self-reflection is one of the century's hallmarks. Here it suffices to recall *Phänomenologie des Geistes*, published in 1806, which takes as its problem "how the new is born" (Nobre 2018). The fact that this new has been ceaselessly explored in minute detail ever since, from sociology to poetry, is itself no novelty. "Modern" (as noun and adjective) and "modernity" have never ceased to circulate. Multiple moderns and modernities (Eisenstadt 2007), conceived in a variety of registers, sometimes emphasizing social aspects, sometimes economic, sometimes political, sometimes cultural, resulting in a tangled web whose historical concreteness defies any attempt at definitive interpretation.

GEORG SIMMEL REFLECTS ON MONEY

This broad and variegated spectrum of transformations is clearly correlated with reflection and the evolution of ideas. But how so? It has long been an aim to design models that allow us to think about the connections between social structure, reflection, and self-reflection. Given this back history, we can imagine that the reflection on money has accompanied these transformations in a mediated and complex form. In thinking about money, the ideas surrounding money also transform the transformations at the same time as they investigate and respond to them.

Acceleration and mobility have been present in economic and monetary thought since the "classical" period with the theme readily encountered in the works of the "classics" of so-called "political economy." Summarizing this history here would be impossible. Instead I look to show how, in the work published by Georg Simmel (1858–1918) in 1900, *Philosophie des Geldes* [in English, *The Philosophy of Money*], we find a consistent and nuanced elaboration of the problem of money informed by nineteenth-century experience. In other words, Simmel's work is an analysis of money rooted in the experiences enabled by the contemporary transformation of the world. Nonetheless, its relevance to our own present enables a discursive approach located in two time frames: now and during the moment of its formulation, such that the experiences of the nineteenth century, which more immediately informed Simmel's thinking, are compared to the experiences of readers today.[2]

It is difficult to identify the dialogues in which Simmel is implicitly engaged while he reflects on money given that many of his interlocutors have since vanished under the waves of time. The same does not apply to the historical experiences and phenomena, though, making it much easier to see how Simmel's reflection was rooted in his own period, in his historical present, than to specify the interlocutors with whom he discussed and debated. Obviously, there were the classics of economics—Smith, Ricardo, Mill, already translated over the century into German and incorporated, to varying degrees, into local discussions in which cameralism remained for a long time present.³ Simultaneously, we can note the emergence of a German political economy belonging to the so-called "historical school," which the literature tends to divide into three generations: the first, born around the 1820s, whose main representatives were Bruno Hildebrand (1812–94), Wilhelm Roscher (1817–94), and Karl Knies (1821–98); the second, born around the 1840s, including Gustav Schmoller (1838–1917), Lujo Brentano (1844–1931), Karl Bücher (1847–1930), and to some extent Georg F. Knapp (1842–1926); and the third, among whom Max Weber (1864–1920) and Werner Sombart (1863–1942) stand out. Simmel, a contemporary of the third generation and a student of Schmoller, but trained in philosophy, was heavily affected by the Völkerpsychologie (a mixture of social anthropology, comparative linguistics, cultural history, and sociology) of his professor, Moritz Lazarus (1824–1903), as well as by an eccentric contemporary of the first generation, Karl Marx (1818–83). This mix of classical political economy, critique of political economy, the German historical school, academic and extra-academic German Philosophy (Kant especially, but also Nietzsche), Völkerpsychologie, the Austrian school of economics (Carl Menger, 1840–1921; Friedrich von Wieser, 1851–1926; Eugen Böhm-Bawerk, 1851–1914): all this and much more formed the intellectual context in which Simmel's work appeared. Moreover, a number of other German authors were very important, sufficing to recall here Adam Müller (1799–1829), whose monetary theory presents many aspects in common with Simmel (see Altmann 1908; Palyi 1916; Winkel 1977; Stadermann 2000). The development of capitalism in Germany at the end of the century, the increasing masses of the new factory workers, social issues, urbanization, changes to social hierarchies, new production systems, new behaviors and uses, new demands for management and state intervention—all of this occurred in a particularly rapid fashion in German lands. The German Empire was proclaimed in 1871, finally unifying the diverse territories and potentates into a nation state. A single currency, the "mark," was immediately created, initiating monetary unification in the territories then united under the "Reich." Living through these changes undoubtedly stimulated the ideas of Simmel, who began to conceive and write his book on money at the end of the 1880s.

It would be naive to imagine or pretend that any single object or idea could synthesize by itself all the transformations and experiences that the century afforded and that defined it. Nevertheless, the attempt to condense a general image, a cluster of meanings, in one single idea may have some cognitive yield. Such is the case of money. Because it spread everywhere. And even in those places it was still unable to reach—poverty and destitution—it was still right there, *in absentia*. Always pulsating, always moving. Perhaps nothing in the material world is quite so omnipresent in human life. Even when it comes to the virtual world, it is not far behind. However, it is not found in the material and virtual worlds alone, but also, and perhaps primarily, in the mental world. Simmel discussed these questions extensively in *Philosophie des Geldes*, the aim of which was, no more or less, to relate money to the whole of existence, demonstrating how money shapes human life and how human life shapes money. Pursuing this plurivocal relation, then, he could investigate a double object, money and humans—gaining an understanding of the world in which we live. Not just in terms of their unity or abstraction, but in terms too of their differences and concreteness. The one and the many, the singular and the plural, both one and the other. Humans and money: therein lies the problem. What though is the solution?

Simmel ventured along more than one path. Not out of any eclecticism or indecision, but from an understanding that, adopting the viewpoint of the whole of existence, all paths lead to money, or set out from it. While he sought "to make the essence of money intelligible from the conditions and connections of life in general," he also wanted "to make the essence and organization of the latter intelligible from the effectiveness of money" (Simmel 1900 [2005]: 52). This programmatic formulation was transformed into a lengthy book, organized in two parts, each pursuing one of these directions. Nevertheless, the secret resides in—and the term is deliberately audacious—the dialectic inaugurated as a form of problematization. Dialectic in a rigorous sense: not the academic sense of thesis, antithesis and synthesis, which indeed is present too, but the dialectic that, through its movement, determines the different in its difference in order, through and with difference, to highlight a becoming as a movement of differentiated and even contradictory forces, which result in the concrete.

It is precisely difference and concreteness that make Simmel's thought a stimulus to our own thinking today. Whether we turn to distant places or those close at hand, we find money—in some of its thousand and one forms. In different forms, sometimes even without form, but nonetheless always there.

Let us turn then more closely to some of Simmel's developments. His best known text, the lecture "Die Großstädte und das Geistesleben" (The Metropolis and the Mental Life) (Simmel 1903), which is a derivative of *Philosophie des Geldes*, systemizes in concentrated form some of the topics discussed in the book or develops the theme based on the viewpoint opened up by it. Simply reading the paper immediately allows us to identify the connection with the description made by historians, summarized above.[4] The second chapter of *Philosophie des Geldes*, for its part, is entitled "The Substantial Value of Money." Here Simmel begins by arguing that money need not have its own value. In fact, the historical process indicates that initially object-money possesses its own value, but gradually loses it as it transforms into money. The more complete the transformation of the object into money, the more it loses its own or intrinsic value. The function of money is to measure values, not to possess its own value (becoming established, therefore, as a unit of account). Simmel describes, then, the transition from money as a substantial value to money as a functional value: a transition from the concrete and immediate to the abstract and mediated. Ultimately money converts into a symbol by becoming pure function. In this process, there is a diminution of the qualitative in favor of the quantitative, since the qualitative is related to substance. The next step of his argument demonstrates what could be called a dialectic of money's functional value; by foregoing its other possible functions, what turns into money acquires its own specific value—in other words, it acquires a value by foregoing values. Money possesses a relational value, made concrete in the process of exchange. Nonetheless, money never completely attains the condition of a pure symbol of economic values and some remainder of substantial value is inevitable in order for money to be able to perform its function. We can note, therefore, the analytic-argumentative procedure: Simmel begins by developing the transition from money's substantial value to its functional value and asserts that it eventually turns into pure symbol, losing its substantial value. Subsequently, however, while exploring the life of money's functional value, he ends up asserting that some substantial value always persists. Academic dialectics might see this as a movement of thesis-antithesis. But his analysis does not stop here and in the third and final part of the chapter (the chapter indeed has three parts, as though evoking the thesis–antithesis–synthesis triad) Simmel deconstructs the distinction between substantial value and functional value, on the basis that ultimately substantial value is also functional.

Pursuing this line of argument, Simmel explores various developments in parallel that prove decisive to our understanding of how he conceives "society," providing a clear insight into the processual and relational nature of his analysis and thinking, which nowadays returns, though very often disguised and without recognition of its Simmelian roots. For this reason, it is worth hearing his own voice:

> The interaction between individuals is the starting point of all social formations. [. . .] Further development [of this social formation] replaces the immediacy of interacting forces with the creation of higher supraindividual formations, which appear as independent representatives of these forces and absorb and mediate the relations between individuals. [. . .] The interactions between the primary elements that produce the social unit are replaced by the fact that each of these elements establishes an independent relation to a higher or intermediate organ. Money belongs to this category of reified social functions. The function of exchange, as a direct interaction between individuals, becomes crystallized in the form of money as an independent structure. [. . .] exchange is one of the functions that creates an inner bond between men—a society, in place of a mere collection of individuals. Society is not an absolute entity which must first exist so that all the individual

relations of its members—super—and subordination, cohesion, imitation, division of labour, exchange, common attack and defence, religious community, party formations and many others—can develop within its framework or be represented by it: it is only the synthesis or the general term for the totality of these specific interactions. [. . .] It is, therefore, almost a tautology to say that exchange brings about socialization: for exchange is a form of socialization. It is one of those relations through which a number of individuals become a social group, and 'society' is identical with the sum total of these relations.

—Simmel 1900 [2005]: 173–74

We can note that although in our present-day world exchanges occur primarily through the mobilization of money, his argument applies generally: the role of money in the world in which we now live is indeed decisive, since it becomes the very production of society.

Another of Simmel's important analytic developments is the eschatology presented in the final pages of *Philosophie des Geldes*, in which the world is comprehended simultaneously as duration and non-duration, fixity and motion. It is only within this eschatology that the full significance of money emerges, making it the most perfect and complete symbol of the mobile and malleable dimension of the world, a world image founded on movement: "There is no more striking symbol of the completely dynamic character of the world than that of money" (Simmel 1900 [2005]: 517).

Hence why Simmel makes money the object of his philosophy: exploring the topic of money implies an inquiry into everything that moves. Money is motion in simultaneously concrete and abstract form. It is the modern as mobility and acceleration. Given its exemplary symbolic quality, money allows Simmel to characterize the universal through the singular, in line with his underlying cognitive procedure, his "aesthetic pantheism" (see Waizbort 2000: 75–112).

Money is nothing but the vehicle for a movement in which everything else that is not in motion is completely extinguished. It is, as it were, an *actus purus*; it lives in continuous self-alienation [Selbstentäusserung] from any given point and thus forms the counterpart and direct negation of all being in itself [Fuersichsein].

—Simmel 1900 [2005]: 517

The same self-alienation that characterizes money as a pure act also characterizes modern life. The direct negation of every "being in itself" is the absolute "being for the other": money, something that only has meaning in relation to its exterior, since it is always in search of more objects through which it can demonstrate its value. The more objects, in quantity and quality, come face-to-face with money, the more it can exercise its quality as a universal equivalent.

Yet while money symbolizes motion, it also symbolizes stability. It can combine within itself the two world images outlined by Simmel, mobility and stability, as the basis of his eschatology. Insofar as it can be exchanged for all manner of things, even for everything, money is revealed as something fixed and immutable in the face of the infinite number of things that circulate ceaselessly around it:

> As a tangible item money is the most ephemeral thing in the external-practical world; yet in its content it is the most stable, since it stands as the point of indifference and balance between all other phenomena in the world. The ideal purpose of money, as well as of the law, is to be a measure of things without being measured itself [. . .] Money expresses the relationship that exists between economic goods. Money itself remains stable with reference to the changes in relationships [. . .].
>
> —Simmel 1900 [2005]: 517

We can discern, then, the double character of money (or its double role), which expresses the two world images that anchor and characterize the modern—and here we can also see the proximity of Simmel's eschatology to the one depicted by Baudelaire in "Le peintre de la vie moderne." The frantic life described by Baudelaire is also a theme of Simmel's reflection, since the expansion of the monetary economy precipitates an acceleration in the pace of life, something that a phenomenology of money must necessarily acknowledge and explore: the more money assumes its functional character and frees itself from its substance, the more it speeds up life. Even in substantial form, like a round coin, money "symbolizes the rhythm of the movement that money imparts to transactions" (Simmel 1900 [2005]: 512–13). But it is above all the extreme case of concentration of money, the stock exchange, that reveals the acceleration of the pace of life to its maximum intensity:

> [. . .] the stock exchange is the centre of monetary transactions. It is, as it were, the geometrical focal point of all these changes in valuation, and at the same time the place of greatest excitement in economic life. Its sanguine-choleric oscillations between optimism and pessimism, its nervous reaction to ponderable and imponderable matters, the swiftness with which every factor affecting the situation is grasped and forgotten again—all this represents an extreme acceleration in the pace of life, a feverish commotion and compression of its fluctuations, in which the specific influence of money upon the course of psychological life becomes most clearly discernible.
>
> —Simmel 1900 [2005]: 512

Simmel comments on the New York Stock Exchange and certainly had his eye on the Berlin Stock Exchange, which was beginning to flourish at the time Simmel was writing—indeed its regulation had become a topic of heated debate. Here we can note Simmel's capacity to articulate exterior and interior, the events of the stock exchange with the agitation of the soul, such as when he relates the city and the life of the spirit. Money, increasingly present, symbolizes all of this dynamism, making it the perfect symbol of the modern. Not only the modern economy, but the modern lifestyle and even, with its rationalism and abstraction, modern ways of thinking. The life of bodies and minds shapes and is shaped—such is Simmel's program—by money, encompassing the whole of existence.

The questions examined by Simmel are innumerable and their relevance testified during his own era and our own, exploring themes that cut across diverse fields of knowledge. Contemporary sociologists, for example, are interested in how money mediates social relations and how social relations mediate money; how it represents values, whether these are "monetary" or not; how we possess money and how we are possessed by it; how money creates its own temporality and what temporality this is. They explore the symbolic dimension of money and how it realizes both means and ends, develops teleological series, defines a mode of action directed towards ends. Money is both an objective and a subjective value. It creates social ties, promotes freedom, gives form to subjectivity, attributes personality and impersonality to social relations, enables the emergence of social types like the poor, the greedy, the ambitious, the blasé, the ascetic, the cynical, the squanderers. It both is and implements tool and technique, drains feeling of color and is in tune with the intellect.

Economists, meanwhile, are interested in value, the theory of value, the processes that constitute values and the values that constitute processes (especially economic processes); the relations between object and value, conscience and value; the problems of scarcity, utility, prices, wages, production, and circulation; money as a substance and a function; currencies and the genesis of means of exchange; the historical development of money and the problem of the equivalent. They wish to understand credit, the concentration and dispersion of value, means of payment, and how money mediates the economy.

Anthropologists, for their part, inquire into how representations of money are formed and transformed; how local, regional, and universal means of exchange are created socially, as well as forms of counting and accounting; what the status of exchange actually is and how money constitutes and/or is constituted by it; how money is spent, saved, and squandered; how money informs conceptions of quantity and quality. They want to know who buys and who sells, how they buy and how they sell; how money circulates and how things, persons, and immaterialities circulate with it.

Obviously this distribution by discipline is arbitrary and incomplete. Many of the questions, if not virtually all of them, encounter reverberations in some form or other in all three disciplinary fields and others too, including philosophy, psychology, law, political science, history (and especially monetary history), and numismatics, just to mention the most obvious. All of these questions are present in and lend substance to *Philosophie des Geldes*, reflecting the diversity of phenomena that Simmel sought to contemplate and, in some form, synthesize into a "philosophy"—the very idea that, for him, offers the possibility for this synthesis. Nothing prevents us from thinking differently, of course, leaving synthesis to one side and diving into the raw concreteness of the particularities and differences. But we can also look for synthesis in other modalities, since each discipline can, each in its own way, offer possible syntheses.

Simmel's reflection thus offers a space of debate and discussion for themes and problems that affect the everyday life of everyone and are subject to the reflections of many. Since all of us need money to live, though some live just for money, the theme is familiar to everyone. But the ways in which it can be approached, and its amplitude, less so.

The topic is inexhaustible. Not a day goes by without it appearing to us in one of its infinite forms. Simmel may very well offer the initial stimulus. But neither do we need to remain scholastically bound to him: the paths are various and we can become lost on any. And it is precisely then that we can truly evaluate Simmel's enterprise, because no one who becomes lost can fail to find a signpost in the pages of *Philosophie des Geldes*.

We can take an example significant to the anthropology of past and present. Much of Marcel Mauss's reflection on what he called "systems of total prestations" was an immediate continuation of what Simmel had formulated in *Philosophie des Geldes*, although this was not made explicit by the French sociologist. In this sense, those total social facts that "set in motion [. . .] the whole of society" (Mauss 1923 [1974]: 179) are a generalization of Simmel's argument, formulated years earlier. Seeking to summarize the "heuristic principle" evoked by Mauss, Claude Lévi-Strauss formulated it as "the attempt to understand social life as a system of relations" (Lévi-Strauss 1960 [1974]: 26, 27). Here we encounter Simmel's program and realization, including in a more acute and radical form, since the social is formulated as no more or less than the system of relations. We can verify, therefore, how Simmel remains alive and well in anthropology through his derivations in the work of Mauss and Lévi-Strauss, or even in the relationisms of diverse extraction that have today gained ground in the body of the discipline.

In any event, money perhaps has a logic, albeit one that is highly complex, variable and processual. Rather than deciphering this logic *in abstracto*, Simmel looks to reveal it *in concreto*. It is not worth trying to summarize the argument, therefore: neither would it be productive, nor would it summarize it. All those interested in "relationisms" have much to gain from an attentive and unprejudiced reading of the way in which Simmel discusses the "concrete universal," society, as a "functional unit" constituted in the set of relations established between the elements and, more precisely, that establishes these relations as elements: a radical "methodological relationism," expressed and made concrete in money. Money, for Simmel, is relation, but also has relations (Simmel 1900 [2005]: 123).

Simmel elaborates a theory of exchange that presumes a theory of sacrifice and develops into a theory of value. Setting out from this complex, it becomes possible to construct an anthropology/sociology of giving, receiving, and exchange (and also a psychology, or an economics and so on, of the same). This problematic takes us to the core of the book and concepts like *Wechselwirkung* ("interaction") and the ideas of relationism, function, and "society" as relations, of which we have already seen one formulation.

Another aspect is that money continues to be even more present and active than in Simmel's era. When he was writing, the German mark had just been created and still coexisted alongside other currencies within the German Empire. There is no doubt that the process of diffusion of the monetary economy, investigated in *Philosophie des Geldes*, has spread in capillary fashion even further. Today money really is everywhere, even though its regime of presence is one of absence: whether as poverty and destitution misery, which are comprehended primarily as the absence of money (though not only), or when we consider that "live money" ("cash") is used today in around eighty-five percent of financial transactions, yet represents just one percent of their total value (Ingham 2004: 5).

The insistence on considering money not only as an object of the material world but, first and foremost, of the mental world, highlighting the extent to which it shapes thought, so to speak, is an old theme and problem when it comes to exploring the connection between social form and the form of thought ("Gesellschaftsform und Denkform": Mannheim,1931: 662; see Sohn-Rethel 1989; Luhmann 1980–99)—in this case, money as a codeterminant/conditioning factor of forms of thought, worldviews, world images and thus images of the human being.

All of this is directly connected to money's diffusion and expansion, a process that still continues and which thus evinces the eminently modern logic identified in the book. Certainly, the forms taken by money have developed since then and its virtual forms especially reflect the mobile, ambiguous and relational character of money, as well as the consummation of its functional value over its substantial value. This aspect—the relation between substantial and functional values—is one of those that became the most clearly realized with the definitive loss of the back of metal currency, in widespread use in 1900 when Simmel was writing. Or looking at the flip side of the coin: how in periods of crisis metals appear as a secure asset (at the peak of the euro crisis there were cash machines in Europe in which the customer inserted a euro note and received a little gold bar).

The recent euro crisis demonstrated the nexus of money as both a real and a mental thing, since it involves the introduction of a unified currency in a non-unified social space—or put otherwise, the introduction of a currency that homogenizes in a non-homogenous social, political, economic, and above all mental space, generating mismatches, inequalities, and conflicts (most clearly evident in the regional economic disparities within the eurozone, resulting in the tension between a no longer national money and a set of nation states: see Dodd 2005). Although on one level the common currency flattens differences—as familiar to tourists who no longer need to exchange and convert currencies every time they cross a national border—on another level it seems to presume and demand an equally unified monetary (and thus political, economic, social, and mental) regime. And it is here that the differences, or rather the problems, start to emerge. While money and the financial economy derived from it have long ruptured the state and national frameworks, political decision-making spaces remain strongly conditioned to national space.

Today in the European Community there is eleven times more virtual money circulating between banks than real money in the possession of people, banks, and governments. The same phenomenon came to the fore in the 2008 financial crisis, which was related to the problem of futures markets; in other words, a problem characteristic of the temporality established by the money form: a temporality that opens up to future operations, since money can be utilized as a promise of payment at a future time (Esposito 2011). After all, "credit and credit alone is money" (Innes 1913: 392, also 402). As the economists never tire of telling us, reaching back to Aristotle, the money form is a promise of payment and a store of value. As a result, the future was opened up to monetary and credit operations in which we increasingly encounter a triple alliance: money as mere function without substance, combined with the technical facilities of electronic communication and circulation, as well as the fact that financial operations evade traditional control institutions (linked to nation states): all of which enables operations of promises of payment *mise en abyme* for which no one is responsible and, for this very reason, when it finally comes to paying the bill, everyone is. There is a memorable phrase of Peter Solomon, senior executive at Lehman Brothers at the time and who today has his own successful investment consultancy firm: "Computers have shown us how to manage risk" (apud Spivak 1985: 88). We have seen and can still see just how much they control . . . Or again turning over the coin, just how much they allow to go uncontrolled.

Obviously, Simmel was not the first to underscore the extent to which money is a mental construct and how far it is eminently social. One of his merits, though, is precisely to have taken this knowledge as a lever for problematization, offering an understanding in which the *symbolic dimension* binds these two aspects. In this sense, Simmel's emphasis on money as a symbol, and moreover as a symbol of the modern, signals a recognition that modern money is pre-eminently mental and social, detaching it definitively from substantialist connections and articulating it with an idea of money as credit.

This knowledge is indispensable if we wish to comprehend, or observe, the universe or system of the economy. We do not need to adhere to modern systems theory to accept the claim that the future is defined by uncertainty. We have already known as much ever since we were expelled from paradise. But if money allows us to gain time, it also enables us—as the economists and sociologists teach—to "defer and search" (Shackel apud Esposito 2011: 50–1): decisions are shifted to a future time and meanwhile one can seek out more and better information in order to make a more informed decision, or in other words, a better deal. If I have time, I can use it to find the best offer and buy more cheaply or sell more expensively. This capacity to coordinate present and future is what Keynes had in mind when asserting: "For the importance of money essentially flows from its being a link between the present and the future" (Keynes 1936: 293).

When it comes to virtual forms, money is perhaps its first historical concretization. Today it is not just a question of Paypal, e-Bay, bitcoin and the like, on-line transfers and flights to fiscal paradises and hells, but even the forms of "virtual interaction" and "social networks," in which the form of producing value clearly remains active behind the marvels of new friendships and the re-encounter with old acquaintances: in all of this, money is anticipated, and this is precisely the issue.

Another approach of interest is a phenomenology of money and its derivatives in the everyday and highly concrete world in which we live, also something very close to what Simmel undertook in his time—since, as I cited earlier, one of his goals was "to make the essence and organization of [life] intelligible from the effectiveness of money." This can be ascertained in what modern sociology has labelled a new economic sociology, or in what anthropology has identified as the social life, or even biography, of objects and merchandise. On these two fronts we encounter contemporary investigations derived from a Simmelian approach, even when their authors do not make this source explicit. Some do so. Such is the case of Appadurai, who in a well-known text took Simmel as a starting point for "exploring the conditions under which economic objects circulate in different regimes of value in space and time" (Appadurai 1986: 4).

As we saw, this phenomenology of the concrete world, which provides the foundations for an eschatology that identifies money with rest and motion simultaneously, is one of the most striking aspects of Simmel's book. He showed us how everything turns on money, fixed, immobile, sovereign; but also how money is what circulates unceasingly around what exists. Life in the big city, acceleration, objective culture, accuracy, fashion, intellectualism, socialism, distinction, greed, dissipation, the blasé and the cynical, symmetry and rhythm, meals, intimacy, the nervous system, prostitution, shock, the poor, diverse monetary instruments, the diversity of styles, regimes of subjectification—all of this approached in connection with the diffusion of the monetary economy. There is no harm in repeating that Simmel offers us an approach that simultaneously exposes what he called the synthetic and analytic dimensions of money: how it is produced socially and how it produces society—and, in particular, the modern form of society and those who live, survive, and die in it.

The resonances between Simmel and current thinking are strong. In the areas of contemporary sociology (for example, Niklas Luhmann), contemporary anthropology (for example, Keith Hart), and contemporary economics (for example, G.L.S. Shackle) we encounter a shared understanding of money as meaning, time, and memory—that is, as a symbolically generalized means of communication inscribed in temporal nexuses (a theme suggested by Polanyi in comprehending money as a semantic system). Human communities need to exchange information, and thus memory, in order to exist and subsist, and money is a decisive instrument in this process (Hart 2006). Since individual identities are also necessarily social identities, here too we can derive a connection with money: not coincidentally, Simmel heavily stressed how money enables individual freedom, differentiates interiority and makes the exterior indifferent, as well as how the dynamics of differentiation and indifferentiation create double-binds, so to speak.

To resume: since exchange roots and develops the market, and the market and state (in the broad sense) possess a symbiotic relation (which leads us to the genesis of the modern) mediated by money, the radius of this problematization has a considerable potential for diffusion. Here it suffices for us to consider the state as an institution regulating various chains of interdependence, creating operational rules in certain chains, which potentially spread stability beyond themselves (for example, by guaranteeing the money used or, put another way, reducing complexity). Money, for its part, as a symbol, meaning, time, and memory, not only benefits from this stability, it is also reproduces and implements it. Perhaps one of the reasons why money is indispensable.

Earlier I mentioned the problem of poverty. Money is connected to power since, as we have seen, it provides the possibility of waiting, choosing, and deciding. Those without money can neither wait nor choose. Hence, they are condemned to the worst deals, while the rich gain the best. In citing the rich and the poor, we arrive at the question of the social types configured by money. Others also appear, like the blasé, the squanderer and the greedy (which are united by their absolute valorization of money, only one with the aim of spending it, the other of hoarding it), the cynical (subjective equivalent of the objectification that reduces differentiated values to the form without qualities of money), and the ascetic (which inspired Max Weber) to cite just a few. Readers of Weber are delighted by the treatment given to the nexus of rationalism and modern, and even to the professional worker, while those of Sombart recognize the identification of the calculability as a decisive trait of the modern (Weber 1920–21; Sombart 1902).

Simmel teaches us that money is the hub of the modern universal eschatology: god or devil, or god-devil. It reigns supreme under the sign of ambivalence: it is what *it is* and what *it is not*. By being indifferent, functional, formal, quantitative, its characteristic being to not possess characteristics, money is magnificently suited to ambiguous relations. At the same time as it separates, it unites. As it approximates, it pushes apart. Money separates those individuals who exchange it by being an intermediary element in the exchange, interposing itself between the exchanging agents. The exchange shifts from simple to mediated and the relation, which without money is direct, becomes indirect through its use. Money is thus an important figure of distancing. Its role and its mediating position—which explains why money functions relatively well in resolving conflicts, settling them by paying—appears as an element of separation. But at the same time money unites since it binds those involved in the exchange: it relates them to each other and brings them closer together. It creates, potentializes and concretizes interdependencies. As a universal equivalent, it facilitates exchange and approximates things that were initially distant. It performs its role of a universal equivalent more perfectly the more things can be exchanged for it, as though everything were gravitating around it.

From this ambiguous situation of money, innumerable questions emerge. For example: is it money that circulates between people or people who circulate around money? Who chases who? Do people go after money or money after people? History shows us that whenever there is a concentration of people, money becomes a necessity. But where there is money, likewise there is a concentration of people.

Money realizes the idea of a universal Esperanto, a language that everyone speaks and understands. It was, then, the most perfect language coined by humans, so perfect that we could ask whether it is not, in fact, the divine language, the Word, the voice of god—or of the devil? With its universal circulation and language, money drastically shortens the distances of the world. It was, still is and probably will be the most advanced frontier of the old, forever renewed, a process of globalization. A single world is a world that speaks the language of money, its local accents mattering little. It shrewdly circumvents the global–local difference: money is singular and unique, but possesses an infinite number of masks, forms, formats, and names. However, at the last moment, the difference of the local always accommodates the equality of the universal. Whether a shell or a stone, a metal disk, a piece of paper, a plastic card, a chip, an electronic impulse, a blockchain: money is always the same, the eternal return of the same.

As money is indifferent by its very nature, it is one of the most suitable and persuasive mediums of understanding among humans: however different they are, people find something in common through money. Money removes things and, to a large extent, people from mutual inaccessibility. It transports things and humans from their original isolation to a realm of relationality, comparability, and interaction. This is why money symbolizes the modern world so well (but not only it): a world where all that was solid became mobile and fluid like smoke (others prefer to say liquid). What was substance converts into relation.[5] Nothing demonstrates so completely the relational nature of the modern world than money, which does nothing other than relate subjects and objects.

Schopenhauer supposedly claimed that money was human happiness *in abstracto*. Hence those who are incapable of being happy *in concreto* tend to adopt money as a form of happiness. In creating Uncle $crooge, Walt Disney seems to have drawn inspiration from Schopenhauer. The question is less innocent than it seems: can anyone be completely happy without money?[6] Even though we still find corners of the planet where people barter (and there are many), and despite the attempts to reconstitute economies based on simple exchange, money spreads along many links of long and varied chains of interdependencies waiting to strike at any moment.

Nothing, then, would appear more natural than the fact that money becomes the god of the modern world. Nothing approximates so closely and so well the idea of god: omnipotent, omniscient, and omnipresent. The god–money overlap is especially elucidative not only because both signify peace, tranquility, and happiness, but because both are ideas that give a unity to multiplicity and a sense of meaning to the world's idiosyncrasies. Both involve an extremely high level of abstraction, perhaps the highest of all.

Money is characterized by being a means sought to achieve all kinds of ends. Consequently, it becomes a point of intersection for the most varied teleological series, a common point at which everything and everyone can potentially meet. For everything and everyone, money is the mirror that tells each what it is—"Mirror, mirror on the wall." It puts each person and thing in its place. Wherever money is present, it facilitates the conversion of everything into numbers and consequently into calculations (the utopia of a fully calculable world does not belong to physics but to money). But what precisely does this mean? Following Simmel, Sombart identified the impulse to calculate as one of the central elements of modern capitalism, and on the basis of his work Weber elaborated his reflections concerning the spirit of capitalism and rationalism.

When money is the common denominator to everything, what matters is no longer "what" but "how much." "What" concerns the qualitatively different, the individual and unique. What is specific and incomparable becomes subsumed when money arrives, since it equalizes everything on the basis of quantity: the only difference that persists is having more or less money. Indecent proposals always provoke money and people by showing how far each dare go.

The impersonal character of money and its anonymity are fundamental traces that are not limited to it, but to everything with which it enters into contact with its Midas touch. A complete domination of money would signify the expulsion of everything that cannot be counted monetarily—that is, whatever is not quantitively measurable, whatever concerns the actual qualities of things. For this reason, whenever personal values are at stake, money seems to be so inappropriate as a form of compensation and reparation.

This is why today the law no longer allows a murder to be compensated by a penalty paid solely in money, a simple fine. Human life is something too singular and unique to be compensated by something so indifferent and "vulgar" as money. But it was not always so. In other eras and other societies, very often a murder could and indeed had to be compensated by a sum in money, paid by the killer (and his family) to the victim's family. Yet it suffices to think of the civil compensations that abound today to see that the problem is still highly topical: to what point can money compensate for the loss of someone? Or in its own clear and direct language: *how much* money can compensate for such a loss? And there is much more. To give just one example: with the development of new reproductive technologies, a similar question is raised at the opposite pole: in the purchase and management of human eggs and sperm. How much is a life worth? A question that could only be formulated in current terms in the nineteenth century when the monetary economy became consolidated and widespread (Zelizer 1985).

No doubt money has something diabolical about it. Innumerable proverbs exist in many different languages that express the double nature of money, its heads and tails. It is a means of symbolic communication with an irresistible colonizing impetus: it tends to replace other forms of communication and other forms of reciprocity, which fall into disuse and lose their meaning and efficacy (Luhmann 1994: 230–71). In the process of becoming a universal symbol, money suffocates the existence of other competing symbols. There is no doubt that money is more than familiar with violent means. And here too it reveals its ambiguity through pacification and violation.

Money's anonymity, the fact that neither it nor anyone knows where it comes from, nor where it will go, possesses a very close affinity to forgetting and memory loss. It is highly volatile and voluble; it was here just a moment ago, but it has already gone. Other types of property exist—a house, a farm, furniture, clocks, jewelry, a dress, a toy—that facilitate memory. Money, though, facilitates forgetting. It goes the same way that it comes: without any history written on its body, without leaving any traces.

It disappears without trace not only from our current accounts and wallets (physical and virtual) but also from the bank stocks and national reserves. From the micro to the macro and the macro to the micro, money circulates without pause and makes us rush around it unceasingly. Today more than ever we know just how right Alice's White Rabbit was: to stay still, we must keep running. Is this not the inhabitant of the big modern city, as Simmel characterized it, precisely under the sign of money?

CONCLUDING REMARKS

In the nineteenth century, responsible for this transformation of the world, the dematerialization of money became increasingly perceived and thematized. It was not only Simmel who highlighted this fact, certainly (in his discussions on the affinity between money and abstraction, money as a function and the loss of its substantial value). During the same period, debates like the one following the American Civil War between greenbackers and bullionists (Carruthers and Babb 1996), the subjective theories of value—in contrast to the objective theory of labor value—developed by Simmel and by the so-called Austrian School (Wieser 1891), followed soon after by Innes' discussion, on the eve of the Great War, that money is no more than credit (Innes 1913; 1914), were all developments indicating that dematerialization, despite the strength of the gold standard, was now prevalent. Since then, this process has never ceased to spread and deepen.

There is little doubt concerning the importance and significance of money in the modern world and its various configurations. From a historical perspective, few social technologies have performed and continue to perform such a significant role and have such an impact on the way humans live, perhaps only comparable to writing and numbers (Ingham 2004: 3). However, the evaluation of the importance of money and its significance—that is, its varied significations—is multifaceted and controversial. For this reason, we have never ceased to inquire into money, seeking a clearer understanding of its importance and the diverse meanings, sometimes contradictory, aporetic, or paradoxical, which it assumes, or which are attributed to it. Basing his ideas about money on the experiences of the nineteenth century, Simmel's work has proven to possess an unexpected contemporary relevance, because even today his formulations remain provocative, stimulating, and enlightening. A good example is the contemporary discussion of acceleration and its various modalities: technological acceleration, the accelerating pace of life, the acceleration of the speed of social change. Long seen as a decisive element in the process of globalization, acceleration is also viewed as a key concept for thinking about the modern

(Rosa 2013). But all of this also contemplates the transformation of the world over the course of the nineteenth century, as well as Simmel's endeavor in *Philosophie des Geldes*: money and its philosophy provide a possibility for exploring the world in transformation, the totality of existence, and this because money is a symbol, a singularity expressing the universal. In this sense, the book is also a powerful and multifaceted diagnosis of its time, establishing its own unique perspective to describe it: through money, transformed into a symbol of the period.

CHAPTER SEVEN

Money and the Issues of the Age

NIGEL DODD

In this chapter I will survey the various debates concerning the nature and governance of money that characterized the nineteenth century, specifically the period 1820–1920 that is covered by this volume. While a comprehensive treatment of these debates is not feasible in the space available, I will try to give an overview of what I consider to be the major thematic concerns of this age. I will, accordingly, divide the discussion into five main sections, dealing with (i) gold and silver, (ii) monetary union, (iii) banking and credit, (iv) land and sea, and finally, (v) debates about new and experimental forms of money. I particularly want to emphasize the spirit of monetary experimentalism that prevailed throughout the nineteenth century: whether these took the form of practical and actually existing monetary arrangements such as the greenbacks used in the United States during the Civil War, or more utopian schemes such as the "labour money" proposed by John Ruskin and others, I argue in this chapter that such experiments with the nature and form of money offer some insight into the "issues of the age" that were held by economists, politicians and others to call for changes in the production, governance and use of money in order to be addressed. All of the schemes discussed were designed to address a number of economic, political and social issues that characterized the nineteenth century: the need to find forms of money that could circulate widely and in sufficient quantities during a period of growing economic prosperity (bimetallism and paper money); war financing (greenbacks); social justice (labor money); hoarding (rotting money) and inequality (social credit).

GOLD AND SILVER

Bimetallism was widely used—and its administration hotly debated—during the second half of the nineteenth century in many European countries, the US and India. The system was attractive because with growing prosperity, there arose the problem of finding a metal that was appropriate for wider and larger monetary circulation: gold was not up to this task because its supply was limited and its distribution uneven. Bimetallism typically took the form of the unrestricted circulation of two forms of metallic coinage, usually gold and silver.[1] The main technical difficulty with bimetallism concerns the ratio between the two metals: the idea of Gresham's Law (named after the sixteenth-century English financier, Thomas Gresham), coined in 1860 (although there were earlier versions such as the Copernicus Law), is that when the ratio gets out of line (e.g. when the commodity versus face value of one metal is less favourable than the other), the "good" money (which has more intrinsic value) will be hoarded and its circulation will grind to a halt.[2] Another problem arose with arbitrage, wherein the entrepreneurially minded could exploit disparities in the official ratios between the two metals in different countries (e.g. if silver is valued more highly relative to gold in, say, England compared to France) (Chown 1994: 75–6). For this reason, it was desirable for governments to enforce a fixed ratio between the two metals, although attempts to do so often failed.

While the monetary use of silver continued to have some very serious advocates in many countries during the latter half of the nineteenth century, bimetallism fell out of "official" favor almost everywhere. The reasons were clear. Arbitrage was becoming increasingly attractive as transactions costs declined. As the price of silver rose, moreover, the metallic value of silver coins was higher than their face value: they were melted down or exported, sometimes leading to an acute shortage of smaller denominated coins. The problem was reversed when the gold price rose. The inevitable result was a somewhat chaotic system of coinage. In the face of major price fluctuations in the price of various metals including silver, bimetallism had been formally rejected in Britain in 1774, although it was fiercely debated (and had strong advocates such as William Huskisson) during the first half of the nineteenth century until the adoption of gold standard in 1844. Germany's decision to followed suit and move to a gold standard in 1871—the US officially adopted gold two years later—led to a collapse in the silver price.

In the US, bimetallism continued to be debated after 1873 because the gold standard was strongly associated with economic recession. The so-called Long Depression ran from 1873 to 1896 (sometimes the dates are 1873–79, if different metrics are used) in the US, during which time the price of wheat fell from $2.95 in 1866, to $1.40 in 1875, and $0.56 in 1894, and industrial production dipped markedly in the US, Germany and the UK. The Long Depression was triggered by the "Panic of 1873," wherein the decision in Germany and the US to abandon the monetary use of silver led to a crash in its price, a drastic reduction in the domestic money supply, and an increase in interest rates that harmed both agriculture and industry alike. As Myers notes, the populist case for a resumption of a silver standard seemed to be self-evident to the agricultural and industrial workers who took the brunt of these events: "It is so clearly a matter of common sense that more money is good for the individual that it seems to follow as a matter of logic that more currency is good for the country" (Myers 1970: 199). In the US, raising the silver price and increasing the money supply became closely-linked causes; indeed, silver's remonetization was recommended by the 1876 Commission of Enquiry instigated by Congress. The question of bimetallism continued to resonate, with especially strong advocacy from William Jennings Bryan (who was the Democratic Party's Presidential candidate in 1896, 1900, and 1908), the People's Party (also known as the Populist Party, which merged with the Democratic Party during the 1896 campaign), and the Free Silver movement, which flourished during the early 1890s.[3]

MONETARY UNION

It is against this background—the technical problems associated with maintaining bimetallism versus the apparent recessionary consequences of a gold standard—that the merits of moving towards a unified, transnational form of money began to be taken more and more seriously. The logic for monetary union seems simple enough on the face of things. For travelers, it is a question of convenience (especially when different coinage systems had the same underlying metallic standard). For economic policy-makers, the case for unifying different monetary systems would be attractive as a means of circumventing the kind of arbitrage I described above, where entrepreneurs exploit different gold–silver ratios from one country to another. This was the logic behind the Latin Monetary Union, established in 1866 (it was finally disbanded in 1927).

The Latin Monetary Union was established by treaty between France, Belgium, Italy, and Switzerland. The treaty was signed on December 23, 1865, coming into effect on August 1, 1866. The States of the Church joined the union in 1866, with Greece and Bulgaria joining one year later. (Spain and Romania also considered joining, while Austria-Hungary rejected the union specifically because of its abandonment of bimetallism.) Centered around the French gold Franc introduced by Napoleon in 1803, the Latin Monetary Union essentially put an end to bimetallism, by ending the free minting of silver. Under the treaty, each member nation would mint only specific denominations of gold coins (100, 50, 20, 10 and 5 francs) and silver coins (5, 2, 1 franc and 50 and 20 centimes).

According to Chown, in a practical sense the union "was in fact no big deal, as the countries concerned already had, in substance, a common currency" (Chown 1994: 86). But in political terms, it is the principle of monetary union itself—and to some degree the theory of what such an arrangement might ultimately lead to—that stands out as emblematic of money's embroilment in the "issues of the day" during this period. Just prior to the period we are discussing in this volume (1820–1920), monetary arrangements in Europe were highly fragmentary. To some degree, money was an expression of politics in this regard. Italy was yet to become a nation, and Switzerland (which lacked a common currency) was merely a loose Federation. In Germany, as many as six different monetary standards were in operation until the 1838 Dresden Convention (in which twenty states adopted the fourteen thaler or twenty-one gulden standard) (Del Mar 1895: 395; Chown 1994: 84). According to Del Mar, the key political concern with monetary standards at this stage was about inflation: "the fear [was] that so much gold would be produced in the mines and pass into the form of money, that disastrous rise of prices ... will ensure sufficient to shake the foundations of society" (Del Mar 1895: 393). For this reason, gold was not legal tender.

Silver, however, was over-valued, leading to the disappearance of silver coins. With debasement by different countries promising further chaos, a conference in Paris held in 1865 called for "the adoption of a uniform and universal coinage" (Barbour 1885: 14; cited in Chown 1994: 85), leading to the Latin Monetary Union later that same year. Besides the clear practical advantages of ruling out confusing standards and competitive debasement, the idea informing monetary union was to establish a more unified, *joint* currency shared by separate nations. This was the explicit focus of the 1867 conference held in Paris during the Paris Exhibition (this was followed by further monetary conferences, held in 1878 and 1881 in Paris and 1892 in Brussels). Félix Esquirou de Parieu, a French statesman, was instrumental in the discussions, urging those countries present to adopt a single gold standard and a decimal system. Unsurprisingly, politicians worried about the damage to national pride should they be seen as adopting the currency system of another state, effectively "Frenchifying" their own currencies: Bismarck, for example, dismissed the whole enterprise as a "Napoleonic dream" (Russell 1898: 117; cited in Chown 1994: 87). The Americans were more enthusiastic about joining a union, arguing for a twenty-five franc gold coin that "will circulate side by side everywhere and in perfect equality with the half eagle of the United States and the sovereign of Great Britain" (Russell 1898: 76; cited in Chown 1994: 87). The French resisted this, fearing that their own gold standard—the twenty-franc napoleon—would be compromised. Meanwhile, the British delegates in

Paris merely observed proceedings, because they were under instructions not to vote in any way that would bind the British government, nor to "express any opinion to induce the belief that Great Britain would adopt the convention of 1865" (Russell 1898: 74; cited in Chown 1994: 88). A Royal Commission on International Coinage was appointed the following year in Britain, which drew quite positive lessons about the advantages of international money for both manufacturers and the general public. Despite this, the Committee expressed caution because any step towards union would entail a slight reduction of the gold content of its own coinage—the twenty-five franc coin contained 0.83 per cent less gold than the sovereign—meaning that entering into union "would be tantamount to a legal permission for every creditor to rob his debtor of 2 pence in the pound" (cited in Chown 1994: 89).

The Latin Monetary Union continued on through the nineteenth century and was not formally disbanded until 1927 (although in practical terms it came to an end well before that). But the intervening years were fraught with difficulties, not the least of which were associated with bimetallism: the price of silver dropped significantly in 1873, leading to increases in silver imports in those countries where it was profitable to mint silver coins in order to exchange them for gold. The minting of silver coins was finally abandoned in 1878, effectively leaving the Latin Monetary Union on a gold standard. The problems with metal, it seems, were difficult to surmount—a gold standard was deflationary, bimetallism was unstable—while monetary unions were bound to be characterized, and often undermined, by political contestation.

BANK MONEY

While the monetary history of the nineteenth century was characterized by debate and experimentation with metallic currency, paper money—freely convertible into metal—did circulate in a number of countries. Throughout the period we are discussing in this volume, banks—in particular, bank deposits—became an increasingly pivotal feature of the monetary system. To the wealthy, coinage was increasingly unnecessary for settling most monetary obligations except for small everyday transactions: one simply instructed one's banker to make a transfer. In Britain, the increasing prominence of banks in the production and use of money provoked a debate between the so-called Currency and Banking "Schools." On the one side, those adhering to the Currency School position—led by Samuel Jones Lloyd, George Warde Norman and Robert Torrens—argued that while it was perfectly legitimate for paper money to circulate, its overall value should never exceed the value of the country's bullion reserves. On the other, proponents of the Banking School view—led by Thomas Tooke—argued that any expansion of the supply of paper money was acceptable (and sustainable) as long as it was in order to meet the needs of trade.

In practical terms, the debate between the Currency and Banking Schools was about how best to regulate the money supply: whether, for example, the Bank of England should monopolize the issue of paper currency. Philosophically, this was a debate about the nature of money itself, raising questions about the status of bank deposits and the quantity theory of money. The debate lasted around a quarter of a century—1819–1844—a period that included the "panic of 1825," a stock market crash that drew a period of excessive speculation in South America to a spectacular close. The crisis began with the Bank of England (which was not yet a full-fledged central bank), and culminated in the closure of six London banks and over sixty country banks. The London *Times* described the rush on the Bank of England on December 1, 1825 as being like "the pit of a theatre on the night of a popular performance" (cited in Chown 1994: 152). By mid-December, the Bank literally ran out of notes, as the difference between the market price of gold and its mint price grew ever wider. According to Lord Bentinck at the time, Britain came close to a condition in which only barter would have been possible (Chown 1994: 153). The crisis served as a focal point for debating the true nature of money and the role of the banking system in regulating its supply. From the Currency School side, the banks—the Bank of England foremost among them—were widely held responsible for printing too much money. From the Banking School side, it was alleged that they had not printed enough. Both sides of the debate were still being heard a few years later, in the run up to the 1833 Bank Act, which renewed the charter of the Bank of England. To the opposition between the Currency and Banking Schools was added a third position—supported for example by Henry Parnell, an Irish writer and Whig politician—which argued for "Free Banking." Both the Currency and Banking Schools accepted that the Bank of England should monopolize the issue of notes, but with one crucial difference: while the former argued for a legal restriction to be imposed that limited notes to metal reserves, the latter allowed for discretionary monetary policy, meaning that the note supply could be increased when the business cycle appeared to require it. Those who supported Free Banking, on the other hand, argued that no institution whatsoever should have a monopoly over the issue of notes.

In the US at this time, the "Second Bank of the United States" was chartered in 1816 and modelled on the First Bank that Alexander Hamilton had established in 1791. The Bank's charter involved similar conditions to those that had been granted to the Bank of England and the Bank of France, although in contrast to its wholly private European counterparts, one fifth of the Bank's capital was government-owned. The Second Bank was the government's exclusive fiscal agent, charged with processing tax payments, holding and transferring all US deposits, and paying and receiving all monies associated with government business. It was also charged with a regulatory function, which was to prevent the uninhibited issue of private bank notes. It did this through its dealings with local banks, by imposing on them a restriction wherein their lending strategies had to be aligned with metal reserves held with the Second Bank. Initially, however, the Bank struggled to achieve this regulatory aim: the "Panic of 1819" was widely attributed to its failure to tighten controls over the supply of money and credit, particularly in the West and South. The Bank subsequently over-corrected this error, tightening monetary policy so much the US was plunged into a recession that lasted until 1822. Although the Bank subsequently enjoyed a period of monetary stability under the Presidency of Nicholas Biddle, the politics around it were anything but stable as Andrew Jackson—US President from 1829 until 1837—advocated the non-renewal of its charter and its replacement by a bank with far more limited powers: Jackson's bank would be controlled by the central Treasury and prohibited from issuing notes or making loans. Although Jackson did not get his way completely, and the Bank's charter was in fact renewed, the so-called "hard money" enthusiasts with whom he associated—unusual as this might seem for a left-wing populist, when viewed from a present-day perspective—continued to move to restrict the Bank's powers. The Bank was forced into a retreat: it became a private entity in 1833, ran into liquidity problems in 1839 and ceased trading in 1841.

Thus, while the arguments of the Banking School seemed to be holding sway in Britain, in the US the hard money arguments of Jackson's "anti-bank" forces were in the ascendant. In this context, the US government faced some serious difficulties after the Second Bank was transformed in 1833, not the least of which was that it now had *no* central bank through which to conduct its business. Moreover, monetary policy and credit regulation had been placed beyond its reach. Banking law did not exist at the Federal level, and banking regulation was seen as a matter for local states, not central government. Private banks proliferated, and a system of quasi free banking—the so-called Free Banking Era—evolved. It was "quasi" free banking because although banks had the power to issue their own notes, they did so under strict restrictions: they were unable to establish branch networks and had to secure their notes by lodging securities with state authorities. "Central" banking was sometimes undertaken locally: for example, by the New York Safety Fund (which provided deposit insurance), and by the Suffolk Bank in Boston (which acted both as a clearing house and a guarantor of the notes of banks that maintained accounts there). This fact was celebrated by John Jay Knox, who became Comptroller of the Currency in 1872, for demonstrating that "private enterprise could be entrusted with the work of redeeming the circulating notes of the banks, and it could thus be done as safely and much more economically than the same service can be performed by the Government" (cited in Rothbard 2002: 120). Yet bank failures were frequent at this time: the average lifespan of a bank was five years, and around half of all new banks failed, many of them because they could not redeem their notes.

While the free banking era involved paper currency that was convertible into gold and silver coins, the situation changed dramatically during the American Civil War. On both sides, inconvertible paper was used as a method of war financing.[4] In July 1861, when Salmon P. Chase was Treasury Secretary, Congress authorized the production of fifty million dollars' worth of Demand Notes that were redeemable for gold and silver coins on demand, and could be used to pay customs duties (at which point they would be taken out of circulation, meaning that by 1863 around ninety-five percent of these notes no longer circulated). This was insufficient, and the first "greenbacks"—so called because (unlike private and state banknotes up until then) they were printed on both sides, with a green reverse side—were issued following the passing of the Legal Tender Act in February 1862. The Act authorized an issue of 150 million dollars' worth of notes which were to be treated as "lawful money." This was unbacked (or inconvertible) paper money. The "obligation text" on the majority of these notes read as follows: "This note is a legal tender for all debts, public and private, except duties on imports and interest on the public debt, and is receivable in payment of all loans made to the United States." The Second Legal Tender Act authorized the issuance of a further 150 million dollars in July 1862, as did the Third Legal Tender Act in March 1863 (Mitchell 1903). In all, greenbacks accounted for 644 million dollars—28 percent—of the North's total wartime debt of 2.3 billion gold dollars (O'Brien 1988). The greenbacks era was brought to a close with the passing the *Specie Payment Resumption Act* in January 1875, which required the government to redeem the notes for gold on demand from 1 January 1879 onwards. In effect, greenbacks resembled "zero coupon bonds" at a cost of 7.94 percent (Chown 1994: 254).

LAND AND SEA

By the end of the nineteenth century and the first decade of the twentieth century, there was a period of relative monetary stability. Discoveries of gold in South Africa, Alaska and Colorado almost doubled the supply of the yellow metal during this period, and most countries switched from bimetallism to a gold standard. In the US, the Gold Standard Act was passed in 1900, with the gold dollar declared as the standard unit of account (while greenbacks, silver certificates and silver dollars were all redeemable into gold). In Britain, where the gold standard had been operating since much earlier in the nineteenth century, there was a brief run on sterling during the "Panic of 1907" (Bruner and Carr 2007), a crisis triggered by the failure of the Knickerbocker Trust Company, which was once one of the largest American banks. But it was the onset of the First World War that really threw the gold standard into chaos, because it highlighted the principal weakness of a system in which the majority of banks simply refused to redeem notes into gold coins at the first signs of panic, which is exactly what happened during the summer of 1914. Thus, abruptly, ended the period of the "classical gold standard." Gold would return after the war, with some spectacularly bad consequences, but that is a matter for the next volume of this book.

Marx once said that money "wears different national uniforms" (Marx 1987: 139). The belief that money "naturally" comes in national units reinforces the argument that states are best equipped to look after money: to manage its production, regulate its supply and guarantee its value. But as the discussion so far demonstrates, the relationship between money, state, and society is contingent and contested, not natural. Up until the nineteenth century, a mixture of domestic and foreign currencies was in use throughout Europe, while in the United States silver coins from Mexico and Spain dominated the domestic money supply. Likewise in Canada, Latin America, East Asia and the Middle East, foreign currency circulated freely until well into the nineteenth century. The monies used in these largely cosmopolitan monetary systems were usually coins with *some* kind of inherent value, although paper money issued by states and banks also circulated across state borders. Historically, as I hope I have shown, debates about the precise nature of the connection between money and government—such as that which took place between "bullionists" and "greenbackers" in Postbellum America (Carruthers and Babb 1996)—were often bound up with disputes about the quality of the monetary medium itself, as well as the social consequences of alternative systems of monetary governance.

Most arguments about money and space focus on *land*. Yet the development of the global economy has been hugely dependent on the organization of power in relation to the *sea*. As Casarino argues, "During the emergence and consolidation of industrial capitalism, the sea became an increasingly turbulent, contradictory, and contested terrain" (Casarino 2002: 4). Nietzsche once portrayed the ocean as lying "like silk and gold and dreams of goodness" (Nietzsche 2001: 119). Gold is crucial to the history of the seas, not only in relation to trade, but also to the forms of primitive accumulation that Marx described. Both the discovery of America and the rounding of the Cape "opened up fresh ground for the rising bourgeoisie," and trade with the colonies gave commerce, navigation and industry "an impulse never before known" (Marx and Engels 1848 [2004]: 220). Water, not just land, has always been crucial for capitalism's spatial configuration, above all its capacity for expansion. The sea is of pivotal importance in the history of slavery (Gilroy 1993). As Frederick Douglass observed in 1852, "The arm of commerce ... makes its pathway over and under the sea, as well as on the earth. Wind, steam, and lightning are its chartered agents. Oceans no longer divide, but link nations together" (Douglass 1852: 205). Still today, more than ninety percent of the world's trade takes place by sea. The thinker who grasped the geopolitical resonance of this most clearly, perhaps, was Carl Schmitt, whose conception of the territorial division of the world—*nomos*—has important ramifications for the theory of money.

According to Schmitt, the ideal of "an economy of free world trade and a free world market, with the free movement of money, capital, and labour" developed against the background of the invasion of the New World, subsequently shaping the territorial ordering of the world between 1492 and 1890. There is a "historical and structural relation between concepts of the free sea, free trade, free world economy, and those of free competition and free exploitation" (Schmitt 2003: 99). What made the connection between growth and free trade conceivable was the opening up of a huge land mass: a "free space, an area open to European occupation and expansion" (Schmitt 2003: 87). But the sea was crucial to this. The *jus publicum Europeaum* specified that the sea "was neither state or colonial territory nor occupiable space," and it "had no borders other than coasts" (Schmitt 2003: 172). This antithesis of land and sea had been the universal foundation of international law and the site of legal debate: while the English viewed the seas as *res omnium* (things belonging to everybody), "a crossroad common and open to all" (Schmitt 2003: 176), the French viewed the seas as *res nullius* (things belonging to nobody). This spatial order was not derived from internal European land-appropriations, but rather from "the European land-appropriation of a non-European new world in conjunction with England's sea-appropriation of the free sea" (Schmitt 2003: 183). Initially the New World was *terra nullius*, no man's land, and a space of territorial indeterminacy. This was the "designated zone of free empty space" (Schmitt 2003: 98) against which positive territorial discriminations had to be made, both legally and politically. What Hobbes described as the state of nature was not the spaceless dystopia it is often held up to be, but a representation of the New World, and Americans were exemplars of the men he describes as having a wolf-character—*homo homini lupus est* (Schmitt 2003: 96). The discovery of the New World initiated a European struggle for territory, leading to a "new spatial order of the earth with new divisions" (Schmitt 2003: 87). Gold, imported from the Americas to Europe through Lisbon and Seville, was integral to this (Vilar 2011: Ch. 8; Bernstein 2004: Ch. 9). The struggle began as a division of surface area, and subsequently deepened into a practical–political project, with Europe at its center.

Schmitt's political theory presupposes that a group's political identity always rests upon a friend–enemy distinction. The enemy does not need to be evil or ugly, nor in economic terms a competitor, but merely *other* "in a specially intense way, existentially something different and alien, so that in the extreme case conflicts with him are possible" (Schmitt 2007: 27). Schmitt was concerned with how different political communities with distinct identities—which are therefore potential enemies—can coexist under a shared international legal order. The function of such an order would be to align extant friend–enemy distinctions with territorial boundaries: in other words, to spatialize them. Money—especially the "national uniforms" it wears, to borrow Marx's phrase—is an important expression of this process of spatialization, as well as a means of reinforcing it.

Throughout the modern era, war has placed the ever-present uncertainty of our relationship with paper money (which, ideally, would be unlimited) in stark relief. At the outbreak of the First World War, gold reserves were expected to determine the outcome, although their role in anchoring the value of money was immediately suspended just about everywhere. In France, 38,000 gold ingots and 1,300 tons of gold coins were shipped out of Paris to pre-arranged locations in the Massif Central and the south almost as soon as fighting began (Ahamed 2009: 71). As "sound" money, gold was meant to ensure that war could be fought without runaway inflation. Even if inflation did occur, it would be short-lived because the available resources for fueling it would be used up after about one year. But experts appear not to have heeded the lessons of money's historical relationship with war, which has invariably been inflationary as states have raised funds through borrowing, taxation, and the printing presses in order to meet their escalating military costs. What stands out here is the possibility that, as with counterfeiting, money relies for its positivity on specific forms of *negativity*: not only appropriated land, but free sea; not only sovereign territory, but *terra nullius*; not only law, but the absence of law; not only order, but lack of order.

UTOPIA AND REFORM

I have so far discussed a number of nineteenth-century developments in the use, production and regulation of money that emerged—or were widely discussed and problematized—in the nineteenth century: bimetallism, monetary union, and inconvertible paper currency. Although political ideals were not completely absent from these arrangements—monetary union is a case in point—they were frequently driven by pragmatism: for example, by the need to ensure a sufficient supply of stable coinage (bimetallism), to prevent international arbitrage (monetary union), and to finance war (inconvertible paper). Perhaps because such experimental arrangements existed, many of them quite short-lived, the nineteenth century was characterized by a high degree of debate about the nature of money, and a plethora of schemes from pamphleteers and others for "improving" it emerged. In this final section of the chapter, I will discuss three such proposals, because they shed further light on aspects of money that were rendered especially interesting or problematic in the arrangements discussed so far. These were both attempts to make money more efficient in some largely technical way—literally, to "improve" money—and to engage with money's relationship to wider questions of equality and social justice. I will focus on three such schemes: the idea of "labour money" advocated by Ruskin; Proudhon's proposals for a Bank of the People; and Silvio Gesell's arguments in favor of "decaying" money.

John Ruskin was an English art critic, social thinker and philanthropist. His "labour money" scheme was outlined mainly in the collection of essays written during the mid-nineteenth century, serialized in *Cornhill Magazine* in 1860 and published as a book in 1862, *Unto This Last* (Ruskin 1997). According to Ruskin, money is essentially "a documentary promise ratified and guaranteed by the nation to give or find a certain quantity of labour in demand" (Ruskin 1997: 185 n.). Given this connection with labor, to issue money based on its "intrinsic value" is a "barbaric" remnant of barter: what matters to money, Ruskin argues, is what it can acquire, not what it is alleged to contain (Ruskin 1928: 169). And what money can acquire, first and foremost, is labor. For this reason, people—not goods—are manipulated when money changes hands. Therefore, an intrinsic connection exists between price and social justice. Ruskin characterizes the payment of wages as "giving time for time" (Ruskin 1997: 195). That is to say, a just wage "will consist in a sum of money which will at any time procure for [the worker] at least as much labour as he has given" (Ruskin 1997: 196). According to Ruskin, this fundamental equation—giving time for time—is a perfectly sound basis on which to organize a system of money and prices. Moreover, a monetary system that is organized on this basis will carry significant social benefits because it automatically prevents the concentration of wealth: it "gives each subordinated person fair and sufficient means of rising in the social scale," hence removing the "worst disabilities of poverty" (Ruskin 1997: 199–200). Those who have wealth do so not simply because they have accumulated money, but because they have successfully ensured that others have less. Ruskin refers to this as "the art of contriving the maximum inequality in our favour" (Ruskin 1997: 182). A system of labor money makes this almost impossible because it is designed to ensure that workers are paid a just wage.

Read from a present-day perspective, Ruskin's arguments may seem naive and simplistic, but the basic principle of "giving time for time" still resonates; indeed it forms the basis of a number of more recent monetary schemes such as local exchange and trading schemes, or LETS, and time dollars (e.g. Ithaca hours). While neither of these more contemporary incarnations of Ruskin's fundamental idea has been massively successful—that is to say, they remain quite marginal within the social contexts in which they arise, are often short-lived, and tend to be characterized by difficulties such as hoarding—the number of schemes in which time is used as the fundamental unit of monetary value continues to proliferate. In the UK, contemporary examples include "Spice," which is a paper currency system paying people in units of hours for work that would otherwise be taken up by volunteering—thereby incentivizing them to "give" their time in exchange for notes that can be redeemed for various services—and "Echo," which is a scheme in which businesses exchange services measured (and paid for) by "hours" rather than paid for by mainstream currency.

What Ruskin's arguments highlight above all is that key questions about the basis of money's value—raised elsewhere in this chapter in relation to gold, silver and credit—were also being taken into more socially and politically rich terrain and connected to human effort, and beyond this, social justice. This was true of Marx, too, of course, although his arguments are often misconstrued because he had so much to say about gold. It is worth noting that in the *Grundrisse*, Marx himself doubted whether "the different civilized forms of money—metallic, paper, credit money, labour money (the last-named as the socialist form)—can accomplish what is demanded of them without suspending the very relation of production which is expressed in the category money" (Marx 2005: 123). We may make piecemeal reforms to money, he says, and "one form may remedy evils against which another is powerless," but no single solution is capable of "overcoming the contradictions inherent in the money relation, and can instead only hope to reproduce these contradictions in one or another form" (Marx 2005: 123). As for the basic idea of labor money, Marx simply argues that the distinction between value and price—that is, "between the commodity measured by the labour time whose product it is, and the product of the labour time against which it is exchanged"—calls for a "third commodity to act as a measure in which the real exchange value of commodities is expressed" (Marx 2005: 139–40). That commodity is money, of course, but—by definition—it cannot be labor.

A similar fundamental concern with the relationship between money and social justice characterized Proudhon's arguments about the banking system. Like Ruskin, Proudhon's arguments focused on the connection between money and work, indeed his expressed aim was to hand control of economic relations over to workers, taking power away from capitalists and financiers. The notion of social or mutual credit was at the core of his proposals, which were laid out in *Solution of the Social Problem* (Proudhon 1927), completed one year after the 1848 revolutions in France. Proudhon envisaged the Bank of Exchange as a replacement for the existing central bank, the Bank of France. Having participated in the 1848 revolutions, Proudhon had misgivings about the provisional government, which he believed was neglecting matters of economic importance. Proudhon's argument is broadly in line with the view that most key problems with money and credit systems as constituted during the modern era derive from their dependence arrangements that place core institutions (e.g. the state and/or banks) at the top of a hierarchy, responsible for issuing and regulating money. Critics of such a system advocate a horizontal arrangement. Proudhon's proposal for a Bank of the People is a good example. His arguments are intriguing because they touch upon one of the most prominent and controversial themes in contemporary discussions of financial regulation and monetary reform, namely, the issue of disintermediation.

Proudhon's idea for a "Bank of Exchange" was premised on the idea that it should be possible to avoid using metallic currency altogether. As with the use of greenbacks to provide cheap war finance, Proudhon's reasoning drew on a close equation between money and credit. Proudhon agreed that money is essentially a form of credit, but he argued that this relationship requires reform if the needs of social justice are to be served. For Proudhon, the problem with most conceptions of money as credit is that they equate money itself with property: money is not capital, he argued, but simply a medium of exchange. In other words, the primary purpose of money is not to earn interest but rather to facilitate exchange. Money is not something that needs to be accumulated as capital because of the interest it earns. On the contrary, money should simply be exchanged and passed on. This had fundamental implications for banking. In Proudhon's scheme, banks would issue exchange notes—basically, a coupon or mortgage note—rather than traditional bank notes. These exchange notes would serve as loans against property. The loan would be set for a number of years, whereupon it would be repayable to the bank by the original borrower. In the event of default, the property on which the note is secured can be sold, and the rights over it passed to the last holder of the note. Compared to traditional bank notes, what goes missing with such an arrangement is the "parasitic middleman, usurping, like that State, the rights of the labourer, and absorbing, like the capitalist, a part of his product" (Proudhon 1927: 92).

Proudhon was fundamentally concerned with two things. In technical terms, he wanted to keep both money and property in motion, to stop them either from stagnating or from being accumulated as wealth: the purpose of exchange notes was "to convert property itself into money; to free it, to mobilize it, to make it circulable like money" (Proudhon 1927: 90). Whereas a traditional bank note contains a guarantee that it could be redeemed in metallic currency, an exchange note, as Proudhon conceived it, would simply be a credit note being passed around and accepted at face value. Credit is thereby viewed as a "simple exchange in which one of the parties delivers his product at one time, the other remits his in various instalments, without interest, without any other costs than those of accounting" (Proudhon 1927: 93). Politically, Proudhon was concerned with social justice. His proposals were premised on a particular understanding of property, labor, and capital. Capital, he argued, is unproductive, and rent, interest and profit are essentially forms of theft (Proudhon 1927: 88). According to Proudhon, mutual credit was a means of abolishing rent and interest because it made the fundamental idea of capital—and thus the capitalist himself—redundant. In a system of interest-bearing property, a creditor was essentially a parasite, to whom the debtor—to wit, the worker—had to pay "tribute" in order to use capital which he or she owned in the first place. In a mutual system, by contrast, there would be no intermediary lender who extracted usury, hence credit would be redefined as the giving of the product of one's labor in consideration for the product of another's future labor. In the interest-bearing system, there could only be one debtor and one creditor. In the mutual system, by contrast, "every creditor or mortgagee becomes a debtor in his turn" (Proudhon 1927: 85). Given this emphasis on the exchange of labor for labor, the resonance with Ruskin is clear.

In an era of bank failures, Proudhon—like Ruskin—could be praised for his optimism and good faith, as much as criticized for over-simplification and naivety. In contrast to the traditional bank, the mutualist association as he saw it would have capital. Proudhon's banks were meant to exist only for the purposes of exchange. Their membership would be unlimited and perpetual, just like one's membership of humanity itself. Moreover, membership of such a bank would not bind us to each other in the sense of joint liability, but only be a form of general insurance. Finally, of course, a bank conceived along Proudhon's lines would make no profit, because "labour produces everything out of nothing" (Proudhon 1927: 87–8). Proudhon argued that his banks could form the financial basis and core of a system of social economy based on two principles: production without capital, and exchange without profit. In such a system, credit would be taken out of the hands of unproductive intermediaries and placed directly into the hands of producers themselves. Credit would thereby be restored to its proper social function: it would cease being a tool of speculation, and would be managed by the community of producers. Such, according to Proudhon, was the principle of mutualism in which wealth came purely from within the community.

Proudhon also proposed a "Bank of the People" that seemed to operate along more pragmatic lines than the Bank of Exchange; indeed he actually established a society of this name in 1849, although it lasted only a matter of months. Whereas the Exchange Bank would lend at zero interest, the Bank of the People would lend at low rates of interest (initially fixed at 2 percent, falling to a minimum of 0.25 percent). While the Bank of Exchange was to have no capital, the People's Bank would begin with five million francs of capital, divided into shares of five francs each. Finally, the People's Bank would issue notes in exchange for specie: although these were not payable in coin, they were simply "orders for delivery, invested with social character, made perpetual and payable at sight by every member or support in the products of services of his industry or profession" (Proudhon 1927: 99). While Proudhon intended that the Bank would eventually be turned into a joint-stock company, initially it operated as a partnership, with a General Manager, a Supervising Council consisting of thirty delegates and General Assembly with one thousand members. Should the Bank fail, assets would be divided "among those who are entitled to them" (Proudhon 1927: 112). The People's Bank did fail: after just three months, Proudhon announced that the experiment was coming to an end: events, he said, had "proved too strong for it."

As with labor money, there are some intriguing parallels between what Proudhon was proposing in the middle of the nineteenth century, and a plethora of subsequent attempts to reform money and banking according to the principles of mutualism that he originally outlined. Credit unions, mutual savings banks and cooperative banks are extremely common in the present day, and although one would be hard pushed to find any operating in quite the "pure" form that Proudhon imagined—loans are interest bearing for one thing—the fundamental principles of mutualism that he outlined are certainly in evidence in all such cases. There are also some wider resonances between Proudhon's conception of mutualism and political philosophy. Mutualism as Proudhon conceived it involves removing the state from the credit system: he resorted to anarchist principles as justification for his banks. In Proudhon's schemes it was the state's absence, above anything else, that should define the future of money. In this specific respect, although his banks failed, Proudhon's arguments turned out to be quite in tune with the present-day age of stateless digital currencies such as bitcoin.

The third reformist thinker under discussion in this section is Silvo Gesell. Gesell (1862–1930) was a theoretical economist, as well as a social activist, whose major work, *The Natural Economic Order* (1906) contained long and detailed sections on "free" money; or as he put it, "money as it should be." Gesell published several other writings on the subject, including *Currency Reform as Bridge to the Social State* (1891) and *The Nationalisation of Money* (1892), as well as founding a monthly periodical, *Geld- und Bodenreforn (Monetary and Land Reform)* in 1900. Gesell's arguments are especially intriguing because of the context in which they were written, namely, the "classical" gold standard as discussed at the end of the last section of this chapter. He defined free money as "an instrument of exchange and nothing else," whose sole test of usefulness was the "degree of security, rapidity and cheapness with which goods are exchanged." Good money as Gesell understood it should secure, accelerate and cheapen the exchange of goods. By contrast, the introduction of the gold standard to Germany had been a "disaster" because it had "over improved" money, considering it only from the point of view of its holder. Gesell's proposal was disarmingly simple: make money less attractive to hold on to. Money, he argued, should age, just like commodities. The latter, he observed, have a definite—material—relationship with time: for example, they rot, decay, break, and rust. Money must have the same properties: it, too, must go out of date like a newspaper, rot like potatoes, rust like iron, and evaporate like ether. If it does not, the relationship between money on one side, and goods on the other, will always be asymmetrical—and insofar as people prefer money to goods, and they are more likely to hoard it. Gesell concludes that money ought to be made worse as a commodity if it is to be improved as a medium of exchange. The gold standard achieved precisely the opposite.

The practice of deliberately reducing money's value over time unless stamped is known as demurrage, although Gesell himself never used this term. The idea is to charge a fee for not using money within a specified time: for hoarding. Although Gesell's scheme was intended for national currency, the practice has been widely adopted within alternative currency schemes, and was a feature of Fisher's stamp scrip as well as Keynes's bancor. Demurrage was taken up in a number of schemes during the Great Depression, albeit not at the level of state currency. In Germany, Austria, Switzerland, and France, and in a number of American towns, demurrage-based "emergency money" was issued. Rates of depreciation varied, although the precise level appeared to make little difference to whether a specific scheme succeeded or failed. The central measure of perceived success in most cases was whether the velocity of money increased, stimulating the local economy. The results were mixed. Godschalk lists four American schemes—in Santa Cruz, California; Okmulgee, Oklahoma; Mason City, Iowa; and Carmel, California—in which money's velocity does appear to have increased significantly as a result of demurrage (Godschalk 2012). Demurrage subsequently returned on a widespread scale with the expansion of the LETS movement during the 1990s; it was used in the Austrian Waldviertler system, Regiogeld in Germany, Abeille in France, and the Stroud Pound in the United Kingdom. In Germany, the Bavarian Chiemgauer applies demurrage to cashless currency via a negative interest rate. Again, these monies often have a velocity of circulation that is notably higher than that of mainstream currencies (as measured by M1) such as the euro (Gelleri 2009; Godschalk 2012).

CONCLUDING REMARKS

We are used to thinking of our own age as a period of increasing plurality and diversity in the forms that money takes: from local currencies that grew from the 1980s onwards, to cryptocurrencies such as bitcoin, to the explosion of new payments systems that has characterized the first two decades of the twenty-first century. This is often contrasted with a "modern age" in which the dominant form of money was national currency regulated by central banks and governments, and managed in conjunction with commercial private banks. In these terms, the nineteenth century has more in common with our own age than with the twentieth century: having one currency circulating within a national territory was not the norm during this period. We are often told that we have entered an unusually fluid and exciting moment in the history of money, as we witness an explosion in the variety of payment systems on offer, and the emergence of new and alternative monetary systems, both locally (with community currencies) and globally (bitcoin and other cryptocurrencies). But as I hope I have shown in this chapter, not only are alternative monies by no means new, but viewed in historical perspective, it is not clear what they are "alternatives" to—or to express this in another way, what "non-alternative" (or "normal") money is supposed to be. Besides the quite well-known reformers we have been discussing here—from Ruskin, Proudhon, and Gesell—there is a host of committed monetary radicals who argue not only that it is possible to create better and alternative monies than those we already have, but that these monies genuinely will enrich our social and economic existence. The chorus of voices calling for monetary reform has certainly grown since the 2007/8 banking crisis. But as we have seen in this chapter, it has never really been silent.

NOTES

Introduction

1. Geographers and social theorists sometimes refer to such changes as time–space convergence or compression, and emphasise their cumulative importance for accelerating the movement of goods, people, and information, effectively reducing the experience of distance (see for example Giddens 1984, Harvey 1989, May and Thrift 2001). See also Wajcman and Dodd 2017 and Waizbort, this volume, Chapter 6.
2. From Nietzsche to Simmel, following Dodd (2012a, 2012b), for example. On the acid nature of money, see Maurer 2006, and on the monetary valorization of life in the US during the period, see Zelizer 1979.
3. In *Capital* Volume 1, Marx's brilliant discussion of the working day includes the following citation from a Dr Richardson, whose article, "Work and Over-Work" appeared in the *Social Science Review*, July 18, 1863: "If the poets were true, there is no man so hearty, so merry, as the blacksmith; he rises early and strikes his sparks before the sun; he eats and drinks and sleeps as no other man. Working in moderation, he is, in fact, in one of the best of human positions, physically speaking. But we follow him into the city or town, and we see the stress of work on that strong man, and what then is his position in the death-rate of his country. In Marylebone, blacksmiths die at the rate of 31 per thousand per annum, or 11 above the mean of the male adults of the country in its entirety. The occupation, instinctive almost as a portion of human art, unobjectionable as a branch of human industry, is made by mere excess of work, the destroyer of the man" (cited in Marx 1867 [1976]: 366).
4. Marx and Engels refer once to money in the *Manifesto*, quoted above (Marx and Engels 1848 [2004]), to denounce the disbanding power of bourgeois money: "The bourgeoisie has torn away from the family its sentimental veil, and has reduced the family relation to a mere money relation."
5. This seems to be one of the main characteristics of the concept of landscape itself, its multiscalar form, and its constitutive relation to the concept of perspective: a

particular synthesis between what is seen through the lens of the observer and what the analyst manages to observe of the landscapes seen by the agents involved in the processes under analysis (Filippuci 2016; Hirsch and O'Hanlon 1995; on the sociogenesis of the concept of landscape at the end of the eighteenth century and the beginning of the nineteenth, see Elias 1933 [1983], Chapter 8).

6. As well as facilitating trade, the fixed gourde–franc parity allowed calculation of the debt that Haiti was obliged to acknowledge with the old metropolis, identified as the first example of an "external debt" in world monetary history (Graeber 2011: 6).
7. Debates like this remained alive in new forms through the concept of the Optimal Currency Area (OCA), for example (Mundell 1961), and the debates that led to the implantation of the euro (Helleiner 2013a).
8. Both the monetary unification processes in the new metropolises—see Carruthers and Babb (1996) on US greenbacks—and the colonial spaces—see Balachandran (1996) on Keynes in India in the context of the First World War—proved to be fertile terrains for the formulation of monetary ideas.
9. Zelizer 1994: Chapter 4, "Poor People's Money."
10. The relation between cash machines, department stores, and the affective economy of individuals and families in US and British cities can be observed in the sociogenesis of the ritual of Christmas (including the giving and receiving of presents), a transmutation of cold and anonymous money into personalized affects that took place in the second half of the nineteenth century (Carrier 1995).

Chapter 4

1. Benton and Clay quoted in *Niles' National Register* (Washington DC, 1838) pp. 278–9. The debate took place on December 30, 1837.
2. *The Congressional Globe*, Second session, volume VI, (Washington, DC 1838) p. 19.
3. On the mixed money of the antebellum economy see Mihm (2007) and O'Malley (2012).
4. "Fiscal History of Texas," *DeBow's Review* 14, no. 4 (April 1853): 381.
5. *Chicago Daily Tribune*, Jan 4, 1858, p. 2.
6. *Baltimore Sun*, July 25, 1848, p. 4.
7. *Baltimore Sun*, May 12, 1838, p. 1.
8. *Baltimore Sun*, Mar 2, 1838, p. 1.
9. *Baltimore Sun*, Jul 14, 1837, p. 2.
10. *The United States Magazine and Democratic Review*, vol. iv (Washington DC 1838), p. 30.
11. *Baltimore Sun*, Jul 14, 1837, p. 2.
12. *New York Morning Herald*, Oct. 12, 1837, p. 1.
13. On gold and circulation see Benn Michaels 1987, and Henkin 1998: Chapter 4.
14. *The Baltimore Sun*, June 17, 1839, p. 2.
15. *Baltimore Sun*, June 19, 1839, p. 2.
16. *Baltimore Sun*, June 19, 1839, p. 2.
17. *New York Times*, Oct 15, 1857, p. 1.
18. *Dublin University Magazine*, vol. xiv, (1839), p. 515.

19. "Tobacco currency—furnished by the manufacturers Pearl & Obreight," (1863), Library of Congress Prints and Photographs Division Washington, DC, 20540 USA.
20. *Western Reserve Chronicle*, December 3, 1862, p. 1.
21. *The Baltimore Sun*, Nov 21, 1839, p. 2.
22. On the origins of the term "carpetbagger," see O'Malley 2012: Chapter 4.
23. Albany, New York *Atlas and Argus*, January 19, 1863, quoted in Wood 1970: 44.
24. *Hooley's opera house songster: containing a choice selection of sentimental, comic, & Ethiopian songs* (NY 1863), p. 21.
25. Frederick Douglass, "Address at a Meeting for the Promotion of Colored Enlistments," Philadelphia, July 6, 1863. Frederick Douglass Papers. Library of Congress, Manuscript Division, http://memory.loc.gov/ammem/doughtml/doughome.html.
26. "The Broker's 'Stamp Act' Lament", July 1862; Monographic. Available at: https://www.loc.gov/item/amss.cw200330/ (accessed November 14, 2018).
27. Some might point to bitcoin, and other alternative currencies, as shinplaster-like currencies. Indeed, they thrive in specific sub-communities in defiance of elite/nationalist efforts at control. Unlike shinplasters, however, bitcoins were conceived as a limited resource, a unit of money with a limit on its final amount. In that sense, they are much more like gold, which derives its value from its scarcity and the finite amount of gold that exists on earth. Bitcoins were similarly always imagined as finite. Shinplasters on the other hand, were as limitless as human creativity itself.

Chapter 5

1. https://www.theguardian.com/media/2010/jan/22/barclaycard-waterslide-rollercoaster
2. https://www.coloribus.com/adsarchive/outdoor/american-express-card-come-fly-with-me-15338355/
3. http://www.campaignlive.co.uk/article/lloyds-tsb/884735
4. C.J. Taylor's "Coxey's Paternalism" of 1894, for example, is a disparaging representation of the protest march of the "army" of the unemployed led by the supporter of greenbacks that depicts Presidential candidate: *Puck*, 35, no. 893 (April 18, 1894). In "The Fool and his Money" from 1899, Louis Dalrymple returns to this theme but it is a stockbroker, rather than a politician, who dispenses fraudulent wealth: *Puck*, 45, no. 1155, (April 26, 1899).
5. Post-structuralist critics such as Marc Shell have explored how the story reveals how in the "institution of paper money, sign and substance—paper and gold—are clearly disassociated, much as word is disassociated from meaning in punning," while literary historians such as Gerald Kennedy and Liliane Weissberg emphasized the subdued history of slavery suggested by the story's geographical setting on Sullivan's Island. See Shell 1982 and Kennedy and Weissberg 2001.
6. Although allegorical readings of the story sometimes gesture to the connections between the Emerald City, Washington DC and the greenbacks of the 1860s (and some acknowledge that Jacob Coxey was himself a proponent not of silver but of greenbacks) the interpretations are constrained by their own historical literalism, the wizard needs to be matched to an actual historical counterpart and the difficulty of

finding an obvious match confounds the analysis. For Henry Littlefield "The Wizard [. . .] might have been any President, from Grant to McKinley" (Littlefield 1964: 54), for Hugh Rockoff he is "Marcus Alonzo Hanna," the Chairman of the National Republican Committee (Rockoff 1990: 750), and for Gretchen Ritter he is the "political charlatan who promised too much and gave too little," the group fears him as emblematic of how "political reform movements of the time were also scarred by their attempts to change the political centre" (Ritter 1997: 182).

7. Michael O'Malley, for example, associates the growth of consumer culture with "leafing through the Sears catalog" in the 1890s, where "one found goods of all imaginable kinds for sale, each an identical perfect copy of some distant unknown original" (O'Malley 2012: 127).

8. "Exciting Balloon Ascension," *Springfield Daily Republican*, Friday July 11, 1862; "Battle watched from air," *Springfield Daily Republican*, Monday June 2, 1862.

Chapter 6

1. The exposition in this text is intentionally based around the narratives of Osterhammel and Bayly, though there is not space here to discuss these in detail. Consequently, the more distinct views that these two authors have of the period will appear smoothed over.

2. Perhaps it is no coincidence, then, that the two historians who informed the description of the nineteenth century, Bayly and Osterhammel, reinforce the nexus between that time and our historical present in various ways.

3. "Cameralism" designates the field of scientific knowledge relating to state administration, especially with respect to finances, economics, and law, as understood in the German states and territories during the eighteenth and nineteenth centuries. Later, economics and administration (especially of the state) came to occupy its place.

4. Those interested can access a large proportion of Simmel's writings in German, as well as various texts in English, on the following website: http://socio.ch/sim/.

5. Cassirer explored the problem, in his own way but in Simmel's wake, in his 1910 book *Substanzbegriff und Funktionsbegriff*.

6. On April 19, 2018, the newspaper *O Estado de São Paulo* reproduced the social network post of a civil servant accused of corruption: "Money does not bring happiness, but a sensation so like it that an expert would be needed to tell the difference". Available from: http://politica.estadao.com.br/blogs/fausto-macedo/dinheiro-nao-traz-felicidade-mas-da-uma-sensacao-tao-parecida-que-e-necessario-um-especialista-para-ver-a-diferenca/ (accessed April 19, 2018).

Chapter 7

1. We can further distinguish between (a) full bimetallism (gold and silver are both legal tender and circulate without restriction); (b) so-called "limping standard" bimetallism, in which gold and silver both circulate as legal tender but only one metal is coined without restriction; and (c) "trade" bimetallism, in which both

metals are coined without restriction but only one is legal tender, whereas the other is used primarily for trade.
2. Here is a dictionary definition of Gresham's Law: "Where by legal enactment a government assigns the same nominal value to two or more forms of circulatory medium whose intrinsic values differ, payment will always, as far as possible, be made in that medium of which the cost of production is least, and the more valuable medium will tend to disappear from circulation" (Palgrave's Dictionary, 1926; cited in Chown 1994: 76).
3. L. Frank Baum's *The Wonderful Wizard of Oz*, first published in 1900, is sometimes reputed to have been an allegory that contributed to this wider discourse about metallic money and the "fake" value of greenbacks (see Rockoff 1990). In Baum's tale, the cowardly lion is sometimes identified as Williams Jennings Bryan, while the Emerald City may have represented the "fake" value associated with paper money, especially greenbacks.
4. Besides greenbacks, there were a number of other notable instances of the use of inconvertible paper money during the nineteenth century. These include "Il Corso Forsoto" (forced currency) as used in Italy between 1866 and 1881 (Clough, 1971: 51–75), the Austrian florin of the 1870s, the Argentine peso and Brazilian real (intermittently) throughout the century, and the Chilean suspensions of convertibility in 1865, 1867 and 1879 (de Soto, 2006: 704).

BIBLIOGRAPHY

Addison, J. 1854. *The Works of Joseph Addison: The Spectator*. New York: G. Putnam.
Ahamed, L. 2009. *Lords of Finance: 1929, the Great Depression and the Bankers Who Broke the World*. London: Windmill Books.
Altmann, S.P. 1908. "Zur deutschen Geldlehre des 19. Jahrhunderts" in S.P. Altmann et al. *Die Entwicklung der deutschen Volkswirtschaftslehre im neunzehnten Jahrhundert*. Leipzig: Duncker and Humblot, Vol. 1, Ch. 6.
Appadurai, A. 1986. "Introduction: Commodities and the Politics of Value" in A. Appadurai (ed.), *The Social Life of Things: Commodities in Cultural Perspective*. Cambridge: Cambridge University Press.
Appadurai, A. 2016. *Banking on Words: The Failure of Language in the Age of Derivative Finance*. Chicago, IL: University of Chicago Press.
Appleby, J. 1976. "Locke, Liberalism and the Natural Laws of Money," *Past and Present*, 71: 43–69.
Ascoli, P.M. 2006. *Julius Rosenwald: The Man Who Built Sears, Roebuck and Advanced the Cause of Black Education in the American South*. Bloomington, IN: Indiana University Press.
Bagby, G.W. 1885. *Selections from the Miscellaneous Writings of Dr. George W. Bagby*. Richmond, VA: Whittet & Shepperson.
Balachandran, G. 1993. "Britain's Liquidity Crisis and India, 1919–20," *Economic History Review*, 46 (3): 575–91.
Balachandran, G. 1994. "Towards a '*Hindoo* Marriage'? Anglo-Indian Monetary Relations in Interwar India," *Modern Asian Studies*, 28 (3): 615–47.
Balachandran, G. 1996. *John Bullion's Empire: Britain's Gold Problems and India between the Wars*. London: Routledge.
Balachandran, G. 1998. *The Reserve Bank of India, 1951–67*. Delhi: Oxford University Press.
Balachandran, G. 2008. "Power and Markets in Global Finance: The Gold Standard, 1890–1926," *Journal of Global History*, 3 (3): 313–35.
Barbour, D. 1885. *The Theory of Bimetallism*. London: Macmillan.
Bassett, C.F. 1901. "Mechanical cashier." US Patent 678,218, issued July 9, 1901.

Bátiz-Lazo, B., Haigh, T. and Stearns, D.L. 2014. "How the Future Shaped the Past: The Case of the Cashless Society," *Enterprise and Society*, 15 (1): 103–31.

Baucom, I. 2005. *Spectres of the Atlantic: Finance Capital, Slavery and the Philosophy of History*. Durham, NC: Duke University Press.

Baum, F. 2000. *The Wizard of Oz: The Centennial Edition*. Ed. Michael Patrick Hearn. New York: W.W. Norton.

Bayly, C.A. 2013. *The Birth of the Modern World, 1780–1914*. Malden: Blackwell.

Baynes, F.W. 1904. "Cash-till." US Patent 754,961, issued March 22, 1904.

Beaumont, F.J. 1900. "Coin-controlled lavatory-lock." US Patent 656,082, issued August 14, 1900.

Beckert, J. 2016. *Imagined Futures*. Cambridge, MA: Harvard University Press.

Benn Michaels, W. 1987. *The Gold Standard and the Logic of Naturalism*. Berkeley, CA: University of California Press.

Berg, O. 2014. *Making Money: The Philosophy of Crisis Capitalism*. London: Verso Books.

Bernstein, P.L. 2004. *The Power of Gold: The History of an Obsession*. Chichester: John Wiley and Sons.

Birla, R. 2008. *Stages of Capital: Law, Culture, and Market Governance in Late Colonial India*. Durham, NC: Duke University Press.

Blitz, A. (Antonio Van Zandt). 1872. *Life and Adventures of Signor Blitz*. New York: T. Belknap.

Bowler, K. 2013. *Blessed: A History of the American Prosperity Gospel*. Oxford: Oxford University Press.

Boyd, S.S. 1900. "Coin assorting, delivering, and recording apparatus." US Patent 655,544, issued August 7, 1900.

Brant, C. 2011. "The Progress of Knowledge in the Regions of Air?: Divisions and Disciplines in Early Ballooning," *Eighteenth-Century Studies*, 45: 71–86.

Brown Jr., W.A. 1929. *England and the New Gold Standard, 1919–26*, New Haven, CT: Yale University Press.

Bruner, R.F. and Carr, S.D. 2007. *The Panic of 1907: Lessons Learned from the Market's Perfect Storm*. Hoboken: John Wiley and Sons.

Bryan, D. and Rafferty, M. 2007. "Financial Derivatives and the Theory of Money," *Economy and Society*, 31 (1): 134–58.

Bryan, D. and Rafferty, M. 2016. "Decomposing Money: Ontological Options and Spreads," *Journal of Cultural Economy*, 9 (1): 27–42.

Burke, K. 2002. "Money and Power: The Shift from Great Britain to the United States" in Y. Cassis (ed.), *Finance and Financiers in European History, 1880–1960*. Cambridge: Cambridge University Press.

Burton, C.M. 1900. "Prepayment attachment for gas-meters." US Patent 647,803, issued April 17, 1900.

Calder, L. 1999. *Financing the American Dream: A Cultural History of Consumer Credit*. Princeton, NJ: Princeton University Press.

Carrier, J. 1995. *Gifts and Commodities: Exchange and Western Capitalism Since 1700*. London: Routledge.

Carruthers, B.G and Babb, S. 1996. "The Color of Money: Greenbacks and Gold in Postbellum America," *American Journal of Sociology*, 101 (6): 1556–91.

Casarino, C. 2002. *Modernity at Sea: Melville, Marx, Conrad in Crisis*. Minneapolis, MN: University of Minnesota Press.

Castagnaro, M. 2012. "Lunar Fancies and Earthly Truths: The Moon Hoax of 1835 and the Penny Press," *Nineteenth-Century Contexts*, 34: 253–68.

Castel, R. 2017. *From Manual Workers to Wage Laborers: Transformation of the Social Question*. London: Routledge, Transaction Publishers.
Cherny, R. 1996. *The Cross of Gold, by William Jennings Bryan*, Omaha, NE: University of Nebraska Press.
Choonara, J. 2009. "Interview: David Harvey—Exploring the Logic of Capital," *Socialist Review*, April (335).
Chown, J.F. 1994. *A History of Money From AD 800*. London and New York: Routledge.
Clavin, P and Wessels, J-W. 2004. "Another Golden Idol? The League of Nations' Gold Delegation and the Great Depression, 1929–1932," *International History Review*, 26 (4): 768–73.
Clough, S.B. 1971. *Storia dell'economia italiana dal 1861 ad oggi*. Bologna: Cappelli.
Coeckelbergh, M. 2015. "Money as Medium and Tool: Reading Simmel as a Philosopher of Technology to Understand Contemporary Financial ICTs and Media," *Techné: Research in Philosophy and Technology* 19 (3): 358–80.
Comaroff, J and Comaroff J. 1991. *Of Revelation and Revolution, Vol. 1: Christianity, Colonialism, and Consciousness in South Africa*. Chicago, IL: University of Chicago Press.
Comaroff, J. and Comaroff, J. 1997. *Of Revelation and Revolution, Vol. 2: The Dialectics of Modernity on a South African Frontier*. Chicago, IL: University of Chicago Press.
Conant, C.A. 1909. *History of Modern Banks of Issue: With an Account of the Economic Crises of the Nineteenth Century and the Crisis of 1907*. New York: G.P. Putnam's and Sons.
Connor, S. 2008. "Thinking Things," Lecture given at the European Society for the Study of English (ESSE), Aarhus, Denmark, August 25, 2008. Available at: http://stevenconnor.com/thinkingthings/thinkingthings.pdf (accessed November 14. 2018).
Corbridge, S. and Thrift, N. 1994. "Introduction" in S. Corbridge, N. Thrift and R. Martin (eds.), *Money, Power and Space*. Oxford: Blackwell.
Croteau, W. 1875. "Moneybox," US Patent USD8655, Washington: US Trademark and Patent Office.
Cushing, F.W. 1902. "Means for forming beaches." US Patent 715,557, issued December 9, 1902.
Darnton, R. 1989. "What Was Revolutionary about the French Revolution?" *New York Review of Books*, January 19.
De Cecco, M. 1975. *Money and Empire: The International Gold Standard, 1890–1914*, London: Rowan and Littlefield.
De Cock, C., Fitchett, J., and Volkmann, C. 2009. "'Myths of a near Past': Envisioning Finance Capitalism Anno 2007," *Ephemera: Theory and Politics in Organization* 9 (1): 8–25.
De Soto, J.H. 2006. *Money, Bank Credit and Economic Cycles*. Auburn, AL: Mises Institute.
Del Mar, A. 1895. *A History of Monetary Systems*. London: Effingham Wilson.
Dick, A. 2013. *Romanticism and the Gold Standard*. London: Palgrave.
Dickinson, E. 2016. *Collected Poems of Emily Dickinson*. London: Lerner Press.
Dodd, N. 2005. "Reinventing monies in Europe," *Economy and Society*, 34 (4): 558–83.
Dodd, N. 2012a. "Simmel's Perfect Money: Fiction, Socialism and Utopia in The Philosophy of Money". *Theory, Culture and Society*, 29 (7/8): 146–76.

Dodd, N. 2012b. "Nietzsche's money," *Journal of Classical Sociology*, 13 (1): 47–68.
Dodd, N. 2014. *The Social Life of Money*. Princeton, NJ: Princeton University Press.
Doty, R.G. 1998. *America's Money, America's Story*. Washington, DC: Whitman Publishing.
Douglass, F. 1852. "What to the Slave Is the Fourth of July?" *Frederick Douglass: Selected Speeches and Writings*. Chicago, IL: P.S. Foner, pp. 188–206.
Drake, P.W. 1994. *Money Doctors, Foreign Debts, and Economic Reforms in Latin America from the 1890s to the Present*. Washington, DC: Scholarly Resources Inc.
Dreyell, J.S. and Frykenberg, R.E. 1982. "Sovereignty and the 'Sikka' under Company Raj: Minting Prerogative and Imperial Legitimacy in India," *Indian Economic and Social History Review*, 19 (1): 1–25.
Durkheim, E. 1912. *The Elementary Forms of the Religious Life*. London: George Allen and Unwin, Ltd.
Eagleton, C. (mimeo), "How and Why Did the Rupee Become the Currency of Zanzibar and East Africa?".
Eagleton, C. (2019 forthcoming), "Currency as Commodity, as Symbol of Sovereignty and as Subject of Legal Dispute: Henri Greffülhe and the Coinage of Zanzibar in the Late 19th Century." in G. Campbell and S. Serels (eds), Indian Ocean Currencies. London: Palgrave.
Eisenstadt, S.N. 2007. *Múltiplas modernidades*. Lisbon: Horizonte.
Elias, N. 1933 [1983]. *The Court Society*. Dublin: University College Dublin.
Ellison, C.E. 1983. "Marx and the Modern City: Public Life and the Problem of Personality," *The Review of Politics*, 45 (3): 393–420.
Esposito, E. 2011. *The Future of Futures*. Cheltenham: Edward Elgar.
Evard, J.E. 1901. "Apparatus for Distinguishing Genuine from Spurious Coins." US Patent 688,839, issued December 17, 1901.
Filippucci, P. 2016. "Landscape," in *The Cambridge Encyclopedia of Anthropology*. Available at: http://www.anthroencyclopedia.com/entry/landscape (accessed November 6, 2018).
Flandreau, M. 2003. *Money Doctors: The Experience of International Financial Advising 1850–2000*. London: Routledge.
Ford, C. 2005. *Divided Houses: Religion and Gender in Modern France*. Ithaca, NY: Cornell University Press.
Foster, R. 1999. "In God We Trust? The Legitimacy of Melanesian Currencies," in D. Akins and J. Robbins (eds.), *Money and Modernity: State and Local Currencies in Melanesia*. Pittsburgh, PA: University of Pittsburgh Press, pp. 214–31.
Foucault, M. 1978. *The History of Sexuality, Vol. 1*. New York: Random House.
Franklin, B. 1969. "A Modest Inquiry into the Nature and Necessity of a Paper Currency," in H.E. Krooss (ed.), *Documentary History of Banking and Currency in the United States*. New York: Chelsea Publishing House.
Fuller, H. 2009. "From Cowries to Coins: Money and Colonialism in the Gold Coast and British West Africa in the Early 20th Century" in C. Eagleton, H. Fuller, and J. Perkins (eds.), *Money in Africa*. London: British Museum Research Publications, pp. 54–61.
Gamble, R.J. 2015. "The Promiscuous Economy" in B.P. Luskey and W.A. Woloson (eds.), *Capitalism by Gaslight. Illuminating the Economy of Nineteenth-Century America*. Philadelphia, PA: University of Pennsylvania Press, Ch. 2.
Geertz, C. 2004. "What Is a State If It Is Not a Sovereign? Reflections on Politics in Complicated Places (The Sidney Mintz Lecture for 2003)," *Current Anthropology*, 45 (5): 577–93.

Gelleri, C. 2009. "Chiemgauer Regiomoney: Theory and Practice of a local Currency," *International Journal of Community Currency Research*, 13: 61–75.
Germana, M. 2009. *Standards of Value: Race and Literature in America*. Iowa City, IA: University of Iowa Press.
Gernaert, J. 1910. "Manufacture of paper." US Patent 964,014, issued July 12, 1910.
Gesell, S. 1891 [1951]. *Currency Reform as a Bridge to the Social State* (trans. P. Pye). Typescript.
Gesell, S. 1892. *The Nationalization of Money*. Buenos Aires: Typescript.
Gesell, S. 1906 [2007]. *The Natural Economic Order*. Frankston, TX: TGS Publishers.
Giddens, A. 1984. *The Constitution of Society: Outline of the Theory of Structuration*. Cambridge: Polity Press.
Gilbert, E. 2005. "Common Cents: Situating Money in Time and Place," *Economy and Society*, 34 (3): 357–88.
Gilroy, P. 1993. *The Black Atlantic: Modernity and Double Consciousness*. London, Verso.
Gilson, F.H. 1901. "Time-Check." US Patent 689,301, issued December 17, 1901.
Godschalk, H. 2012. "Does Demurrage Matter for Complementary Curriencies?" *International Journal of Community Currency Research*, 16: 58–69.
Golway, T. 2014. *Machine Made: Tammany Hall and the Creation of Modern American Politics*. New York: W.W. Norton and Co.
Goodwin, J. 2003. *Greenback: The Almighty Dollar and the Invention of America*. London: Penguin.
Goux, J-J. 1990. *Symbolic Economies: After Marx and Freud*. Ithaca, NY: Cornell University Press.
Graeber, D. 2011. *Debt: The First 5,000 Years*. New York: Melville House.
Green, E.H.H. 1988. "Rentiers versus Producers? The Political Economy of the Bimetallic Controversy c. 1880–1898," *English Historical Review*, 103 (408): 588–612.
Green, E.H.H. 1990. "The Bimetallic Controversy: Empiricism Belimed or the Case for the Issues," *English Historical Review*, 105 (416): 673–83.
Green, S.K. 2010. *The Second Disestablishment: Church and State in Nineteenth Century America*. Oxford: Oxford University Press.
Greenberg, J.R. 2015. "The Era of Shinplasters," in B.P. Luskey and W.A. Woloson (eds.) *Capitalism by Gaslight. Illuminating the Economy of Nineteenth-Century America*. Philadelphia, PA: University of Pennsylvania Press, Ch. 3.
Gregory, C.A. 1996. "Cowries and Conquest: Towards a Subalternate Quality Theory of Money," *Comparative Studies in Society and History*, 38 (2): 195–217.
Guyer, J. 1995. "Introduction: The Currency Interface and Its Dynamics," in J. Guyer (ed.), *Money Matters: Instability, Values and Social Payments in the Modern History of West African Communities*. Portsmouth: Heinemann.
Guyer, J. 2004. *Marginal Gains: Monetary Transactions in Atlantic Africa*. Chicago, IL: University of Chicago Press.
Hall, J. 1877. "Improvement in Toy Money-Boxes." US Patent RE7,614, issued April 17, 1877.
Hamnett, B. 1999. *A Concise History of Mexico*. Cambridge: Cambridge University Press.
Hardacre, H. 1989. *Shinto and the State, 1868–1988*. Princeton, NJ: Princeton University Press.
Hart, K. 1986. "Heads or Tails? Two Sides of the Coin," *Man*, 21: 637–56.

Hart, K. 2001. *The Memory Bank: Money in an Unequal World*. Knutsford: Texere Publishing.
Hart, K. 2006. "The Euro: A Challenge for Anthropological Method". Available at: http://thememorybank.co.uk/papers/the-euro-a-challenge-for-anthropological-method/ (accessed October 18, 2018).
Harvey, D. 1989. *The Condition of Postmodernity: An Enquiry into the Origins of Cultural Change*. Oxford: Wiley-Blackwell.
Hays, S.P. 1957. *The Response to Industrialism, 1885–1914*. Chicago, IL: University of Chicago Press.
Helleiner, E. 1998. "National Currencies and National Identities," *American Behavioral Scientist*, 41 (10): 1409–36.
Helleiner, E. 2003a. *The Making of National Money Territorial Currencies in Historical Perspective*. Ithaca and London: Cornell University Press.
Helleiner, E. 2003b. "Dollarization Diplomacy: US Policy Toward Latin America Coming Full Circle?" *Review of International Political Economy* 10 (3): 406–29.
Heller, M.A. and Eisenberg, R.S. 1998. "Can Patents Deter Innovation? The Anticommons in Biomedical Research," *Science*, 280 (5364): 698–701.
Henkin, D. 1998. *City Reading: Written Words and Public Spaces in Antebellum New York*. New York: Columbia University Press.
Hirsch, E. and O'Hanlon, M. (eds.) 1995. *The Anthropology of Landscape: Perspectives on Space and Place*. Oxford: Oxford University Press.
Hirschman, A. 1982. "Rival Interpretations of Markets Society: Civilizing, Destructive, or Feeble?" *Journal of Economic Literature* 20 (4): 1462–88.
Hobsbawm, E. 1989. *Nations and Nationalism since 1780. Program, Myth, Reality*. Cambridge: Cambridge University Press.
Holmes, R. 2013. *Falling Upwards: How We Took to the Air*. London: William Collins.
Holt, T.C. 1991. *The Problem of Freedom: Race, Labor, and Politics in Jamaica and Britain, 1832–1938*. Baltimore, MD: Johns Hopkins University Press.
Hughes, I.M. 1978. "Good Money and Bad: Inflation and Devaluation in the Colonial Process," *Mankind*, 11 (3): 308–18.
Ingham G.K. 2004. *The Nature of Money*. Cambridge: Polity Press.
Innes, A.M. 1913. "What Is Money?" *The Banking Law Journal*, 377–408.
Innes, A.M. 1914. "The Credit Theory of Money?" *The Banking Law Journal*, 151–68.
Jevons, W.S. 1896. *Money and the Mechanism of Exchange*. New York: D Appleton and Company.
Johnson, A. 1920. "The Promotion of Thrift in America," *The Annals of the American Academy of Political and Social Science* 87 (1): 233–42.
Johnson, M. 1970. "The Cowrie Currencies of West Africa Part II," *Journal of African History*, 11 (3): 331–53.
Kaminsky, A.P. 1980. "'Lombard Street' and India: Currency Problems in the Late-Nineteenth Century," *Indian Economic and Social History Review*, 17 (3): 307–27.
Kane, R.F. 1876. "Money Box," US Patent USD9231S, US Trademark and Patent Office: Washington.
Kazin, M. 2006. *A Godly Hero: The Life of William Jennings Bryan*. New York: Anchor Books.
Kennedy J.G. and Weissberg, L. 2001. *Romancing the Shadow: Poe and Race*. Oxford: Oxford University Press.
Kepley, A.H. 1884. "Traveler's Treasure-Belt." US Patent 297,268, issued April 22, 1884.

Keynes, J.M. 1936. *The General Theory of Employment Interest and Money*. London: Macmillan.
Keynes, J.M. 1971. *Indian Currency and Finance* (1913), republished as *Collected Writings of John Maynard Keynes*, E. Johnson and D. Moggridge (ed.), Vol 1. Cambridge: Cambridge University Press.
Khan, B.Z. 2005. *The Democratization of Invention: Patents and Copyrights in American Economic Development, 1790–1920*. Cambridge: Cambridge University Press.
Konings, M. 2014. *The Development of American Finance*. Cambridge: Cambridge University Press.
Kosambi, D.D. 1981. *Indian Numismatics*. Delhi: Orient Longman.
Koselleck, R. 2000. *Zeitschichten*. Frankfurt: Suhrkamp.
Koselleck, R. 2010. *Vom Sinn und Unsinn der Geschichte*. Frankfurt: Suhrkamp.
Krippner, G.R. 2005. "The Financialization of the American Economy," *Socio-Economic Review*, 3: 173–208.
Kuper, A. 2001. "Fraternity and Endogamy. The House of Rothschild," *Social Anthropology* 9 (3): 273–87.
Kuroda, A. 2007. "The Maria Theresa Dollar in the Early Twentieth-Century Red Sea Region: A Complementary Interface between Multiple Markets," *Financial History Review*, 14 (1): 89–110.
Kuroda, A. 2008. "Concurrent but Non-Integrable Currency Circuits: Complementary Relationships among Monies in Modern China and Other Regions," *Financial History Review*, 15 (1): 17–36.
Kuroda, A. 2009. "The Eurasian Silver Century, 1276–1359: Commensurability and Multiplicity," *Journal of Global History*, 4 (2): 245–69.
Leach, W. 1993. *Land of Desire: Merchants, Power and the Rise of a New American Culture*. New York: Vintage Books.
Leer Weiss, B. 2005. "Cowries, Coffee, and Currencies: Transforming Material Wealth in Early 20th Century Bukoba" in P. Geschiere and W. van Binsbergen (eds.), *Commodification: Objects and Identities (The Social Life of Things Revisited)*. Berlin: LIT Verlag.
Leibbrandt, G. 2009. *A Billion Here, a Billion There: The Statistics of Payments*. London: Swift Institute.
Lepler, J. 2013. *The Many Panics of 1837: People, Politics, and the Creation of a Transatlantic Financial Crisis*. Cambridge: Cambridge University Press.
Lévi-Strauss, C. 1960 [1974]. "Introdução" in M. Mauss, *Sociologia e antropologia*. São Paulo: Epu/Edusp.
Limebeer, A.J. 1935. "The Gold Mining Industry and the Gold Standard," *The South African Journal of Economics*, 3 (2): 145–57.
Linick, A. 1900. "Coin-Controlled Electric Battery." US Patent 641,309, issued January 16, 1900.
Littlefield, H.M. 1964. "The Wizard of Oz: Parable on Populism," *American Quarterly*, 16: 53.
Luhmann, N. 1980–99. *Gesellschaftsstruktur und Semantik, 4 Vols*. Frankfurt: Suhrkamp.
Luhmann, N. 1994. *Die Wirtschaft der Gesellschaft*. Frankfurt: Suhrkamp.
Lumsden, J. 1844. *American Memoranda, by a Mercantile Man*. Glasgow: Bell and Bain.
Lurie, A. 2000. "The Oddness of Oz," *New York Review of Books*, December 21.

Macleod, H.D. 1855–56. *Theory and Practice of Banking*. London: Longman, Green, Reader and Dyer.

Mannheim, K. 1931 [1959]. "Wissenssoziologie" in A. Vierkandt (ed.), *Handwörterbuch der Soziologie*. New Ed., Stuttgart: F. Enke.

Martínez-Piva, J.M. 2009. *Knowledge Generation and Protection*. New York: Springer.

Marx, K. 1844. "On the Jewish Question." Online edition, Marxists.org. Available at: https://www.marxists.org/archive/marx/works/1844/jewish-question/ (accessed December 31, 2016).

Marx, K. 1849. "Wage Labour and Capital", originally published in *Neue Rheinische Zeitung* April 5–8 and 11, 1849. Available at: https://www.marxists.org/archive/marx/works/1847/wage-labour/ (accessed August 19, 2018).

Marx, K. 1867 [1976] *Capital: Critique of Political Economy, Vol. 1*. Harmondsworth: Penguin.

Marx, K. 1987. *The Poverty of Philosophy*. London: Lawrence and Wishart.

Marx, K. 2005. *Grundrisse: Foundations of the Critique of Political Economy*. Harmondsworth: Penguin.

Marx, K. and Engels, F. 1948 [1982]. "Manifest der Kommunistischen Partei", in *Ausgewählte Schriften in zwei Bänden*. Berlin: Dietz.

Marx, K. and Engels, F. 1848 [2004]. *The Communist Manifesto*. Harmondsworth, Penguin.

Maurer, B. 1999. "Forget Locke? From Proprietor to Risk-Bearer in New Logics of Finance," *Public Culture*, 11 (2): 365–85.

Maurer, B. 2006. "The Anthropology of Money," *Annual Review of Anthropology*, 35 (1): 15–36.

Maurer, B. 2015. *How Would You Like to Pay?: How Technology is Changing the Future of Money*. Durham, NC: Duke University Press.

Mauss, M. 1923 [1974]. *Sociologia e antropologia*. São Paulo: Epu/Edusp.

Maxon, R. 1989. "The Kenya Currency Crisis, 1919–21 and the Imperial Dilemma," *Journal of Imperial and Commonwealth History*, 17 (3): 323–48.

May, J. and Thrift, N. (eds.) 2001. *Timespace: Geographies of Temporality*. London: Routledge.

May, W. 2015. "The Ballooning Tradition of American Poetry" in T. Stubbs and D. Haynes (eds.) *Navigating the Transnational in Modern American Literature and Culture*. Abingdon: Routledge.

McLeod, K. 2015. *Pranksters: Making Mischief in the Modern World*. New York: New York University Press.

McQuade, M. 2007. "Fair-Y Tale: The Wizard's Souvenir," *The Journal of the Midwest Modern Language Association*, 40: 115–29.

Mengis, M.C. 1889. "Mechanical Depository." US Patent 631,024, issued August 15, 1899.

Metzler, M. 2006. *Lever of Empire: International Gold Standard and the Crisis of Liberalism in Prewar Japan*. Berkeley, CA: University of California Press.

Mihm, S. 2007. *A Nation of Counterfeiters: Capitalists, Con Men, and the Making of the United States*. Cambridge: Harvard University Press.

Mill, J.S. 1894. *Principles of Political Economy*. New York: John W. Parker.

Mill, J.S. 2015. *On Liberty, Utilitarianism and Other Essays*. Oxford: Oxford University Press.

Mintz, S. 1961. "Standards of Value and Units of Measure in the Fond-des-Negres Market Place, Haiti," *Journal of The Royal Anthropological Institute of Great Britain and Ireland*, 91 (1): 23–38.

Mintz, S. 1964. "Currency Problems in Eighteenth-Century Jamaica and Gresham's Law" in R. Manners (ed.), *Patterns and Processes in Culture*. Chicago, IL: Aldine, pp. 248–65.

Mintz, S. 1984. *Sweetness and Power: The Place of Sugar in Modern History*. New York: Viking.

Mitchell, W.C. 1903. *A History of Greenbacks*. Chicago, IL: University of Chicago Press.

Montgomery, J. 1861. *Poems by James Montgomery*, London: Routledge, Warne and Routledge.

Morris, E.R. and Bawtree, A.E. 1911. "Means for Detecting Counterfeit Bank-Notes, Bonds, Coupons, and the Like." US Patent 1,002,600, issued September 5, 1911.

Mortimer, T. 1776. *A New and Complete Dictionary of Trade and Commerce*. London: printed for the author.

Mundell, R.A. 1961. "A Theory of Optimum Currency Areas," *The American Economic Review*, 51 (4): 657–65.

Mwangi, W. 2001. "Of Coins and Conquest: The East African Currency Board, the Rupee Crisis, and the Problem of Colonialism in the East African Protectorate," *Comparative Studies in Society and History*, 43 (4): 763–87.

Myers, M.G. 1970. *A Financial History of the United States*. New York: Columbia University Press.

Nason, H.E. 1901. "Means for Locking and Sealing Money-Bags." US Patent 688,671, issued December 10, 1901.

National Research Council. 1993. *Counterfeit Deterrent Features for the Next-Generation Currency Design*. Vol. 472. Washington DC: National Academies Press.

Neiburg, F. 2010. "Sick Currencies and Public Numbers," *Anthropological Theory*, 10 (1): 96–102.

Neiburg, F. 2016. "A True Coin of Their Dreams: Imaginary Monies in Haiti (The Sidney Mintz Lecture for 2010)," *Hau: Journal of Ethnographic Theory*, 6 (1): 75–93.

Neiburg, F. and Guyer, J. 2018. "The Politics of the Real," *Hau. Journal of Ethnographic Theory*, 8 (1/2): 236–8.

Neiburg, F. and Guyer, J. 2017. "The Real in the Real Economy," *Hau. Journal of Ethnographic Theory*, 7 (3): 261–279.

Nelson, A. 1902. "Checking Apparatus for Restaurants or the Like." US Patent 715,122, issued December 2, 1902.

Nelson, E.W. 1987. "The Gold Standard in Mauritius and the Straits Settlements between 1850 and 1914," *Journal of Imperial and Commonwealth History*, 16 (1): 48–76.

Nicholson, F.E. and Blanchard, G.I. 1902. "Hog-Killing Bed." US Patent 712,579, issued November 4, 1902.

Nietzsche, F. 2001. *The Gay Science: With a Prelude in German Rhymes and an Appendix of Songs*. Cambridge: Cambridge University Press.

Nobre, M. 2018. *Como nasce o novo*. São Paulo: Todavia.

O'Brien, P. 1988. *The Economic Effects of the American Civil War*. Atlantic Highlands, NJ: Humanities Press International Inc.

O'Malley, M. 1994a. "Specie and Species: Race and the Money Question in Nineteenth-Century America," *American Historical Review*, 99 (2): 369–95.

O'Malley, M. 1994b. "Response to Nell Painter," *American Historical Review*, 99 (2): 405–8.

O'Malley, M. 2012. *Face Value: The Entwined Histories of Money and Race in America*. Chicago, IL: University of Chicago Press.
Oastoe, T. 1874. "Improvement in Street-Cars." US Patent RE6,059, issued September 22, 1874.
Osborn, F.C. 1906. "Cash-Register." US Patent 817,725, issued April 10, 1906.
Osterhammel, J. 2011. *Die Verwandlung der Welt. Eine Geschichte des 19. Jahrhunderts*. München: C.H. Beck.
Pallaver, K. 2009. "A Recognized Currency in Beads. Glass Beads as Money in 19th-Century East Africa: The Central Caravan Road" in C. Eagleton, H. Fuller, and J. Perkins (eds.), *Money in Africa*. London: British Museum Research Publications, pp. 20–9.
Pallaver, K. 2015. "'The African Native Has No Pocket': Monetary Practices and Currency Transitions in Early Colonial Uganda," *International Journal of African Historical Studies*, 45 (3): 471–99.
Palyi, M. 1916. "Romantische Geldtheorie," *Archiv für Sozialwissenschaft und Sozialpolitik*, 42: 86–116.
Parrinder, P. 2014. *Science Fiction: A Critical Guide*. London: Routledge.
Petternel, A. 1900. "Protective Device against Burglary." US Patent 657,672, issued September 11, 1900.
Pocock, J.G.A. 1979. *Virtue, Commerce, and History: Essays on Political Thought and History, Chiefly in the Eighteenth Century*. Cambridge: Cambridge University Press.
Poe, E.A. 2001. "The Gold Bug" in *Edgar Allan Poe: Complete Tales and Poems*. New York: Castle Books.
Polanyi, K. 1941 [2001]. *The Great Transformation: The Political and Economic Origins of Our Time*. Boston: Beacon Press.
Polanyi, K. and MacIver, R.M. 1957. *The Great Transformation*. Vol. 5. Boston, MA: Beacon Press.
Poovey, M. 2008. *Genres of the Credit Economy: Mediating Value in Eighteenth and Nineteenth Century Britain*. Chicago, IL: University of Chicago Press.
Proudhon, J-F. 1927. *Proudhon's Solution of the Social Problem*. New York: Vanguard Press.
Pruthi, R.K. 2004. *Arya Samaj and Indian Civilization*. New Delhi: Discovery Publishing House.
Ray, R. 1995. "Asian Capital in the Age of European Domination: The Rise of the Bazaar, 1800–1914," *Modern Asian Studies*, 29 (3): 449–554.
Ritter, G. 1997. "Silver Slippers and a Golden Cap: L. Frank Baum's The Wonderful Wizard of Oz and Historical Memory in American Politics," *Journal of American Studies*, 31: 171–202.
Ritter, G. 1999. *Goldbugs and Greenbacks: The Antimonopoly Tradition and the Politics of Finance in America, 1865–1896*. Cambridge: Cambridge University Press.
Rivers, W.H.R. 1914. *The History of Melanesian Society*, Vol. 2, Cambridge: Cambridge University Press.
Robinson, M.R. (ed.) 2012. *Lesser Civil Wars: Civilians Defining War and the Memory of War*. Cambridge: Cambridge Scholars Publishing.
Rockman, S. 2009. *Scraping By: Wage Labor and Survival in Early Baltimore*. Baltimore, MD: Johns Hopkins University Press.
Rockoff, H. 1990. "The 'Wizard of Oz' as a Monetary Allegory," *Journal of Political Economy*, 98: 739–60.
Rosa, H. 2013. *Social Acceleration*. New York: Columbia University Press.

Rosenberg, E.S. 2003. *Financial Missionaries to the World: The Politics and Culture of Dollar Diplomacy, 1900–1930*. Durham, NC: Duke University Press.
Rothbard, M.N. 2002. *History of Money and Banking in the United States: The Colonial Era to World War II*. Auburn, AL: Mises Institute.
Ruskin, J. 1928. *Time and Tide and Munera Pulveris*. London: Macmillan.
Ruskin, J. 1997. *Unto This Last and Other Writings*. Harmondsworth: Penguin.
Russell, H.B. 1898. *International Monetary Conferences, Their Purposes, Character and Results, with a Study of the Conditions of Currency and Finance in Europe and America during Intervening Periods, and Their Relations to International Action*. New York and London: Harper Brothers.
Rydall, R. 1993. *World of Fairs: The Century of Progress Expositions*. Chicago, IL: University of Chicago Press.
Sahlins, M. 1996. "The Sadness of the Sweetness: The Native Anthropology of Western Cosmology (The Sidney Mintz Lecture for 1994)," *Current Anthropology* 37, 3: 395–428.
Schmitt, C. 2003. *The Nomos of the Earth: In the International Law of the Jus Publicum Europaeum*. Candor: Telos Press.
Schmitt, C. 2007. *The Concept of the Political*. Chicago, IL: University of Chicago Press.
Schweikart, L. 1987. *Banking in the American South from the Age of Jackson to Reconstruction*. Baton Rouge, LA: Louisiana State University Press.
Shell, M. 1982. *Money, Language and Thought*. Baltimore, MD: John Hopkins University Press.
Shell, M. 2005. "Buying into Signs: Money and Semiosis in Eighteenth-Century Language Theory" in M. Osteen and M. Woodmansee (eds.), *The New Economic Criticism: Studies at the Interface of Literature and Economics*. London: Routledge.
Siddiqi, A. 1981. "Money and Prices in the Earlier Stages of Empire: India and Britain 1760–1840," *Indian Economic and Social History Review*, 18(3–4): 231–62.
Simmel, G. 1900 [2005]. *Philosophie des Geldes*. 2nd. ed., Berlin: Duncker and Humblot. English transl.: *The Philosophy of Money*. London: Routledge.
Simmel, G. 1903. "Die Großstädte und das Geistesleben" in *Die Grossstadt*. Dresden: v. Zahn and Drensch, pp. 186–206.
Simmel, G. 1903 [2002]. "The Metropolis and Mental Life" in G. Bridge and S. Watson (eds.), *The Blackwell City Reader*. Oxford and Malden: Wiley-Blackwell, pp. 11–19.
Simmel, G. 1905. "A Contribution to the Sociology of Religion," *American Journal of Sociology*, 11 (3): 359–76.
Simmel, G. 1908 [2011]. *The Philosophy of Money*. London: Routledge.
Simmel, G. 1910 [1945]. "The Sociology of Sociability," *American Journal of Sociology*, 55 (3): 254–61 (translated by Everett C. Hughes).
Skocpol, T. 1995. *Protecting Soldiers and Mothers: The Political Origins of Social Policy in the United States*. Cambridge, MA: Harvard University Press.
Sloterdijk, P. 2011. *Bubbles*. London: Semiotexte.
Smith, A. 1982. *The Wealth of Nations: Books I-III*. London: Penguin.
Sohn-Rethel, A. 1989. *Geistige und Körperliche Arbeit*. Ed. rev., Heidelberg: VCH.
Sombart, W. 1902. *Der moderne Kapitalismus*. Leipzig: Duncker and Humblot.
Sova, D.B. 2007. *Critical Companion to Edgar Allan Poe: A Literary Reference to His Life and Work*. New York: Facts on File Publishing.
Spivak, G.C. 1985. "Scattered Speculations on the Question of Value," *Diacritics*, 15 (4): 73–93.

Stadermann, H.J. 2000. "Die Geldtheorie an der Schwelle zum 20. Jahrhundert" in J.G. Backhaus and H.J. Stadermann (eds.), *Georg Simmels Philosophie des Geldes*. Marburg: Metropolis, pp. 18–60.

Stearns, D.L. 2007. "'Think of it as Money': A History of the VISA Payment System, 1970–1984". Ph.D. dissertation.

Strathern, M. 1975. *No Money on Our Skins: Hagen Migrants in Port Moresby*. Canberra: New Guinea Research Unit, Australian National University.

Strathern, M. 2001. "The Patent and the Malanggan," *Theory, Culture and Society*, 18 (4) : 1–26.

Streb, J. 2016. "The Cliometric Study of Innovations," *Handbook of Cliometrics*, 447–68.

Swanepoel, N. 2015. "Small Change: Cowries, Coins, and the Currency Transitions in the Northern Territories of Colonial Ghana" in F.G. Richard (ed.), *Materializing Colonial Encounters: Archaeologies of African Experience*. New York: Springer.

Swift, J. 2013. *The Complete Works of Jonathan Swift*. London: Delphi Classics.

Tagore, R. 1917 [2011]. "Nationalism in India" in N. Bhusan and J. Garfield (eds.), *Indian Philosophy in English: Renaissance to Independence*. Oxford: Oxford University Press, pp. 23–6.

Thompson, E.P. 1967. "Time, Work-Discipline, and Industrial Capitalism." *Past and Present*, 38: 56–97.

Tschachler, H. 2013. *The Monetary Imagination of Edgar Allan Poe: Banking, Currency and Politics in the Writings*. New York: McFarland.

Ttjppee, H. 1875. "Improvement in Fare-Boxes." US Patent RE6,689, issued October 11, 1875.

Turnbull D. 1840. *Travels in the West: Cuba; with Notices of Porto Rico, and the Slave Trade*. London: Longman, Orme, Brown, Green and Longmans.

United States Patent Office. 2017. "Patentable Subject Matter". Available at: https://www.uspto.gov/web/offices/pac/mpep/s2104.html (accessed May 20, 2017).

Vilar, P. 2011. *A History of Gold and Money: 1450–1920*. London: Verso.

Vogl, J. 2014. *The Spectre of Capital*. Stanford, CA: Stanford University Press.

Waizbort, L. 2000. *As aventuras de Georg Simmel*. São Paulo: Editora 34.

Wajcman, J. and Dodd, N. (eds.) 2017. *The Sociology of Speed: Digital, Organizational and Social Temporalities*. Oxford: Oxford University Press.

Walker, F.A. 1896. *International Bimetallism*, London: Macmillan.

Weber, M. 1905 [2011]. *The Protestant Ethic and the Spirit of Capitalism*. Oxford: Oxford University Press.

Weber, M. 1917 [1991]. "Science as a Vocation" in H.H. Gerth and C. Wright Mills (eds.), *From Max Weber: Essays in Sociology*. London: Routledge, pp. 129–56.

Weber, M. 1920–21. Gesammelte Aufsätze zur Religionssoziologie. Tübingen: J.C.B. Mohr.

Weber, M. 2002. *The Protestant Ethic and the "Spirit" of Capitalism and Other Writings*. Harmondsworth: Penguin.

Weber, M. 2009 [1919]. "Science as a Vocation" in H.H. Gerth and C. Wright Mills (eds.), *From Max Weber, Essays in Sociology*, 129–56, London: Routledge.

Weiss, B. 2005. "Cowries, Coffee, and Currencies: Transforming Material Wealth in Early 20th Century Bukoba" in P. Geschiere and W.van Binsbergen (eds.), *Commodification: Objects and Identities (The Social Life of Things Revisited)*. Berlin: LIT Verlag.

Welch, J.W. 1999. "Weighing and Measuring in the Worlds of the Book of Mormon," *Journal of Book of Mormon Studies*, 8 (2): 36–45, 86.

Wells Brown, W. 1852. *Three Years in Europe; or, Places I Have Seen and People I Have Met*. London: Charles Gilpin.
Wesley, J. 1744. "The Use of Money." John Wesley Sermon Project Online. General Editors R.N. Danker and G. Lyons (1999–2011). Nampa, Idaho: The Wesley Center for Applied Theology. Available at: http://wesley.nnu.edu/john-wesley/the-sermons-of-john-wesley–1872-edition/sermon–50-the-use-of-money/ (accessed December 31, 2016).
Whalen, T. 1994. "The Code for Gold: Edgar Allan Poe and Cryptography," *Representations*, 46: 35–57.
Wieser, F. 1891. "The Austrian School and the Theory of Value," *The Economic Journal*, Vol. 1.
Winkel, H. 1977. *Die Deutsche Nationalökonomie im 19. Jahrhundert*. Darmstadt: Wiss. Buchgemeinschaft.
Wood, F.G. 1970. *The Black Scare: The Racist Response to Emancipation and Reconstruction*. Berkeley and Los Angeles: University of California Press.
Zelizer, V. 1979. *Morals and Markets: The Development of Life Insurance in the United States*. New York: Columbia University Press.
Zelizer, V. 1985. *Pricing the Priceless Child*. New York: Basic Books.
Zelizer, V. 1994. *The Social Meaning of Money: Pin Money, Paychecks, Poor Relief, and Other Currencies*. New York: Basic Books.
Žižek, S. 1989. *The Sublime Object of Ideology*. London: Verso.
Zook, G.F. 1920. "Thrift in the United States," *The Annals of the American Academy of Political and Social Science*, 87 (1): 205–11.
Zuijderduijn, J. and van Oosten, R. 2015. "Breaking the Piggy Bank: What Can Historical and Archaeological Sources Tell Us about Late-Medieval Saving Behaviour?" *Working Papers* 0065. Utrecht University: Centre for Global Economic History.

INDEX

Italic numbers are used for illustrations.

air, money as 99, 102–3, 120–1
alternative money 158–63
    See also shinplasters
Anderson, Maurice 28–30, *31*
anthropological studies 79–81, 135
Appadurai, A. 139
Appleby, Joyce 40, 41
arbitrage 84, 148
art and representation, seeing and satire 97–122
    balloons of money 104–9, 120–2
    bubbles of money 102–4
    consumerism 119–20
    credit in literature 110–16
    images of money 99–102
    The Wizard of Oz 116–18
authenticity of currency 20–1

Bagby, George 93
balloons and money 104–10, *107–9*, *111*, 120–1
bank money 151–4
Bank of the People 161–2
Banking School 151, 152
banks, trust in 24, 32
Barclaycard 98
barter 48, 70, 80–1
Baucom, Ian 102

Baum, Frank L., *The Wonderful Wizard of Oz* 42, 116–18, *118*
Bayly, C.A. 127–8
Beaumont, Frederick John 30
Benn Michaels, Walter 68
Bennett, James Gordon 79
Benton, Thomas Hart "Bullion" 73, 74
Berg, Ole 101
Betton, T.W. 81–2, *81*, 84
bimetallism
    vs the gold standard 8, 42, 148–9, 151
    in the US 18, 66
    and the value of money 40–1
    and *The Wizard of Oz* 117
Bismarck, Otto von 150
Blitz, Antonio 76
Bowler, K. 63
Boyd, Sanford 26, *27*
Britain
    banks 151
    bimetallism 42, 148
    coinage controversy 40–1
    faked US money 20
    gold standard 124
    and monetary union 150–1
    panics 152, 154
Brown, William Wells 89–91
Bryan, William Jennings 66, 69, 149

bubbles and money 10, 102–4
Burton, Charles 30

capitalism 32, 58, 59, 92, 125–6, 160
Casarino, C. 155
cash registers 26
Castagnaro, Mario 115
centralization of money 4, 54
character of money 142, 143
Chase, Salmon P. 154
Chicago World's Fair (1893) 118–19
children 22
China 50
Chown, J.F. 150
class-based society 124–5
Clay, Edward Williams, *The Times* 106, 109, *109*
Clay, Henry 74
Cohen, Isabella 21
coin-operated payments 30
coin sorting devices 26, 27, 28
colonial currencies 46–53
colonialism 6, 39
    See also imperialism
Comaroff, J. 69
Comaroff, J.L. 69
communication networks 127
community currencies 158–63
    See also shinplasters
company scrip 82
compensation for crime 143
concepts of money 2–3, 8–11
consumerism 117, 119–20
Corbridge, S. 36–7
counterfeit money 21, 45, 76
counting of money 26–8, *27*
cowrie shells 48, 51
credit
    belief in 102
    mail order catalogues 119–20
    representation of 97–8, 103–10
    social 159–62
    temporality of money 138–9
    and wealth 99
credit cards 19–20, 98
credit money in America 110, *111*, 112
credit theory 70–1
crime, compensation for 143
crimes and shinplasters 87
criminalization of debt 80

crises 137–8
    See also panics
Croteau, Candide 26
Cruikshank, George, *The Land of Promise!!!* 106, *108*
Cuba 6, 86
currency board systems 6, 7
currency and money, distinction between 43
Currency School 151, 152

Dalrymple, Louis, *The 'advance-agent of prosperity' on the road* 110, *111*
Darwinism 60
Dayananda Saraswati 61
debt and community 79–85
Del Mar, A. 150
dematerialization of money 144
demurrage 163
Denslow, William Wallace 119
Dent, William, *Public credit, or, the state idol* 99, *101*
Dickinson, Emily, *You've Seen Balloons Set* 121
dirty money 77
disestablishment of religion 60
disintermediation 160
Dodd, Nigel 46–7
dollar (United States) 6, 7, 95
domestic sciences 9
Doty, Richard 75, 83
doubloon (Spain) 5, 86
Douglass, Frederick 93, 155
Durkheim, Emile 59

Eagleton, C. 52
East Africa 51–3
economics
    development of 2, 8–9, 69–70, 129–30
    and the study of money 36, 135
efficiency, intensification of 128
emancipation from religion 58–62
Engels, Friedrich 37, 126
Euro (European Union) 49, 138
everyday money in the Antebellum US 73–95
    money and nationalism 85–91
    mutual debt and community 79–85
    shinplasters 75–9, 91–5
exchange relations 80, 137

fare boxes 28
financialization 35
fire company, New York 79
flight, as a symbol of credit 97–8
folk theory about money 36
fractional reserve lending 73
France 46, 150, 157, 159
Franklin, Benjamin 73–4
Free Banking 152, 153
free money 162
free trade 2, 156
Frisby, David 2
functionalist view of money 37–8

Gamble, Robert 84
Germana, Michael 94
Germany 9, 130, 137, 150
Gesell, Silvo, *The Natural Economic Order* 162
Gillray, James, *William Pitt—the national parachute* 106, *107*
Gilson, Franklin 32
god, money as a 141–2
gold
    and imperialism 67–9
    and religious movements 64, 66–7
    during World War I 157
gold rushes 10–11
gold standard 8, 41–2, 124, 148, 154–5
Goodwin, Jason 110
gourde (Haiti) 7–8
Goux, J.-J. 44
Graeber, David, *Debt, the First 5,000 Years* 79–81
greenbacks 18, 20, 45, 92, 154
Gresham's law 8, 148
Guyer, Jane 48

Haiti 7–8
Hall, John 23–4, *25*
happiness and money 142
Hart, Keith 38
Harvey, David 98
hawala trades 53
Hays, Samuel P. 57
heterogeneity of money 3–5
Hinduism 61
history and money 36–40
Hoar, George 66
hoarding of money 163

Hogarth, William, *Some of the Principal Inhabitants of ye Moon* 99, *100*
Holmes, Richard 109
home economics 9

ideas of money 35–55
    colonial currencies 46–53
    illusions of money 40–6
illusions of money 40–6, 100–2
imperialism 67–9, 124
India 39, 42, 44, 47–8, 50, 53, 61
    See also rupee (India)
industrialization 125, 126
Innes, A. Mitchell 70–1, 144
intellectual property. *See* patents
interpretation of money, mobility and acceleration 123–45
    Georg Simmel reflects on money 129–45
    transformation in the imperial age 123–9
invisible causal forces 63
Islam 60
issues of the age 147–64
    alternative money 157–63
    bank money 151–4
    gold and silver 148–9
    land and sea 154–7
    monetary unions 149–51

Jackson, Andrew 74, 153
Japan 60–1, *62*
Jevons, William Stanley 2, 60
Johnson, Alvin 22
Jones, Thomas Howell, *The Reign of Humbug!!* 106, *108*
JP Morgan Chase & Co. 19–20
Judaism, emancipation of 58
Jukes, Francis, *Stock Exchange* 105–6, *105*

Kane, Robert 22, *23*
Kazin, Michael 69
Keynes, John Maynard 44, 46, 139
Khan, Zorina 18
Knox, John Jay 153
Kosambi, D.D. 47–8
Kuroda, A. 43

labour money 158–9
language of money 9, 46–7, 69, 141, 143

Latin Monetary Union 7, 149–51
leakage of money 28
legal status of shinplasters 87
Lévi-Strauss, Claude 136
Lincoln, Abraham 68
Linick, Adolph 30
Littlefield, Henry 117
Locke, John 40, 41
logic of money, Simmel on 136–7
Long Depression, USA 148–9
Lumsden, James 86–7

Macleod, Henry Dunning 8
magic of money 37
mail order catalogues 119–20
Marryat, Frederick 86
Marshall, Alfred 42
Marx, Karl 44, 58, 126, 155, 159
mature money economy 3
Maurer, Bill 36
Mauss, Marcel 136
May, Will 109
McCulloch, Hugh 66
McKinley, William 67, 67
Melanesia 62, 68
Menger, Carl 9
Mengis, Morris 24
Methodism 62–3
Mill, John Stuart, *On Liberty* 2
Minstrel shows 93–4
missionaries 69
modernity 60, 129
monetary reform programs 47, 60, 157–63
monetary standards 42
   See also gold standard
monetary unions 7, 149–51
monetization 30, 32–3
money-boxes 21–6, *23*, *25*
money supply and shinplasters 82–3
money supply, regulation of 152
Montgomery, James 64
moral force of money 63, 67
Mormonism 63, 64
Mortimer, Thomas, *A New and Complete Dictionary of Trade and Commerce* 102
motion and money, Simmel on 133–5, 144
Müller, Adam 130
multiple currencies 47–9, 50–3, 75–6, 85–6, 90, 155

mutual credit 159–62
Myers, M.G. 149

Nast, Thomas 60, 61, 64, *65*
nationalism 8, 85–91
naturalism 68, 69
Nietzsche, Friedrich 155
Noble, Thomas Satterwhite, *The Price of Blood* 85–6, *85*
Nusbaum, Aaron 119

O'Malley, Michael 42, 68–9
Oosten, R. van 22
origin myths 8, 69–71
Osterhammel, J. 128
Ottoman Empire 60

Pallaver, K. 51
panics 152, 153, 154
   See also crises
paper money 6–7, 20, 74, 151–4, 157
   See also shinplasters
Parieu, Félix Esquirou de 150
patents 16–19
   See also technologies of money
phenomenology of money 139–40
pneumatic tubes 28–30, *31*
Pocock, J.G.A. 103
Poe, Edgar Allan 112, 115–16
   The Gold Bug 112–13, 116
   The Unparalleled Adventures of Hans Pfall 113–15, 116
Polanyi, Karl, *The Great Transformation* 11–12
poor people 74–5, 78, 89–95
private money. *See* shinplasters
prosperity and faith 62–4
Proudhon, Pierre-Joseph
   Bank of the People 161–2
   Solution of the Social Problem 159–61

racism 68–9, 74, 78, 92–4
rag money 82
reform programs 47, 60, 157–63
relationships, monetary 38
rents, conflicts over 52–3, 54
RescueTime 33
Ritter, Gretchen 67
Ritty, James 26

ritual and religion 10, 57–71
   emancipation from religion 58–62
   gold and silver 64–7
   imperialism 67–9
   origins of money 69–71
   prosperity and faith 62–4
Rivers, W.H.R. 62
Rockman, Seth 82–3
Rosenberg, Julius 119
rupee (India) 42, 47, 50–2
Ruskin, John 158

satire. *See* art and representation, seeing and satire
savings 21–6, *23, 25*
Scandinavian Monetary Union 7
Schmitt, Carl 156
Schmöller, Gustav 9
schools, religious and secular 60
sea and power 155–6
Sears, Roebuck 119
Second United States Bank 74, 152–3
sending money abroad 52, 53
Shell, Marc 117–18
shillings (England) 40–1
shinplasters (USA)
   ambitions of subaltern groups 91–5
   debt and community 81–5, *81*
   introduction to 73–9
   legal status of 87–9, *88–9*
   nationalism and money 85–7
   and poor people 89–91
   and race 92–5
Shintoism 60–1, *62*
silver
   the money of radicals 67
   price of 151
   in USA 149
   value of 40–1
   See also bimetallism
Simmel, Georg
   background 130
   on exchange 137
   individualism and money 2
   influence of 136–7, 140–1
   The Metropolis and the Mental Life 131
   on motion and money 133–5, 144
   on the phenomenology of money 139–40

The Philosophy of Money 9, 130–1
   on religion 60
   on society 132–3, 140–1
   on the symbolic dimension of money 139
   urbanization and money 3
   on the value of money 131–2
Slawson, John 28
Sloterdijk, Peter 103
Smith, Adam 70, 99
social change 124–5
social credit 159–62
social sciences and money 36–40
society, Simmel on 132–3, 140–1
sociological studies 135
Solomon, Peter 138
sound money 66
South Africa 69
South Sea Company 103–4
specie money 73
Stephenson, John 28, 29
Strange, Robert 78
Strathern, Marilyn 17
streetcars 28, 29
Swift, Jonathan, *The South Sea Project, 1721* 103–4
symbolic dimension of money 139

Tagore, Rabindranath 61
TaskRabbit 33
Taylor, Charles Jay, *Coxey's Paternalism* 110, *111*
technologies of money 15–33
   authenticity of currency 20–1
   coin-operated payments 30
   counting and transfer of money 26–30, *27, 29, 31*
   cultures of money 30–3
   ideas of money 30, 32–3
   materials used 19–20
   money-boxes 21–6, *23, 25*
   patents 16–19
temples and money 71
temporality of money 138–9
territorial division of the world 156–7
thaler (Maria Theresa, Austria) 5, 38, 51
Thomas, Dalby 41
Thompson, E.P. 83
thrift 22
Thrift, N. 36–7

time as a monetary unit 158–9
tobacco notes 87–9
transfer of money 28–30, *29*
transformation in the imperial age 123–9
transport 97–8, 127
Tschachler, Heinz 112
Tupper, Horace 28

ubiquity of money 137–8
Uganda 51
United States of America
    bimetallism 18, 66
    Civil War and Legal Tender Acts 154
    consumerism 119–20
    credit money 110, *111*, 112
    early monetary history 18
    Free Banking Era 153
    and the Latin Monetary Union 150
    Long Depression 148–9
    Mormonism 63, 64
    multiple currencies 75–6
    patent system 17–19
    patents and the definition of money 19–21
    race and money 68–9
    religion and money 66–8
    rights of African-Americans 45
    schools, religious and secular 60
    Second Bank of the United States 74, 152–3
    silver 149
    See also shinplasters
universality of money 42–6
urbanization 3, 126–7

Vallandigham, Clement 68
value of money 40–1, 70, 131–2
variety of money 5–8
velocity of circulation 163
Virgin Money 97
Vogl, Joseph 99–100, 114

wars 154, 157
Weber, Max 2, 58, 141
Wesley, John 63
Whalen, Terence 112
wildcat banks 89
women 9
work 126
world's fairs 119

Zanzibar 51–2
Žižek, Slavoj 99, 100–2
Zuijderduijn, J. 22